SCOTTISH FOOTBALL QUOTATIONS

SCOTTISH FOOTBALL QUOTATIONS

KENNY MACDONALD

Foreword by Ally McCoist MBE

MAINSTREAM
PUBLISHING

EDINBURGH AND LONDON

For Jacquie, Jack & Ben

First published in Great Britain in 1999 by
MAINSTREAM PUBLISHING COMPANY (EDINBURGH) LTD
7 Albany Street
Edinburgh EH1 3UG

ISBN 1 84018 214 8

A catalogue record for this book is available from the British Library

Typeset in AGaramond and Gill Sans
Printed and bound in Finland by WSOY

CONTENTS

Acknowledgements	7	Food	75
Foreword	9	Foreign	77
Age	11	Fury	82
Ally	12	Future	84
Anglos	14	The Game	86
Bosman	17	Gazza	89
Celtic	18	Girls Girls Girls	95
Children	24	Glug Glug Glug	97
Clever Clogs	27	Goalies	99
Clubs	28	Goals	102
Coaching	40	Grounds	103
Craig B.	42	Health	105
Defeat	44	Ho Ho Ho	107
Directors	45	Home Life	112
Doh!	47	Internationals	113
Estonia	51	Jim Farry	116
Euro '96	52	Kenny	119
Euro pe	56	Managers	123
Fame	59	Mark	130
Family	60	Mojo	132
Fans	61	Money	133
Fergie (1)	65	Non-league	141
Fergie (2)	66	Off!	141
Fergie (3)	69	Old Firm	142
Fitness	74	Other Sports	148

Ouch!	149	Stein	193
The Past	155	Style	195
Philosophies	157	Swearing	197
Players	160	Tackling	198
Press	168	Tommy B.	198
Pressure	172	Tragedy	199
Punch-ups	174	Transfers	200
Rangers	175	TV	203
Real Work	177	US	204
Referees	179	Walter S.	206
Religion	182	Weird	208
The Sack	186	The Wife	210
Sarcasm	187	Wise Words	212
Scotland v England	187	World Cup '98	215
SFA	188	The End	218
Souness	191	Index	220

ACKNOWLEDGEMENTS

Thanks:

Doug Baillie, Bill Bateson, Jim Black, John Colquhoun, Gareth Davies, Alan Dick, Jim Duffy, Martin Frizell, John Gahagan, Donald Hallam, Kevin McCarra, Brian McClair, Ally McCoist, Jim McInally, Alastair McSporran, Pat Nevin, Stuart Rafferty, Phil Shaw, Scott Struthers, Jason Tomas.

Hello:

My mother and father, Tim Allan, Gary Armitage, Debbie Begg, David Belcher, Frank Bradford, Graeme Bryce, Agnes Cassells, Liesha Clark, Stuart Cosgrove, Ronnie Cully, Billy Dodds, Kevin Donnelly, Gordon Dryden, Mike Dunn, Tom English, John Fahey, Ray Farningham, David Farrell, Jan-Erik Fjeld, Joyce Gordon, Alexandra Grant, Mark Guidi, Ronnie Gurr, Davie Irons, Nick Jones, Ron Jones, Weldon Kees, Hugh Keevins, Graeme Kerr, Miodrag Krivokapic, Iain King, Leo Kottke, David Leslie, The Loud Family, Lindsay MacDonald, Colin McAdam, Gary McAllister, Ian McCall, Maureen McCarroll, John McCormack, Archie McGregor, Stevie McKenzie, Joe McLaughlin, Susan McLaughlin, Alex McLeish, Alan Mackin, Madeline Mair, Danny Marlin, Michael Marra, Campbell Money, Iain Munro, Eric Musgrave, Ron Newey, Charlie Nicholas, Claire Oldfield, John Peel, S.J. Perelman, Tommy Reilly, Rice University Marching Owl Band, Ian Ross, Fratelli Sarti's, Brian Scott, Neil Scott, Eliphas Shivute, Simon Stainrod, Gregor Stevens, Jose-Luis Velo, David Walker, Steve Welsh, Bobby Williamson, Clare Wood, Ian Wood, Warren Zevon.

FOREWORD

I am delighted to have the opportunity to introduce this second volume of quotations about the game and the country we all know and love.

When *Scottish Football Quotations* was published in 1994, I was pleased to find a section all about yours truly, but somewhat shell-shocked to find the first entry was an extract from a punishment exercise I received from Hunter High School in East Kilbride when I was a fourth-year pupil in 1978 (for bad timekeeping, which probably won't surprise anyone who knows me).

That is an indication of the kind of research and attention to detail which went into the first volume, and the copy you are holding promises more of the same.

Since the first book came out, we in Scotland have been treated to the phenomenon that was, is and always will be Paul Gascoigne, and I'm delighted he not only has a section of his own, but has a few of his inimitable remarks recorded for posterity (see his entry under 'Food' for proof). People will have their own opinion of Paul, but I doubt if anyone will say Scottish football was dull while he was here.

I'm just disappointed Kenny didn't see fit to include a line of my own on the evening I was honoured to be named in the Top Rangers Team of All Time earlier this year. I made my way up to the stage to stand alongside some of the Ibrox greats from the past and I told Walter Smith, 'Yes, Mark Hateley, Brian Laudrup, Paul Gascoigne . . . this team would have scored some number of goals. And looking at the defenders, we'd have had to.' I'd like to give you Richard Gough's quote by way of response but this is a book for all the family.

Maybe it'll make volume three. In the meantime, enjoy this one.

Ally McCoist, MBE

AGE

I lost consciousness 20 minutes from the end.
Tommy Burns on playing for Kilmarnock against Rangers at 37, May 1994.

I had a feeling the day after the Cup final was lost to Raith Rovers that the repercussions would be felt by the older players at Celtic Park first of all. I knew that some of the Celtic support thought I was past my sell-by date and it is at times like those that negative thoughts consume people's minds. It's what a player cannot do that becomes the issue instead of what he might be good at.
Celtic's **Charlie Nicholas**, April 1995.

If I was to finish now I'd think, 'What a waste', because I'm at my peak now. Mentally I'm perfect. Physically I'm perfect.
Former Hibs keeper **John Burridge** at the age of 42, August 1995.

There's nobody fitter at his age – except maybe Raquel Welch.
Coventry boss **Ron Atkinson** on Gordon Strachan, who'd just turned 39, 1996.

If I had my time again, I'd go to Italy earlier. I was 31 when I went to Sampdoria.
Graeme Souness, April 1996.

Morton Olsen was marking me. He must have caught me offside 20 times and he was about 40 at the time.
Steve Archibald recalls winning the 1984 UEFA Cup against Anderlecht, April 1996.

It's a terrible feeling when you've once been paid to keep fit and then you lose it. It's a sobering thought when you climb the stairs and you're out of breath.
Former Scotland defender **Martin Buchan**, January 1997.

Ask Gordon Strachan and the rest who have played through to their mid-30s. The more you work the more you can do.
FA technical director **Howard Wilkinson**, June 1997.

I still feel quite adolescent in my enthusiasm for football.
Craig Brown, April 1998.

I resent any implication I might be on cruise control.
Brian McClair, 34, on signing for Motherwell, July 1998.

The legs aren't doing too bad and the lungs are OK. The liver is rotted and will probably be finished off if we get the right result on Sunday.
Bradford's **Stuart McCall** prior to his team's last First Division match on 9 May 1999. Bradford won 3–2 at Wolves to go back into the top division in England for the first time in 77 years.

ALLY

When he [McCoist] broke his leg against Portugal, he was lying on the table with his leg in a splint and someone said, 'How are you feeling?' and he says, 'It could be worse, we could have lost 5–0.'
Craig Brown, February 1998. Scotland lost the game, in April 1993, 5–0.

You're like dogshit in the box. We don't know you're there until the damage is done.
Celtic defender **John Hughes** to McCoist, December 1995.

Is there a sadder sight in football than watching Ally McCoist watching someone else scoring for Rangers?
Former Celtic director **Michael Kelly** after McCoist, who'd already scored a hat-trick, was clearly distraught as Brian Laudrup selfishly scored Rangers' fifth goal himself rather than pass to him in the 7–2 European Cup win over Alania Vladikavkaz, August 1996.

The greatest Rangers player of all time.
Maurice Johnston on McCoist, December 1996.

Smarter than the average bear.
Headline of an article on McCoist, *The Scotsman*, 25 January 1997.

People say Ally's had it easy playing for Rangers, but the country is full of strikers who couldn't make it at Ibrox.
Dundee United coach **Gordon Wallace** after McCoist passed his post-war league goal record of 264, February 1997.

He is a very nice person. I know because he keeps on telling me.
Rangers' Chilean striker **Sebastian Rozental** on McCoist, February 1997.

At Euro '92 there were calls for McCoist to be dropped from the team.
Someone, in protest, put a giant poster under my door. Under the photo
of Ally was the message, 'Please don't drop me, Andy', signed, 'The
Golden Slipper' (he was the Golden Boot that year). I don't know who was
responsible but like all true Scottish football people, he had a sense of
humour.
Andy Roxburgh in *The Absolute Game* fanzine questionnaire, March 1997.

He was better than Ally McCoist.
Andy Roxburgh on Ferenc Puskas singing, after hearing the Hungarian at a
coaching course in Budapest, April 1997.

A unique player who comes along once every 25 years.
Scotland B-team coach **Tommy Burns** on McCoist, March 1998.

I just love him.
Team-mate **Jorg Albertz** after McCoist had scored in the Tennents Scottish
Cup semi-final against Celtic, 5 April 1998.

People think he's just jolly old Ally, but that's not the guy I know. I know
a guy who works hard and wants to score goals. He doesn't like failure.
Raith boss **Jimmy Nicholl** on McCoist, July 1998.

You've always got a chance when you've got Superman in your team.
Kilmarnock boss **Bobby Williamson** after McCoist scored his first goal for
the club after coming on as a sub against Livingston, August 1998. The following week, in his second game from the start, McCoist scored a hat-trick in the
3–0 win over Hearts.

The '80s were a strange time for music. You went from Sid Vicious
wanting to kick your bollocks to Boy George wanting to kiss them.
Ally McCoist, October 1998.

ANGLOS

I don't think anyone likes Willie. Deep down I think that when he looks in the mirror even Willie dislikes Willie.
Tommy Docherty on former Manchester United player Willie Morgan, November 1997.

He [Kenny Burns] turned up to sign for us in a car without tax or insurance. It's a wonder we weren't arrested.
Brian Clough, His Way, 1993.

We won two European Cups and we never practised a free kick. 'Just give it to Robbo,' was the cry.
Martin O'Neill on life at Nottingham Forest under Brian Clough, quoted in His Way, 1993.

When he got up in the morning, he would lift his legs over the bed, put his feet down and he'd go straight into his socks, shoes, trousers, shirt, tie, everything and pull everything up, like a big zip. That's Robbo.
Kenny Burns on former Nottingham Forest and Scotland team-mate John Robertson, quoted in Mike Wilson, Don't Cry For Me Argentina, 1998.

They clearly resented two newcomers coming down from Scotland to break up the side.
Gary McAllister on early days for him and Ally Mauchlen at Leicester City.

We were presented with this cylindrical art-deco piece of furniture and I didn't want it. I wanted the silver thing.
Andy Gray on the League Championship trophy he won with Everton in 1985.

I stopped working at my game when I got to Highbury and things started to go wrong from there.
Charlie Nicholas, April 1995.

London actually knocked some of the daft ideas about stardom out of my head. There are people who, to this day, are amazed at my ability to remember their first name.
Charlie Nicholas, April 1995.

It was a nice family club and we did our best to ruin it.
Victor Kasule on playing at Shrewsbury, October 1996. His accomplices were Dougie Bell, Alan Irvine and Steve Pittman.

A coach who could crap, but definitely not a crap coach.
John Colquhoun on his coach at Millwall – Steve Harrison – who was sacked by England following an unsavoury party trick involving a cup, September 1996.

When [Steve] Sedgley had gone out for training I got one of his squash socks and had a shit in it. I was careful not to do too much otherwise he'd have noticed the weight. So after training he went to put the sock on, rolled it up and put his thumbs straight in my shit. If that had been anyone else they'd have thrown the socks away but not Sedgley. The filthy bastard emptied the shit out and took them home for his wife to wash.
Former Scotland striker **David Speedie** on dressing-room fun at Coventry, December 1996.

This lad Shearer will have to play some football to keep me out.
Former Scotland striker **David Speedie** to boss Kenny Dalglish, when Dalglish told him he was moving to Southampton as part of the deal to bring Alan Shearer to Blackburn, December 1996.

Gordon Strachan is a good mate of mine but it [training on Stewart's pitch at his Epping home] doesn't seem to be doing him much good at the moment.
Rod Stewart, December 1996. Coventry were struggling near the bottom of the Premiership at the time.

Exeter away was the worst. It was a night match so we travelled down on the day and didn't get away after the game until 10 p.m. I finally made it into my bed at 5.30 the next morning after a round trip of about 1,000 miles and 22 hours. To make it worse, we lost.
Carlisle's **Owen Archdeacon**, who lives in Erskine, Renfrewshire, January 1997.

What right does this guy have to say stick money on Coventry to go down? What is he? A London cabbie? I won't let someone like that criticise our team. He wanted a bit of glory – his 15 minutes of fame. Andy Warhol must have been right.
Coventry captain **Gary McAllister** on Woking goalkeeper Laurence Batty, who'd criticised Coventry after playing them in the FA Cup, February 1997.

McAllister stood there swearing and cursing at me, which I don't think was very dignified for an international captain. He wanted to fight me but I

just laughed at him. He kept on saying, 'We graft, we work hard for our living.' What does he think, that we don't?
Woking goalkeeper Laurence Batty after being confronted by Coventry captain Gary McAllister after Coventry's 2–1 FA Cup win, February 1997.

There was no need for him [McAllister] to come into our dressing-room, using the language he did, but maybe he had a reason.
Woking manager Geoff Chapple on the same incident, February 1997.

They seemed to think Jimmy was Scottish as well. Apparently Danny Baker kept going on about how Jimmy should take his Scots back up the road.
Millwall's Paul Hartley on Jimmy Nicholl's demise at the club, April 1997.

No.8: Brian McClair. Very underrated. To score 100 goals in both England and Scotland is a great achievement. Most successful Scot still playing, if two minutes a week counts.
John Colquhoun picking his top 10 players of all time, October 1997. At the time McClair was often a sub at Manchester United.

He's a big lad. If he said it was Christmas you'd sing carols.
Ian St John on new Scottish cap Matt Elliott of Leicester, November 1997.

5' 10", size ten feet, as elegant as footballers get; totally different to me, in other words.
Coventry boss Gordon Strachan on his son Gavin, November 1997.

All I could hear was these bagpipes and I thought someone had put a bagpipe record on. I stood outside and everyone came outside the marquee and these bagpipes were getting louder and louder. I turned round and there was a bagpiper walking up the hill in full outfit. Oh, I shed tears.
Colin Hendry, recalling Blackburn's 1995 Championship celebration, June 1998.

We'll never win the league. That's an impossibility. You can qualify for Europe, but you need a good run, using a regular squad of the same 15 or 16 players, no injuries or suspensions, plus a bit of luck. That's possible.
Coventry boss Gordon Strachan, February 1999.

In 1989, six weeks before we won the double, I said to Kenny Dalglish that it was the worst Liverpool team I'd ever played in. So maybe I'm not a very good judge.
Former Liverpool defender Alan Hansen, March 1999.

BOSMAN

Football is a resilient animal. It survived two World Wars, so I think we will survive the Jean-Marc Bosman verdict.

Jim Farry, 15 December 1995, after the European Court of Justice ratified that transfer fees at the end of a contract are illegal, as is the three foreigners rule.

After Bosman I envisage greater responsibility being put on players as their rewards increase. They will be held accountable for their performances, for the way they live and for the effort they make to settle. I believe that some who are found wanting could find themselves the subject of litigation by clubs.

Rangers manager Walter Smith, March 1996.

We have been left in limbo because a man with a funny hat in a European court decided that football was like every other walk of business life. But what other business has an unofficial retirement age of 35?

Motherwell boss Alex McLeish after seeing two of his players, Paul Lambert and Rob McKinnon, leave for nothing under the Bosman rule, August 1996.

I think the Bosman thing was very, very good because it all boils down to people being entitled to what they are worth. Why should footballers be treated any differently to anyone else?

Agent Bill McMurdo, *The Absolute Game* fanzine, May 1997.

They cut their own throats. Before the transfer deadline they'd turned down bids of £2.7m from Middlesbrough, Chelsea and Everton, knowing that come June I was away for nothing. They walked the tightrope and fell off.

Everton's John Collins on Celtic's handling of the end of his Parkhead contract, February 1999.

Nobody has come up with a reason why footballers shouldn't be as free in their job as anyone else is.

Clydebank defender and SPFA assistant secretary Fraser Wishart, February 1999.

It [winning the European Cup] might have been for Scotland, but it definitely wasn't for Britain. It was for Celtic.
Lisbon Lions skipper **Billy McNeill**, 1995.

Celtic is a love affair that we take to our deaths.
Celtic rebel leader **Brian Dempsey**, February 1991.

It was even worse after Lou Macari arrived as manager. There was a total collapse of the spirit I had been used to inside the dressing-room. There were no smiles and not so much as a 'good morning' to be heard. He [Macari] made it perfectly clear that he didn't fancy the team he had inherited and would be bringing in his own players and staff.
Charlie Nicholas, April 1995.

Davie is a hard, hard guy and a lovely, totally straightforward and honest bloke. But I don't think he was the right choice to manage Celtic.
Celtic's **Tommy Burns** speaking, while still a Parkhead player, on Davie Hay, quoted in Tom Campbell and Pat Woods, *Dreams, and Songs to Sing*, 1996.

If ever a man was made for a specific club, it was Billy McNeill and Glasgow Celtic. He was never really manager here, or at Aston Villa. His heart was always at Parkhead.
Manchester City chairman **Peter Swales**, April 1989, quoted in Tom Campbell and Pat Woods, *Dreams, and Songs to Sing*, 1996.

He has done the honourable thing in resigning.
Celtic chairman **Kevin Kelly**, the irony of his words presumably lost on him, speaking of Liam Brady's resignation, October 1993.

The rebels have won.
Rebel leader **Brian Dempsey** as the Celtic dynasty falls, 4 March 1994.

Mr McCann is taking the club in the wrong direction. It is because of this that I have decided I will not be back at Celtic as part of his team for the future.
Celtic rebel leader **Brian Dempsey** announces his disenchantment, June 1994.

I can't wait to see my team play again. They're the greatest side in the world. I haven't been able to get to a match for years but that will all change now.
Celtic fan Bishop Roddy Wright, who'd eloped with lover Kathleen McPhee, September 1996.

The way Celtic play you could put Franz Beckenbauer at the back and they would still lose goals.
Former Rangers captain **Terry Butcher,** January 1997.

Are they really better than the Southamptons and Coventrys of this world?
Manchester United chairman **Martin Edwards** on suggestions that Celtic were ready to join the Premiership, January 1997.

I can see where Celtic are coming from because they are a big team in a crap league and they want to move to a bigger stage.
Xavier Wiggins, spokesman for Wimbledon Supporters' Association, on reports linking Celtic with a takeover of his side, February 1997.

I want the supporter to know that he is once again the moral owner of Celtic Football Club.
Former director **Brian Dempsey,** announcing plans to gain control of Celtic when Fergus McCann leaves in 1999, March 1997.

There is surely something uniquely deluded about a persecution complex suffered by supporters of a club whose silverware haul is among the biggest in the world history of the game. But then, that in itself is the source of the complaint: Celtic fans throughout the 1990s have provided the highly entertaining phenomenon of the glory-hunter whose club never wins anything. A century of sucking in prizes like a black hole, and then they hit a decade in which their trophy count is level with Raith Rovers and Motherwell.
Chris Brookmyre, *The Absolute Game* fanzine, May 1997.

You can't have harmony if there are pockets of us and them, but that's the way it is at the moment.
Celtic's **Peter Grant,** May 1997.

While other clubs appeared to be able to identify a player they wanted to buy and then just go ahead and buy him, with Celtic it seemed that the process would take roughly the same time as the gestation of an elephant. It seemed that youngish players who were linked with Celtic had become veterans, completed their careers and moved into pub management before

Magoo was satisfied enough with the small print to authorise the expenditure.
Alastair McSporran, *The Absolute Game* fanzine, August 1997.

I've said all down the line that our position is that Paolo is not for sale.
General manager **Jock Brown** on Paolo Di Canio, 5 August 1997.

He [di Canio] wasn't sold. He was traded. The only way to get [Regi] Blinker was to involve di Canio. He was available as a trading tool to get Blinker.
Jock Brown, 6 August 1997.

I'm not prepared to sit here and be told that I've been leading you up garden paths. I don't accept that I misled you. Every answer I gave I stand by.
Jock Brown responds to criticisms that he had misled the media over the di Canio 'trade', 6 August 1997.

Myself and the board and Jock Brown felt he should not continue long-term. Given the situation we had it would have been unlikely we would have asked him to continue.
Managing director **Fergus McCann** on title-winning coach Wim Jansen's resignation, 11 May 1998, the day Jansen quit.

In March he was asked for an assessment of the players we have and to provide in writing his plans for improving the squad. I've got a memo covering this issue but again he refused to comply. He's a free spirit, an individual who does his own thing. You can't do that in an organisation as big as ours.
Fergus McCann on Jansen, 11 May 1998.

We must be the only team in the world that wins the double then loses the manager almost the next day.
Celtic's **Paul Lambert**, on the day of Jansen's resignation.

When we asked him about a strategy for the future, we weren't talking rocket science.
Fergus McCann on Jansen, 15 May 1998.

I had a problem early on at the Darren Jackson signing. He told the press that I saw videos of Jackson but I didn't see them.
Wim Jansen on Jock Brown, 15 May 1998.

They keep bringing up the fact that I didn't go to watch Harald Brattbakk. Well, I didn't see Jonathan Gould, Craig Burley, Marc Rieper or Stephane Mahe and there was no problem for me.

Wim Jansen, 15 May 1998.

I couldn't understand his behaviour over Brattbakk. He told us when he came here he didn't trust videos. But the first excuse for not going to see him [Brattbakk] was that he was going to see Manchester United against Feyenoord, which I believe was a social event. I said I could fix him up to go to Trondheim for the next Champions' League fixture. He said he didn't want to miss training. We would have hired a private jet to take him over at three o'clock and straight back so no training would be missed but he would not go.

Jock Brown on Jansen, 15 May 1998.

The club didn't even make a phone call to ask [if Borussia Dortmund's Karlheinz Riedle was available]. Two weeks later he was at Liverpool.

Wim Jansen on being thwarted regarding signings, 15 May 1998.

I found out his age. I ascertained what salary he would require. I found out what transfer fee would be involved. I found out all the figures required. I then said to Wim, 'Let's go and look at this guy and see what you think. See if he's still got it.' Wim wasn't interested in anything like that. He just wanted Riedle signed.

Jock Brown's response, 15 May 1998.

He wanted to pick his World XI, pick up a couple of trophies, enhance his reputation and go.

Jock Brown on Jansen, 15 May 1998.

There is no one in football I have ever found it more difficult to work with.

Wim Jansen on Jock Brown, 15 May 1998.

He has no right whatsoever to form a view of me except from the direct dealings we have had. He never wanted to find out anything about me and has no right to have an opinion on what I am like and what I do.

Jock Brown's response, 15 May 1998.

Sometimes I had to fight more against my own people then against my opponents.

Wim Jansen, 15 May 1998.

I do a lot of self-criticism and analysis of myself. There are things I'd have done differently.
Jock Brown, 15 May 1998.

He was quite a nice guy for whom it didn't work out.
Fergus McCann on Jansen, 15 May 1998.

This has been a good week that has just looked bad for Celtic.
Fergus McCann, 15 May 1998.

I've spoken to a lot of football people throughout Europe in recent weeks and every time you mention Celtic they shake their heads.
Simple Minds singer and Celtic fan **Jim Kerr**, July 1998.

Celtic Sign A Blank Czech
Daily Record headline, 18 July 1998, the day after new coach Jozef Venglos's appointment. Initially, Venglos had no work permit and could only operate in an advisory capacity.

Peter McLean, Celtic's public relations manager, showed me the *Daily Record* back page heading: JOKE BROWN. 'There you are,' said Peter. 'For 51 years you have been subjected to generally positive media comment. Now you have joined Celtic. You haven't done anything, you haven't made a decision, but you are now being portrayed as a joke. Welcome to the club!'
Former Celtic general manager **Jock Brown**, in *Celtic-Minded*, 1999.

You told me we had a lot of good players at the club, but we don't.
Celtic coach **Wim Jansen**, quoted in Jock Brown's *Celtic-Minded*, 1999.

Wim could not lose. I could not win. Either he won the championship and became a hero or he lost the championship and it was all my fault.
Former Celtic general manager **Jock Brown**, in *Celtic-Minded*, 1999.

I made towards him and said, 'Congratulations, well done!' He did not acknowledge me and cast his eyes firmly at the floor and walked past towards the dressing-room. A handshake was out of the question. For him to say later I did not congratulate him was entirely out of order.
Jock Brown, in *Celtic-Minded*, 1999.

Murdo [MacLeod] made some reference to Willie [McStay] being 'an empire builder'.
Jock Brown's claim that MacLeod blocked McStay's appointment as Celtic youth development manager, in *Celtic-Minded*, 1999.

The lives of Eric [Black] and Willie [McStay] became a misery.
Jock Brown claims the Celtic coaches were ostracised by coach Wim Jansen, in *Celtic-Minded*, 1999.

By the time 30 June comes round a lot of players are going to be reminded of the Dionne Warwick song, 'Do You Know The Way To San Jose?' That's the one with the line about 'all the stars that never were are parking cars and pumping gas'.
Fergus McCann reveals a hitherto-hidden Bacharach & David passion in a sideswipe at Celtic's four out-of-contract stars, December 1998.

Celtic are primed and ready with massive support, no debts and a fantastic new stadium, all of which is as a result of Fergus McCann. But we must invest to get to the next stage.
Simple Minds singer **Jim Kerr**, one of the consortium looking to take over Celtic, February 1999.

What worried me was that I didn't hear any talk from him [McCann] about football.
Jim Kerr, February 1999.

If you say at the start that you're selling the place in five years, you're hardly likely to add a conservatory and invest in gardening tools, are you?
Jim Kerr on McCann's five-year plan, February 1999.

As for Mr Kerr's pejorative remarks about Fergus McCann having done a standard job with Celtic, he must have been living on a desert island for the past five years, perhaps listening to some of his discs. Does he know nothing of the fact that the club was taken from the edge of bankruptcy by this man who then built a European-class stadium, and did someone not tell him that last season Celtic won the League for the first time in ten years?
Praise for Fergus McCann from Rangers director **Hugh Adam**, in a letter to *Scotland on Sunday* newspaper, 14 March 1999.

No one worth mentioning could give a monkey's for the thoughts of this business dinosaur, or his dim-witted views on what is good for our wee club.
Jim Kerr responds, in a letter to *Scotland on Sunday* newspaper, 21 March 1999.

I think the first error was made very early, when we should have immediately changed the old way of appointing a manager from former players, somebody who had worn the shirt, a so-called 'people's choice'. I think Tommy Burns himself acknowledged that he probably took charge

of a club like Celtic too young and too soon. That was one of those potentially damaging traditions I should have changed right off.
Celtic managing director Fergus McCann looks back as he prepares to quit, April 1999.

Last summer, we were badly let down by a couple of individuals who were serious prospects. Jock Brown was wrongly blamed for the delay, but nobody could have worked harder or travelled more in pursuit of getting that job done. We were strung along by a couple of men.
Fergus McCann, April 1999.

What was it Nixon said? You guys won't have me to kick around any more.
Fergus McCann in his last days as Celtic's managing director, April 1999.

I am not paying for his retirement.
Simple Minds' **Jim Kerr** refusing to buy any shares made available after Fergus McCann's departure, May 1999.

CHILDREN

At the moment kids learn to play the game of football rather than learn to play football. I see it with my own boys. Even at under-10 level they learn to play the offside trap and nonsense like that.
Rangers boss **Walter Smith**, 1994.

I think I'm tuned into kids, to what they think. There is the child in us all. I believe that. I'd hate to lose that feeling inside of being a big kid. The one thing that attracts me to children more than anything is their refreshing innocence and honesty.
Ally McCoist, June 1994.

If one of my girls walked in and said, 'Daddy, I'm going out with a footballer,' I'd say, 'No, you *were* going out with a footballer!'
Former Scotland striker **Andy Gray**, quoted in *The Lad Done Bad – Sex, Sleaze & Scandal in English Football*, 1996.

If I had to choose between having Lauren go through something like that and all the medals and money in the world, I would still be a welder.
Rangers' **John Brown**, *Blue Grit*, 1995. His daughter Lauren required a heart operation in 1995.

I spoil my kids and I get them excited and laughing. That's the kind of father I am. Now I understand that you can't take any of this with you.
Charlie Nicholas, April 1995.

At Kiev youngsters are taught ball skills and nothing else four nights a week by former pros. So when you turn 16 you can do everything with a ball then it's time to deal with physical work. Here I see 10-year-olds running round and round a track. When I arrived at St Johnstone I saw young players who couldn't kick with their left foot. Incredible.
Former Russian international **Sergei Baltacha,** December 1995.

He's got more skill than I had at that age – or maybe even now.
Colin Hendry on his five-year-old son Kyle.

They'd put two or three players on me to man-mark me. I came home crying and said I can't handle it and my mum and dad said, 'OK, go away, play chess, do anything.'
Brian Laudrup on pressures as a youth, 1997.

One of the things you need to get rid of in Britain is schools football. We don't have it in Holland. Youngsters are taught by proper coaches.
Celtic's **Pierre van Hooijdonk,** June 1996.

I'm not the first guy to miss the birth of their kid.
Paul Gascoigne, 1996. He had been drinking with Rangers team-mates when Regan was born.

At 13 I was playing with guys who were 30. I had to go home after the game when they all went to the pub.
Eoin Jess on playing as a youngster in Portsoy, July 1996.

I told my wife that our son would probably be playing. I think she must have gone to the loo at least five times on our way to the ground . . . The thing I really remember was how he changed. Before the kick-off he was my son. When the referee blew the final whistle he had become one of the players.
Bobby Gould on his son Jonathan's Coventry début in December 1992. Coventry won 5–1.

I have a young child myself and I'm outraged some people might think I would make nasty remarks about the Dunblane tragedy.
Rangers' **Charlie Miller** after being cleared of assault, February 1997. Celtic fan John McKee had claimed Miller told him, 'F*** you and f*** Dunblane'.

My little girl wanted to teach me to dance. I told her to bugger off.
Alan Hansen, October 1997.

If I play my son at snooker, I want to thrash him.
Alan Hansen, October 1997.

Forget wee kids standing shivering, not getting a kick of the ball and having some guy screaming at them from the touchline because they are not playing the offside rule properly.
Think tank chairman **Ernie Walker**, January 1998.

I've a two-year-old daughter and another child on the way. I'm not going to go in a wheelchair and try to catch them.
Rangers' **Alan McLaren** announcing he was quitting football because of knee injuries, April 1998.

My father was never the type to praise me. If I scored a hat-trick and he said, 'Well done', I used to ask my mother what was up with him.
Manchester United boss **Alex Ferguson**, November 1998.

It didn't help that my own son gave away the penalty. If it had gone in he'd have been an orphan.
Stenhousemuir manager **Terry Christie** after his son Max gave away a penalty in the Scottish Cup-tie against Whitehill Welfare, 9 January 1999. Whitehill missed and Stenhousemuir went on to a bumper pay-day against Rangers at Ibrox.

[He's] living with his granny, eating at home and his uncles are there to look after him. And I've no worries about his mental strength. He made his début against Aston Villa in the Cup, where Coventry hadn't won in a hundred years, ended up on the winning side, and didn't bat an eyelid.
Coventry boss **Gordon Strachan** on son Gavin, February 1999.

I've got this great dilemma about my grandson: he was born in London, his mother was born in Kenya but her father is Danish. So he could play for Kenya, Denmark, Scotland or England. But he won't be playing for bloody England!
Manchester United boss **Alex Ferguson**, February 1999.

Of the 14 Old Firm games he has played in, I've only been to a couple. I went to his first one but it was horrible. It's such a shame because I love watching him play . . . When Celtic wanted to sign him I definitely had misgivings. I told him that. I hadn't forgotten what it was like.
Former Celtic and Hibs defender **Jackie McNamara** on his son, April 1999.

My skin isn't dark, but it's darker than most of the children. If someone said something, I fought them. That stopped it. That and football.
Celtic's Henrik Larsson remembers growing up black in the Swedish town of Helsingborg, May 1999.

CLEVER CLOGS

Bob has three degrees from universities, including one in North Carolina, Jock is an MA from Cambridge, I'm a BA from the Open University. As a footballer I was the one the manager would turn to last and say, 'Right son, nothing clever from you this week.'
Scotland boss Craig Brown, August 1995.

People are going to think that not only are centre-halves useless and ugly, but we're also thick.
Blackburn's Colin Hendry after losing at Trivial Pursuit in a game set up by Goal magazine, 1996.

As a joke, I'd put a message on it saying 'Choccy is great!' As he is hopeless with anything technical, he couldn't remove it. He was convinced that, like me at the club, the message would be there forever, a thought too hideous for him to cope with.
Brian McClair on high jinks with Alex Ferguson's mobile phone, recalled in Odd Man Out, 1997.

The Gaffer says at the end of his team talk, 'Has anybody got any questions?' and there's never anything. Once I said, 'Yes, I've got a question.' The Gaffer was very pleased until I added, 'Where do babies come from?' I've never tried that one again.
Brian McClair on Alex Ferguson team talks, Odd Man Out, 1997.

Even as a kid he was a real blether and you could never get him to shut up. He was always reeling off a load of statistics about players you'd never heard of and would bore all the other players to tears.
Dunfermline's Ian Westwater on former Hearts team-mate John Robertson, October 1997.

Being a footballer is what I do. It isn't what I am.
Kilmarnock's Pat Nevin, November 1997.

If you have any intelligence [in football] then you get stick. You're supposed to be rough and tough and one of the lads.
Craig Brown, February 1998.

After Kilmarnock had drawn the Bosnian side Zeljeznicar Sarajevo in the UEFA Cup qualifying round, my first thought was, 'I've already played in Baghdad, Beijing and Belfast. All I need is Beirut for the full set.'
Pat Nevin, July 1998.

It is the coronation city of the kings of Moravia.
Celtic coach, **Dr Jozef Venglos**, after being asked by a journalist what he knew about the Czech city of Olomouc, August 1998. The local team had been drawn to play Kilmarnock in the UEFA Cup.

CLUBS

Aberdeen
A bear with a petted lip.
Journalist **Jim Traynor** on Aberdeen boss Roy Aitken, *Daily Record*, 16 January 1997.

Airdrie
I've worn tutus, Kenny Everett-style gloves and posed for pics with a knife through my head. It's all part of the fun. I'm fed up picking up papers and seeing stony faces.
Airdrie keeper **John Martin**, November 1996

They are very big and very strong but they do not play football. Their defenders get the ball and they just turn without looking and hammer it up the field.
St Johnstone's **Attila Sekerlioglu**, not an admirer of Airdrie's tactics, February 1997.

Albion Rovers
The last time I saw a crowd like this was outside the Social Security office in Coatbridge.
Albion Rovers' announcer surveying Cliftonhill's all-ticket capacity crowd of 1,202 for the Coca-Cola Cup tie against Hibs, 3 September 1996.

I admire the fans. We've been to Ross County, a 3½-hour journey in midweek, and there are 12–14 of our fans who won't set home until 2 in the morning. Even if it was just one or two people, you've still got to go out and try for then.

Albion Rovers' John Gallacher, September 1996.

Cowdenbeath, Stranraer and all these sort of clubs. Really, what have they got to offer us? When was the last time that they had good players that came through and were transferred on? Tell me, Albion Rovers. When have they brought players on? You haven't even got kids coming through at Rangers and Celtic so what chance have you got of setting them from Albion Rovers?

Agent **Bill McMurdo**, *The Absolute Game* fanzine, May 1997.

The sun came out from behind the clouds twice in the second half.

Rovers manager **Billy McLaren** remembers the bright spots of the 8–0 home defeat by Ross County, 15 August 1998.

Arbroath

I couldn't stand it any longer. After all the lying and deceptions I couldn't bear seeing Tommy's name there. So I took the car home, hosed it down with hot water and peeled off the offending letters. Now it just has Arbroath FC on it again.

Arbroath committee member **Bill Thomson** on removing former manager Tommy Campbell's name from the club car after his acrimonious departure from the club, May 1997.

Ayr United

I am an Ayr United supporter myself. My happiest memories are standing on the terrace with my father, drinking weak Bovril, eating mutton pie, watching Dandy McLean running rings round the opposition. It made a perfect Saturday.

Artist **Peter Howson**.

We'll play with a new 3–4–3 formation. Three on the goal line, four along the six-yard box and three in line with the penalty spot. And Henry Smith will play behind them as sweeper.

Ayr boss **Gordon Dalziel** outlines his side's tactics for the Coca-Cola Cup tie against Rangers at Ibrox, September 1996.

Caledonian

They let the club down.

Caledonian boss **Steve Paterson**, after his side beat Albion Rovers 6–1, 21 October 1995. Paterson thought his players, 6–0 up at half-time, had soft-pedalled.

Clyde

Too big to be a wee club and too wee to be a big club.
Journalist John Rafferty on Clyde, *The Scotsman*, c. 1960, quoted in *The Absolute Game* fanzine, June 1996.

Clyde are a credit to the game in every respect.
Willie Waddell, 1968.

Half of them were booing and half of them were cheering. The only problem was that the half that were cheering were cheering the half that were booing.
Former Shawfield boss **Craig Brown** recalls a trip to a Clyde Supporters' Club in Castlemilk, quoted in *Official Scotland World Cup Supporters Book*, 1998.

Clydebank

We – the Steedmans – gave birth to the club, we created Clydebank Football Club in our image. It's our baby and we're not letting anyone take it away from us.
Clydebank chairman **Jack Steedman,** after coach Brian Wright quit, April 1997.

Ever since the club was formed in 1965, we, the Steedman family, have always bought and sold every player ourselves. All negotiations with players, all transfers, all bonuses and everything like that are settled by us – not by the coach. Yes, it's a unique structure but it will never change while there's a Steedman at the club.
Jack Steedman, April 1997.

Wimbledon's move to play in Dublin was farcical. This is super farcical.
FAI chief executive **Bernard O'Byrne** on Clydebank's move to relocate in Dublin, February 1998.

Cowdenbeath

The children keep on asking why the minister keeps going on about cows and beef.
Cowden fan and Orkney minister Rev. **Ronald Ferguson,** March 1994. He is the author of *Black Diamonds & The Blue Brazil*, a chronicle of coal, Cowdenbeath and football.

I'm not under any pressure. I've another two years to win our next home game.
Cowdenbeath boss **John Reilly** after their first home win since 25 April 1992 – on 2 April 1994.

We are joint top of the league and they [East Stirling] are bottom, but they are no worse or better than us. We're just carrying a bit more luck.
Cowdenbeath manager **Tom Steven** reflects on Division Three life, October 1996.

Dumbarton
It would have been nice to have met with Cruyff but we did the best we could and it wasn't to be. For us it was a case of nothing ventured, nothing gained.
Then-Dumbarton manager **Sean Fallon** on the 1980 effort of the club to sign Johann Cruyff.

I've spent more money on my car since I became manager than I have on players.
Dumbarton boss **Jim Fallon**, 1995.

Dundee
They probably didn't know they could play as badly as that. They took a deep breath and forgot to exhale.
Jim Duffy on the performance of his players in the November 1995 Coca-Cola Cup final against Aberdeen, January 1996.

I am very interested in acquiring clubs all over the world. I have a lot of African players on my books and I want a stage for them.
Georgia, USA-based Nigerian doctor **Obie Okehi** on reports he was set to buy Dundee, 1996.

I was one of the very few managers who got no stick. If we weren't going well on the pitch, it would just be blamed on Ron Dixon.
Hibs boss **Jim Duffy** recalls working at Dens under Canadian chairman Dixon, January 1997.

His greatest achievement wasn't reaching cup finals or coming close to promotion, it was creating a great youth system.
Former boss **Simon Stainrod** on Jim Duffy's time at Dundee, January 1997.

In Dundee, every census in the last 20 years has shown the city's population is going down. If everyone put their shoulder against the same wheel they'd have a chance. I saw that 20 minutes after I got off the train for the first time. But instead, people would rather go on about ethnic rivalry – in Dundee and elsewhere – and you end up with two clubs in the same street pulling in opposite directions. It's total bullshit.
Former Dundee chairman **Ron Dixon**, February 1998.

If I was a Dundee fan now I would be tearing my hair out.
Proclaimers singer – and honorary president of the Hands On Hibs pressure
group – **Charlie Reid**, as merger talk sweeps Tayside, February 1999.

Dundee United

At Fir Park, during the game between Motherwell and Dundee United,
Tommy McLean, the United manager, was nearing meltdown. He yelled
and threw his arms about as if conducting something composed by
Wagner in a bad mood.
Ian Wood, *The Express*, 18 November 1996.

Our board advised Golac not to sign at least four players but he went and
did it. Was that interfering?
Dundee United chairman **Jim McLean** on accusations of stopping previous
boss Ivan Golac buying players, December 1996.

The only thing I can see stopping the groundshare from happening is Jim
McLean's ego. But he's not going to be around forever.
Dundee chairman **Ron Dixon**, March 1997.

I fall out with the chairman of Dundee United. I make no apology for that
and if I live till I'm 90 I'll continue to fall out with him because he and I
will never agree.
Agent **Bill McMurdo** on Tannadice chairman Jim McLean, *The Absolute Game*
fanzine, May 1997.

I didn't realise I was suspended until Davie Bowman told me after the
game. And when it comes to suspensions he's an expert.
Dundee United's **Andy McLaren**, suspended for the Coca-Cola Cup final
after being booked in the semi against Aberdeen, October 1997.

I wouldn't treat my dog the way I was treated by Tommy McLean at
Dundee United. The man was horrible.
United defender **Julian Alsford**, September 1998. He'd been given a two-week
sick line by his doctor and told to stay away from Tannadice, because playing
there was affecting his health.

Dunfermline

Richard will find it's not like Dunfermline at all.
Kansas City Wizards spokesman **Jim Moorhouse** on the impending arrival of
Richard Gough at the MLS club, February 1997. Gough stayed five months in
America before returning to Rangers – his first game back was a 7–0 win over
. . . Dunfermline!

Andy's the only guy at the club I can't understand. I mean, who's Ken? He keeps talking about him.

Dunfermline's English keeper Lee Butler on team-mate Andy Tod, August 1998.

East Fife

He was wearing a replica short-sleeved shirt and East Fife shorts as well and shouted: 'Call yourself a hard man, MacKinnon', as I tried to wipe the snow out of my eyes.

Kilmarnock's Davie MacKinnon recalls a fan at a match at Bayview in December 1989. The game was subsequently abandoned because of a blizzard.

East Stirling

Three weeks before kick-off I had 8 players and a 15-stone goalkeeper who insisted he had done pre-season training.

Alex Ferguson, recalling his first job as manager of East Stirling.

Falkirk

It was worth it just to see the look on their faces when I said yes. They had a press conference to announce my arrival which was bigger than the one I'd had at Marseille. And anything's got to be better than the sausage factory.

Chris Waddle on signing for Falkirk, September 1996.

Try missing one in the World Cup semi-final.

Chris Waddle, consoling Paul McGrillen on missing a penalty against Airdrie, 28 September 1996.

I want this Cup final to be good. The FA Cup final was over in 42 seconds, just like most men when they're lovers.

Falkirk's Andy Gray before the Scottish Cup final, May 1997.

Forfar Athletic

At the end of the season the manager, Jerry Kerr, came into the dressing-room and said he was going to read out a list of the players that were being freed. Then he stopped and said it'd be easier to read out the players that were to be kept. The list wasn't very long.

Defender Alex Brash, December 1995, on the Forfar side which finished bottom of the Second Division in 1974–75, having won one game out of 38.

Hearts

I was a Hearts supporter. I didn't want to leave but I did, and it was the best thing I've ever done.

Dave Mackay on leaving for Spurs in 1959, April 1997.

33

Justin Fashanu was in the treatment room and the physio asked him if he was injured. Fash said he wasn't, he was just getting a break from the rest of the team.
Hearts striker John Colquhoun, September 1993.

I believe Jim Jefferies was brainwashed into taking the decision to join Hearts.
Falkirk chairman George Fulston, about to be frustrated in attempts to keep his manager at Brockville, 31 July 1995.

He [Jefferies] is a contracted Falkirk employee and there is such a thing as the law of the land.
George Fulston, 1 August 1995.

I became confused as a result of things that were said to me by the chairman and eventually gave in to the pressure. I looked at my performance on television on Saturday night. Standing outside Brockville saying things I didn't mean to the crowd, I realised I resembled a zombie.
Jim Jefferies, 2 August 1995. Two days later he was appointed manager on a five-year contract.

Not being in the team destroyed a little bit of my love for the game. For a few minutes of that day I wasn't even sure I wanted my team to win.
John Colquhoun on being overlooked by Hearts for the 1996 League Cup final against Rangers, 18 May 1997.

There has been the splendid sight of Scotland's third biggest, positively gigantarian Super Club, Heart of Midlothian plc, reclaiming the place which is rightly theirs in the marvellous Bells Premiership, i.e. fourth.
'Bruno Glanvilla,' *The Absolute Game* fanzine, May 1997.

Hibs

Probably the worst strip in the world.
Sun headline on announcement of Hibs' new sponsorship deal with Carlsberg, 28 June 1996. The new strip is a curious shade of purple.

The stage show 'We Are The Hibees' continues to be dogged by controversy as critics question the authenticity of a scene set in the 1990s purporting to show Hibs with more than two forwards in the opposition half.
The Absolute Game fanzine, October 1996.

I know there will be a lot of Hibs fans who don't want me as manager.
Jocky Scott after getting the job on a temporary basis, October 1996.

I had been planning to bring both of them over last week but because of the Festival we struggled to find quality accommodation for them.

Hibs boss Jim Duffy runs into novel problems in his bid to sign Israeli and Portuguese players, August 1997.

Kilmarnock

When I said he'd score 50 goals this season I didn't mean against us.

Killie boss Bobby Williamson after Rangers' Marco Negri scored a hat-trick against them, 1 November 1997. He'd scored twice against them in September.

Livingston

I've told him he won't get an international cap, he'll get a turban.

Boss Jim Leishman after discovering Livingston's Craig Smart was eligible to play for India, 1996.

I had to decide whether I was going to be a tactical genius or just win championships. Now I'll be happy if we're humpty from the weight off all the gold medals hanging round our necks.

Boss Jim Leishman, September 1996.

Morton

When I was at Aberdeen, Morton were my bogey team. I tried everything. I tried two up front, three up front, no one up front. They beat us. I packed the midfield, I tried no wingers, I tried three wingers. Once I played with two outside-lefts. They still beat us. One time I tried everything to stop Andy Ritchie's free kicks. A hole in the middle of the wall. Big guys at the end of the wall. Five in the wall. Six in the wall. On the Saturday what happened? Andy Ritchie scored the winner from a free kick.

Manchester United boss Alex Ferguson on memories of Morton, at Allan McGraw's tribute dinner, 26 October 1997.

Motherwell

I once met a Motherwell supporter in a bar in Fiji. He told me he was going home early so he could watch Motherwell play Airdrie. He said he thought nothing of it. When your heart is claret and amber, the world's a gey small place.

Former Reuters & *Times* foreign correspondent and 'Well fan, Gavin Bell, August 1994.

Brian McLaughlin was one of the few players I have ever seen with the ability to play off his leading foot. He never had to change his stride pattern when a ball was played to him, whichever foot or part of his foot

it arrived at. Whatever pace he or the ball was travelling at, he never broke his stride when he took the ball on. Very few players can do that. Jan Molby is probably the only one I know who can do it now. Hoddle could do it in his day. You can't learn that – you've either got it or you haven't.
Scotland skipper Gary McAllister on his former Fir Park team-mate, April 1996.

Partick Thistle

You've got to remember we were up against a Celtic side quite capable of scoring five goals in one half against anybody. And you've also got to remember that we were Partick Thistle – and quite capable of losing five goals in one half against anybody.
Alan Rough recalling not being confident of success, despite being 4–0 ahead at half-time against Celtic in the 1971 League Cup final, October 1996.

Wee Bertie would wear his European Cup medal round his neck and if you argued with him he'd rip his shirt open and say, 'Hey Higgins, have you got one of these? Eh? Eh?' And I'd say, 'No, and I'm not very likely to win one playing here either.'
Former Thistle striker **Tony Higgins** on playing under Bertie Auld, in after-dinner speaking, 1990s.

Because of our financial situation I spent my first three months here trying to do swap deals. Funny how other managers always want to exchange one of their reserves for your best player.
Partick Thistle boss **Murdo MacLeod**, 1996.

If anyone thinks we're going to give away a company which we've built up over six years at a personal loss to satisfy the wishes of some Indian with a curry shop, they better get real.
Partick chairman **Jim Oliver**, 27 August 1995.

We'd deal with anyone, whether they were Asian, Eskimo, one-eyed black lesbian saxophone player.
Jim Oliver counters allegations of racism, August 1995.

I do not accept Mr Lambie's evidence as either truthful or reliable. I found Mr Lambie to be an unsatisfactory witness, prone to extravagance of manner and expression.
Lord Hamilton in the Court of Session, August 1996, after former Thistle players Ray Farningham and Davie Irons won their court case against non-payment of agreed bonuses by the club.

His testimony was, in my judgement, an invention.
Lord Hamilton on Lambie's assistant Gerry Collins, August 1996.

Every team talk for me now is like a broken gramophone record. I could make a tape of my talks at the start and at half-time of every game and somebody could just play them over and over without me needing to turn up for matches.
Partick boss John McVeigh after bottom-of-the-table Thistle won only one of their first eleven games, 18 October 1997.

Queen's Park

There were about 170 buggers on our doorstep at Hampden that night. Some had no boots, just gym shoes. Others turned up in jeans, two guys played in glasses and one bloke had just one arm.
Former Queens coach Eddie Hunter recalling a newspaper appeal for players, October 1996.

Raith Rovers

I was training at Raith Rovers and I went to Manchester United for a trial and the trainer [at Raith] threw me out. So I went to sign for Rangers. I wasn't even bothered about signing for Rangers. I would rather have signed for Raith Rovers but they wouldn't have me.
Former Rangers and Scotland winger Willie Johnston, now a Kirkcaldy publican, November 1994.

Highlight of my time there was half-time in the Olympic Stadium in Munich. The thought of Klinsmann and the rest in the Bayern dressing-room getting a bollocking because we were beating them 1–0. I have a wee smile when I think about that.
Millwall boss Jimmy Nicholl on his time at Kirkcaldy, 1996. Raith lost 2–1 in Munich.

They were doing things that were affecting the football side, pouring all the money into the stadium. But as soon as I was out the door the players were on £1,000 win bonuses. It wasn't that the money wasn't there, but that they obviously didn't want me to spend it.
Jimmy Nicholl on his Raith days, April 1997. By the time the magazine article quoting him appeared, he was back at Raith as assistant manager . . . and shortly afterwards as boss.

I'll be giving everyone a chance to show what they can do.
Raith Rovers manager Tommy McLean, 3 September 1996. Seven days later he was off to Dundee United.

Thirteen of the sixteen who lost to us were in the squad against Celtic yet we got absolutely no credit for what we achieved. Because it was Raith beating Bayern the impression given was that something must have been wrong with Bayern.

Raith boss Iain Munro after Raith beat Bayern 1–0 the night before the Germans beat Celtic 2–1 in Peter Grant's testimonial, February 1997.

They've lost everyone in the town and if they're too blind to that fact they want to open their eyes.

Jimmy Nicholl after the sacking of boss Iain Munro, April 1997. Nicholl, Munro's assistant, was asked to take the job but initially refused.

The club has gone backwards to 1990. They've got a couple of new stands and a tidy wee stadium but all the progress has been made on the face of it. Behind the scenes it's the same old story.

Jimmy Nicholl on Raith, April 1997.

There was absolutely no way I would have taken it. I'm desperate to work and I could do with the money but I'm not that desperate to work for them.

Jimmy Nicholl on being offered the manager's job, April 1997. On June 20 he took it.

St Johnstone

It's 1976 and in the Premier Division's inaugural season St Johnstone are blazing a trail, with laser-like intensity, towards new depths of ineptitude, setting records that remain unsurpassed to this day despite the efforts of succeeding batches of Premier fodder like Hamilton Accies, Clydebank and Morton. 11 points from 36 games, three wins and a wondrous 27-game sequence without a win that started before the clocks went back and was still gathering momentum when British Summer Time came along again.

Archie MacGregor, *The Absolute Game* fanzine, April 1996.

I did until half-an-hour ago.

Paul Cherry, booked for speeding the day he was freed by the club, on being asked by the traffic cop if he played for Saints, 2 May 1996.

Being a bit-part player at St Johnstone was not how I imagined my career ending, and I readily took the decision which I had been agonising over for so long.

John Colquhoun announcing his intention to quit playing, 18 May 1997.

At St Johnstone I remember going into Alex Totten's office to ask why I had been dropped and he replied, "Cos you're playing rotten.' I loved that. I went out thinking, 'Aye, I'm playing shite, why did I go to his door and annoy Alex in the first place?'
Former Saints striker **Willie Watters**, August 1998.

St Mirren
With St Mirren I'd say, 'My job is to make sure we can climb Mount Everest with our slippers on.'
Former Saints boss **Alex Ferguson**, May 1997.

When I was at St Mirren it was a desolate place. Even the birds woke up coughing.
Alex Ferguson on St Mirren, December 1997.

At St Mirren I was freed as a player, sacked as assistant manager and then I chucked it while I was in charge. So I've got the full set.
St Mirren boss **Jimmy Bone** after quitting in protest at the axing of assistant Kenny McDowall, August 1996.

Stirling Albion
The red of Stirling Albion complemented perfectly the fiery, spotty complexion of an adolescent young footballer. The jersey was, I recall clearly, very nylony. Appearing from the terracing to be a Travoltaesque disco-dancing shimmery kind of fabric, it was, in reality, a nightmare. Running too fast, whilst being pursued by a defender, there was a real danger of producing an electric shock that would stop a rhinoceros in its tracks.
John Colquhoun, May 1997.

Stranraer
Q: Favourite moment from the last decade?
A: Stranraer winning the Challenge Cup final. All the hard work I put in during the mid-80s eventually paid off.
SPFA secretary – and ex-Stranraer striker – **Tony Higgins**, *The Absolute Game* fanzine survey response.

COACHING

We enjoyed soccer better then than today. We never saw a blackboard.
James Brown from Troon, the only Scot to score in the semi-finals of the World Cup, interviewed in June 1994 at the age of 85. Brown emigrated as a teenager and was the last surviving member of the US side which reached the semis in the 1930 World Cup.

We were a shambles and a performance like that is not good enough for a club like Celtic. The players should be in twice a day for training until we learn to pass the ball properly. The bad run we are having has nothing to do with effort or determination. It is about a poor quality of possession. How can you get anywhere if you keep giving the ball to the other side?
Celtic's **John Collins** after a draw at Tannadice meant they'd taken only 3 points out of 18, November 1994.

It saddens me to see the young boys at Celtic Park head for the gym as soon as training is over every day so that they can work with the weights. When do they have their extra practice with the ball?
Charlie Nicholas, April 1995.

The last time I sat in front of a blackboard was at school in Scotland. It certainly never happened in all my years at Liverpool.
Alan Hansen, April 1996.

Even the bulbs in my garden are in formation.
Arsenal boss **George Graham** on getting his defence in order.

If you weren't doing your job properly in the Liverpool first team, the solution was to put you in the reserves.
Alan Hansen, April 1996.

The idea of the miniature game [Soccer Sevens] may be seen as an Ajax invention but Andy Roxburgh launched it in 1981 and the coaches he spoke to at the seminars listened to him. It became known as the Ajax system worldwide whereas it probably should have been called the Andy Roxburgh system. The Dutch listened to Andy. Unfortunately his own countrymen didn't.
SFA community development programme co-ordinator **Jim Fleeting**, May 1996.

40

If you played football on a blackboard, Don Howe would win the World Cup easily.
Former Scotland winger **Willie Johnston**, May 1996.

At the moment, people who've never kicked a ball can coach kids. You wouldn't get someone who'd never swum before to teach kids to swim, would you?
SFA community development programme co-ordinator **Jim Fleeting**, May 1996.

Having no adult intervention makes such a massive difference. If you go to kids' games it's the adults who are roaring at decisions and bawling at the officials. Given the chance, even the youngest of kids can apply the rules fairly.
SFA community development programme co-ordinator **Jim Fleeting**, May 1996.

No one coached me before I was 14 or 15. Before that I could fantasise about being Jimmy Johnstone, Peter Marinello, Pat Stanton or Colin Stein. There was no one trying to organise me. I could run all over the field and play in every position. Now we tell eight-year-old kids they are a right-back.
Coventry boss **Gordon Strachan,** November 1997.

If you're dribbling and you keep getting kicked in the shins you say, 'I think it's about time I passed now.' That's the way you learn. Not by people shouting at you about offside when you're nine. That's nonsense.
Coventry boss **Gordon Strachan**, August 1998.

Clyde had 27 players last year and no reserve team. How can that be? What madman dreamed that up? Maybe I am missing something. Maybe I should go to Largs and learn about it.
Clyde general manager **Ronnie MacDonald**, February 1999.

In 1982 we tried it for four games at Liverpool, with me as sweeper. I could give you a day-long seminar on the sweeper system, but on the pitch we couldn't do it. We didn't know when to come or when to stay.
Former Liverpool defender **Alan Hansen**, March 1999.

CRAIG B.

I was, I suppose, a rough player, a dirty bastard.
Craig Brown, February 1998.

I still consider it a privilege to have the honour and responsibility of managing the finest club in the country.
Then-Clyde manager **Brown,** quoted in *The Absolute Game* fanzine, June 1996.

I'm bilingual. I have the appropriate register for each occasion. Players are smart and they can hang you out to dry, but I can speak their language.
Craig Brown, September 1993.

Craig Brown's most important job is not to manage Scotland but to apply himself to his duties as the SFA's technical director and act as the head of a staff who have experience of playing the game as professionals.
SFA chief executive **Jim Farry,** January 1995.

People expect us to beat everybody we play. The trouble is, so do I.
Craig Brown after losing to the United States, May 1996.

Dignified, shrewd, never resorting to media bullshit, his general demeanour was so impressive he set a standard by which all future Scottish coaches will be judged.
FourFourTwo magazine's verdict on Brown, August 1996.

I don't lose my temper but I've been told that I can have a sharp tongue. Players sometimes mistake kindness for softness.
Craig Brown, November 1996.

I keep getting shown the England goal they scored against us which was a great goal but it was seven passes and they think that's great. We played Austria in a friendly last year and the goal McGinlay scored was about 15 passes.
Craig Brown, *The Absolute Game* fanzine, April 1997.

I never think of him as my brother. He's a guy asking me questions and it wouldn't matter who it is. It's still my job to try and answer them.
Craig Brown on being interviewed by TV commentator Jock, *The Absolute Game* fanzine, April 1997.

Without wanting to sound bombastic, the furthest the under-16s have gone in a tournament, I was the coach. The furthest the under-19 team's gone, in Chile in 1987, I was the coach. The furthest the under-21 team's ever gone, I was the coach. So I had good experience of international football.
Craig Brown, The Absolute Game fanzine, April 1997.

Most embarrassing moment: I was manager of Clyde and we were playing Forfar, whose player-boss was Archie Knox. He stood on one of our players and I ran on to the pitch and chased him to the centre circle. I was escorted off by two policemen and the referee.
Craig Brown, October 1997.

I hate sunbathing. I think it's the biggest waste of time imaginable.
Craig Brown, October 1997.

If a kid sees me getting into my car at a game he'll ask for my autograph and then more of them will turn up. But I know there's always one at the back saying, 'Who is he, anyway?'
Craig Brown, October 1997.

Craig Brown of Scotland has mastered the art of 'lowering expectations'. He learned from the mistakes of then manager Ally MacLeod who took the team to the 1978 World Cup, with the whole country thinking they'd come home champions. Brown's careful not to play up the team's triumphs, the theory being that the impact of their failures will be lessened. Most people agree he's done an excellent job so far.
Professor George Sik, a psychologist specialising in football, November 1997.

You would have thought I had murdered one of their next of kin.
Craig Brown on the reaction to him dropping Paul McStay from a Scotland squad, February 1998.

I've got three points already. This World Cup will be a skoosh.
Craig Brown after being penalised by traffic cops for stopping on the hard shoulder, March 1998.

In the team photograph he'd be very careful about where he positioned you. You knew straightaway from your position how he rated you. The nearer the middle the better. Once you got to the edge you were in trouble. He used to come up to the guy on the end and say, 'You just sit there son, a pair of scissors'll soon get rid of you!'
Craig Brown on former Dundee boss Bob Shankly, March 1998.

When people were on my back about the 'schoolmaster' thing, their comments were hopelessly out of date. I've not actually taught in a school since 1969. There's this inverted snobbery thing in Scotland; you're not allowed to be educated and in football.
Craig Brown, June 1998.

DEFEAT

It might have been 5–1.
Celtic captain **Billy McNeill** on the 1970 European Cup final, which Celtic lost 2–1 to Feyenoord, quoted in Tom Campbell and Pat Woods', *Dreams, and Songs to Sing*, 1996.

The most vivid memory was the silence of the dressing-room. I can still hear it after all these years.
John Colquhoun on Hearts losing the 1985–86 title in the last few minutes at Dundee, May 1996.

Last night I had to go back home and tell my sons that their dad still had nothing to show for 16 years in the professional game. It was a bitter pill to swallow.
Hearts' **John Robertson** after losing 4–3 to Rangers in the Coca-Cola Cup final, November 1996.

I've had only two failures in my life – the *Sunday Scot* newspaper and Rangers in Europe.
Rangers chairman **David Murray**, 6 July 1998.

I saw Dick Advocaat sitting with his head in his hands at 3–0 and that was worth the admission money alone.
Shelbourne boss **Dermot Keely** after the UEFA Cup first leg between the sides. Rangers came back to win 5–3, July 1998.

As a club Rangers were very friendly, but Advocaat was most disrespectful. It's a common courtesy for managers to shake hands at the end of a game but once the whistle went in both matches Advocaat was off like a shot down the tunnel . . . it wouldn't have taken much for him to knock on our dressing-room door and say, 'Well done'.
Shelbourne boss **Dermot Keely**, not a fan of the new Rangers coach, after Rangers had beaten the Irish side 7–3 on aggregate in the UEFA Cup, July 1998.

DIRECTORS

If I had reported what happened at board meetings no one would have believed me. They would have said Basil Fawlty wrote that.
Former Celtic chief executive **Terry Cassidy** on his time at Parkhead, quoted in Allan Caldwell, *Sack The Board!*, 1994.

I had never even been introduced to the man in all the time he was here. He never said hello to anyone or introduced himself to the players. He flew up for games and went away again.
Celtic's **Charlie Nicholas** recalls Celtic director David Smith, quoted in Allan Caldwell, *Sack The Board!*, 1994.

'Graeme, you're going now.' 'Walter, you need Durie.' 'Walter, you need McLaren.' These are the kind of strategic moves the chairman must make to ensure the smooth running of the club.
Rangers chairman **David Murray**, November 1994.

I've probably been to training once in six years, and that was once too often. The role of the chairman is not to milk the glory.
Rangers chairman **David Murray**, November 1994.

I've just filled in a questionnaire for a Celtic fanzine and they asked me, 'If you had £20m to spend on players, who would you buy?' My answer was that I would give the money to my manager because I wouldn't know a good player if he came up and kicked me in the backside.
Kilmarnock chairman **Bob Fleeting**, February 1995.

We've argued all our working life, I've thrown him out of my car and I've thrown him out of his own house. But I like to think the arguments have been for the better of the business.
Falkirk chairman **George Fulston** on manager John Lambie, 1995.

If Celtic never won another game it would be a source of enormous rejoicing to me.
Rangers vice-chairman **Donald Findlay**, March 1996.

It helps keep my feet on the ground to remember that I was on my own personal nine-in-a-row then. The club hadn't won the league since I came to Ibrox in 1978.

Rangers director Campbell Ogilvie, recalling Graeme Souness arriving at Ibrox in 1986, April 1996.

No man could have been more unassuming, more understanding and knowledgeable. He was humble in victory, magnanimous in defeat; he could always see the other person's point of view; he was the essence of courtesy at all time.

Scotland boss Craig Brown on former Clyde chairman Tom Clark, June 1996.

When we score a sublime goal I'm as happy as anyone but you don't get to enjoy a game. You can't possibly. The game's too important to enjoy.

Celtic managing director Fergus McCann, September 1996.

He would ban me from Tynecastle for life and then phone me the same night and say I'll leave you a ticket for Saturday for the Director's box as long as you don't tell the press you got the ticket from me.

Agent Bill McMurdo, recalling dealings with former Hearts chairman Wallace Mercer, *The Absolute Game* fanzine, May 1997.

New people with an entrepreneurial approach bring innovative thinking. They have a contribution to make, but how many of them are committee animals? Most are self-made, have flown by the seat of their pants and are not used to working by committee. It is anathema to ask them to work in the SFA Council. They do their own thing, and if it works for their clubs, that is fine. In the SFA there are 46 guys, not 1, making a collective decision, although the public perception is that it is me. That is entirely wrong.

SFA Chief Executive Jim Farry, August 1997.

When I came here everyone said I would pick the team but it became apparent when I was left out or substituted on more occasions than I wanted to be that I'm actually in the worst position of any player. I can't go and knock down the manager's door because I gave him the job and I trust his judgement.

Motherwell chief executive Pat Nevin, February 1999.

I've never been to a board meeting in my life. My chairman will pop into my house for a cup of tea and a blether. We do our own thing, which is rare.

Coventry boss Gordon Strachan, February 1999.

My initial impression of Fergus was that he was a nasty wee chap, and I think I had good reason.
Former Celtic striker Andy Walker on managing director Fergus McCann, April 1999.

With the previous person here I might as well have spoken to a brick wall.
Celtic's Alan Stubbs compares new chief executive Allan MacDonald with previous managing director Fergus McCann, May 1999.

Morton are 125 years old and he has wrought more havoc in the last two years than anything they had to suffer in the previous 123.
Former Morton manager Allan McGraw on chairman Hugh Scott, May 1999.

[Success] is my responsibility but it is his [David Murray's] money.
Rangers coach Dick Advocaat after winning the title, May 1999.

DOH!

No one seems to remember the goal I scored – a pretty decent header as I recall. I remember walking off at half-time, looking up at the scoreboard and seeing the scoreline, Brighton 1 Manchester United 0, with my name underneath as goalscorer. I remember thinking, 'Well, no matter what happens now I've made my mark, no one can take that away from me.'
Gordon Smith on his 1983 FA Cup final miss for Brighton against Manchester United, June 1996.

For the past 13 years I've been reminded of that miss at least once a day.
Gordon Smith.

Three years after the game I was in Malaysia when an eight-year-old boy came up to me and asked for my autograph. So I scrawled my name on a scrap of paper and handed it back to him. The kid studied it for a few seconds then turned to me and said, 'Excuse me, but are you the Gordon Smith who missed that open goal in the last minute of the Cup final?'
Gordon Smith discovers his fame is now global.

There will be more advantages for me with England.
Bradford City's Stuart McCall, 5 November 1984, after being named in Scotland's under-21 squad for a game against Spain. He'd been picked in

England's under-21 squad the same day. On 16 February 1985 he decided he wanted to play for Scotland.

Celtic should be in Europe every year, and win at least one domestic trophy every season.
New Celtic boss **Liam Brady** makes a rod for his own back, June 1991, quoted in Tom Campbell and Pat Woods' *Dreams, and Songs to Sing*, 1996. Brady failed to win a trophy as boss.

I've been looking round the land at Cambuslang trying to imagine where the first goal will be scored.
Celtic chairman **Kevin Kelly** unveils details of Celtic's prospective £100m home, April 1992.

I couldn't turn my back on Falkirk.
Falkirk boss **Jim Jefferies**, turning down the Hearts manager's job, 29 July 1995. Two days later he announced he wanted the Tynecastle job.

I can drink like a chimney.
Duncan Ferguson, quoted in John Brown's *Blue Grit*, 1995.

Drinking binges on tour. Late nights. Furious managers. Warnings and fines handed out. It all sounds like the Dons are in pretty good shape to me. I'm delighted to see a Scottish team slipping back into our bad old ways.
Rangers striker **Ally McCoist** on Aberdeen's pre-season tour high jinks, 4 August 1996. On the morning the newspaper article appeared, McCoist failed a breath test coming out of a nightclub and was subsequently fined £2,500 and banned from driving for 15 months.

We wanted a few beers so I went out to get them. I didn't realise the car was so powerful and when I came back I attempted to do a handbrake turn and bang, the car was over. It was a write-off. John [McGinlay] wasn't too keen on the car anyway.
Victor Kasule recalls a slight problem with his Shrewsbury team-mate's car, October 1996.

I'm always faintly offended when someone says they've seen the worst penalty and it's not mine.
Pat Nevin recalling a penalty for Chelsea against Manchester City which barely reached the opposing goalkeeper, October 1996.

One of the other guys . . . I'm not going to drop him in it . . . Ian Ferguson, he said it's that . . . so I just went like that. I didn't know anything about it.
Paul Gascoigne on miming playing the flute against Steaua Bucharest, in the TV documentary, *Gazza's Coming Home*, October 1998.

World According To Boy From Barlinnie
Headline in *The Independent* reviewing George Graham's autobiography, 1996. Graham is from Bargeddie, some way from Glasgow's prison.

You can't win titles with kids.
TV pundit **Alan Hansen,** on the opening day of 1995–96 season, after Manchester United's youthful side had lost 3–1 at Aston Villa.

Yes, I was wrong.
Alan Hansen, April 1996, after United won the title.

It doesn't look as if they're going to let me forget that line. It was printed up on a Manchester United T-shirt. Kids still come up to me and ask me to write it down in their autograph books. That's the problem with giving out opinions on the telly. Everyone remembers it when you get it wrong. Not that it bothers me. If that's what I'm remembered for so be it.
Alan Hansen, October 1997.

Which newspaper are you from?
Andy Roxburgh's wife to Rangers' John Brown, before the match against Portugal in October 1992. Brown had been given a message to call Roxburgh, who'd called him into the Scotland squad, quoted in *Blue Grit*, 1995.

Most Embarrassing Moment: Being asked to name three Rangers players with a 'z' in their name and missing out myself.
Ayr United manager **Gordon Dalziel,** newspaper questionnaire, September 1996.

John Collins, who plays for Monaco, we're familiar with, aren't we? Played in Euro '96, formerly played for Rangers and Hibs . . .
BBC's **Des Lynam** at half-time of the Newcastle v Monaco UEFA Cup quarter-final, 4 March 1997. He apologised for his error within five minutes (presumably before the switchboard exploded).

I hate missing any kick-off and have done ever since Rangers played Montrose in the Summer Cup years ago. It was a two-leg affair and Rangers seemed to be cantering to a 2–1 aggregate win. When the whistle

blew I was on the way out when I suddenly spotted the teams lining up again. Montrose had scored an early goal before I'd arrived; it's embarrassing when it turns out a football man doesn't even know the score.
Alex Ferguson, *A Will To Win – The Manager's Diary,* 1997.

How do you think he is? He's scored an own goal at Easter Road and missed a penalty tonight. He'll be all right after a couple of years in Siberia.
Airdrie boss **Alex MacDonald** after striker Steve Cooper's misfortunes in the relegation play-offs against Hibs, May 1997.

I was going past the dug-out and MacDonald gave me a kick. It was on my left leg, my good one. I thanked him for the three points and told him to have a nice journey home.
Dundee's **Dave Rogers** accuses Airdrie boss Alex MacDonald after Rogers had scored in the 1–0 win for Dundee, 4 October 1997.

Anyone who remembers what I was like as a player would know that if I had kicked him he would have been stretchered off.
MacDonald's response, denying Rogers' claims, 4 October 1997.

Allegations which were made at the end of the game have now been shown to be unsubstantiated and unfounded. I don't know why the player made these allegations. Perhaps he was over-excited in the situation at the end of the game.
Dundee manager **John McCormack** apologises and brings an end to one of the season's more bizarre incidents, 6 October 1997.

The only thing they should discuss [in Scotland] is how long they're going to play the League each year before giving the Championship trophy to Rangers.
Former Dundee chairman **Ron Dixon,** February 1998. Celtic won the title three months later.

Shortly after Ian Rush joined Liverpool I said to a friend, 'He can't head it, and he hasn't got a left foot or a right foot.' Five years later he'd broken every goalscoring record there was.
Former Liverpool defender **Alan Hansen,** March 1999.

Whenever I play in London, I always get Seaman rammed down my throat.
Coventry's **Gary McAllister's** unfortunate choice of words, on fan taunts about his penalty miss at Euro '96, March 1999.

I haven't given it much thought. To be honest, I'm more interested in England's game at Wembley.
Former *Magpie* presenter **Tommy Boyd**, after being asked on Radio Five about his preparations for Scotland's European Championship match against the Czech Republic, 27 March 1999. Radio Five thought they were interviewing the Scotland defender.

If you think about them [Scotland] in English terms they are the West Ham of world football – they never quite perform to their full potential.
Sports minister **Tony Banks** calls for a united Britain football team, 28 April 1999.

Tony Banks has been yellow-carded in the past for talking out of turn to the Scottish people but it's obviously made no difference.
SNP spokeswoman **Kim Nicoll** responds to Banks, 28 April 1999.

ESTONIA

We hardly got over the halfway line all day.
Scotland boss **Craig Brown's** dry assessment of the three-second Estonia v Scotland match, October 1996.

If any part of the process or the World Cup organising committee itself was chaired by one of our group rivals then I would have thought FIFA's protocol should have to be reviewed. We spend a lot of money on fair play and that is not just about cards and badges. Fair play is the basic ethos of our whole sport. There will be a time for reflection by certain individuals on whether that tenet of responsibility has been followed.
SFA Chief Executive **Jim Farry** on FIFA's decision to replay the Estonia match – a decision taken with FIFA's Swedish vice-president Lennart Johansson on the committee, November 1996. Sweden were in the same World Cup section as Scotland.

Looking back, it is questionable if I should have chaired or even attended the FIFA meeting but honestly, isn't it irrelevant?
Lennart Johansson on the Estonia decision, December 1996.

I heard the score on the radio and I almost crashed my car.
Lebanon boss **Terry Yorath** on hearing of Scotland's draw in Monaco, February 1997. Lebanon had beaten Estonia 2–0 the previous match.

We heard that some of the Scotland players said it was good that FIFA ordered a replay because then they would score more goals than the 3–0 win in Tallinn. We thought, 'Right, we'll try extra hard – let's see who is the strongest team.'
Estonia goalkeeper **Mart Poom**, March 1997.

It was a horrible game.
Scotland captain **Gary McAllister** on the 0–0 draw in Monaco.

Do you think this was God's revenge for what happened in Tallinn?
Estonian journalist to **Craig Brown** after the draw in Monaco, 11 February 1997.

Scotland deserved to lose after their disgraceful pleading to FIFA.
Estonian newspaper *Eesti Paevaleht* after the 0–0 draw.

They are a bottom-of-the-First-Division side and St Johnstone would rip them to shreds. These players are not international quality at all and if we don't beat them then we may as well give up.
Danny McDermid on Estonia, March 1997. An FA qualified Class 1 referee from Arbroath, he is also a British Army staff sergeant. He'd refereed them in a friendly against Latvians Skonto Riga at their Cypriot training camp.

The floodlights were inappropriate. Not winning the rescheduled game has nothing to do with it. I never complained, I'll make it quite clear. All I said to the observer was could we see the lights on.
Craig Brown, *The Absolute Game* fanzine, April 1997.

As for the SFA, they're full of talk and menace when it comes to sticking a 20-year ban on an under-16 goalie who is having a fly fag when his team is up the other end of the park but oh so ready to tug their forelock at FIFA when they come down shamefully on the side of a bunch of cowboys who could teach the Russian mafia a thing or two.
Alex Horsburgh, *The Absolute Game* fanzine, April 1997.

EURO '96

Bagpipes and claymores won't win us games in the European Championships.
Scotland boss **Craig Brown**, April 1994.

We got off the plane from America and there were hundreds of Press there. It was like 'Scots in Sober Sensation'.
Striker Ally McCoist on England's pre-tournament problems on a flight back from the Far East.

From Princess Anne
To Gavin Hastings
With the strikers on form
Let's dish out the pastings.
Hugh Reid and the Velvet Underpants, in song 'Craig Brown's Tartan Army', before Euro '96.

When we played Holland we were driving to Villa Park in the coach and there was a load of Scotland fans on an embankment. There's a few had cans and the radio on, getting their faces painted with the St Andrew's flag. And Brian Martin, who'd been in the team but he'd been left out of the squad, well, Brian Martin's there with a Scotland flag around his neck and a tartan bunnet on. We all spotted him and everyone on the bus was: 'Hey! it's Brian Martin! Big Buff's out there!' And he's had a couple of drinks, and everyone on the bus is shouting towards this one fella. And the funny thing is we've seen him before he's seen us.
Colin Hendry, June 1998.

I remember leading up to the game Davids and Seedorf had said, 'We don't know any of their players', and I think coming off the pitch there were one or two of our players going, 'Well, you know us now.'
Colin Hendry after the Holland game.

If the truth were known, I didn't particularly want to shake hands with them. We were about to do battle with another nation. There was a lot of pride at stake and a lot of passion at stake. You've got no friends when you play against a team like that.
Stuart Pearce on handshaking with the Scots before the Wembley match. Pearce very publicly looked the other way as he went down the line to shake hands.

The ten minutes at the start of the second-half when they allegedly overran us is a myth.
Craig Brown, *The Absolute Game* fanzine, April 1997.

I thought I actually got the ball. It was a very impetuous thing to do and I don't recommend it. Going back, I'd rather not have done it. That situation was very impulsive and if I'd had time to think I wouldn't have done it, would I?
England's Tony Adams on the tackle on Gordon Durie which brought about Scotland's Wembley penalty.

At the last minute the ball started gently rolling and it flashed through my mind, 'Is he going to stop?'
David Seaman facing McAllister's penalty.

It didn't roll. If you were a golfer on a green on a windy day, it was just a flicker. It didn't really move. I'm not using that as an excuse. That didn't cause me to miss.
Gary McAllister.

I went to blast it high up down the middle and I simply didn't get it high enough. The ball moved. I did notice it. Half an inch higher and it's a goal. So if it made a difference it was unbelievable bad luck. But it wasn't a great penalty. I'll put my hand up and say that.
Gary McAllister, November 1997.

I know there are far more important things in life than football but if you cut me open and had a look inside right now it wouldn't be a pretty sight. I don't know if I can sink any lower.
Gary McAllister after his penalty miss.

I got correspondence that Ally McCoist should have taken the penalty. But here in Scotland Ally McCoist should do everything.
Craig Brown.

He [McAllister] quickly got dressed and got out into the bus and sat there on his own. One of the backroom boys went and sat with him but he didn't feel like talking to anybody. But after an hour or so he came out of the bus and did interviews. I admired him greatly for that.
Craig Brown, *The Absolute Game* fanzine, April 1997.

Gary McAllister missing the penalty against England in Euro '96? He'll never forget about it. He'll put it to the back of his mind but it will always be there.
Don Masson, who missed Scotland's penalty against Peru in the Argentina World Cup, quoted in Mike Wilson, *Don't Cry For Me Argentina*, 1998.

You've got to hold your hands up sometimes and say, 'Yeah, great piece of skill'.
Colin Hendry on Paul Gascoigne's Wembley goal.

There are only one or two players who can do that in the world and Paul's one of them.
Alan Shearer on Gascoigne's goal.

It got him out of jail really, because he had a crap championship.
Colin Hendry on Gascoigne's goal, September 1996.

The first thing that entered my mind was that we'd been representing my country and we'd been beaten by England at Wembley.
Colin Hendry.

The difference between the two teams was Shearer.
Craig Brown, The Absolute Game fanzine, April 1997.

A boxer who's ahead on points and gets knocked out loses the fight.
England boss **Terry Venables** after being told Scotland had won eight corners to England's two and had 55 per cent of the play, June 1996.

The singing of 'Flower of Scotland' in Wembley Stadium, broadcast live around the world, was a wonderful slap in the face of the Union. I was almost moved to join in . . . if we'd been drawn in a group without Scotland I fear the English team performance might never have risen above mollusc level.
Singer **Billy Bragg** during Euro '96.

Q: Favourite moment from the last decade?
A: Ally McCoist's goal against Switzerland at Villa Park.
Craig Brown, The Absolute Game fanzine questionnaire, March 1997.

I suddenly found myself out on the touchline but I don't really know how I got there.
Craig Brown on the goal against Switzerland, August 1996.

Football's a great game but moments like this make it so difficult. There are a lot of tears in the dressing-room.
Colin Hendry as Scotland came close to qualifying for the second round.

My heart bleeds for them. Never mind.
A smiling **Alan Shearer** on Scotland's Euro '96 exit, quoted in Total Sport, August 1996.

I just can't bear to be staying in England while the Championships are still on, especially with the English doing so well.
Colin Hendry speaks for a nation, 1996.

It was a disappointment rather than a hurt when we failed so narrowly. I'd have hated to go down there and lose badly in the games and have ignominious failure. But I don't want glorious failure. I'd rather be lucky and fluke your way there.
Craig Brown.

What went through my mind was that the fans had backed us well for three games. Most of the players weren't feeling sorry for themselves, mostly for people who'd spent good money, because it wasn't cheap to go and watch games in Euro '96. We just wanted a wee bit of glory for them.
Gary McAllister.

I don't honestly think it was a top standard tournament, in terms of quality of play. Even the Germans who won it were very functional.
Craig Brown, *The Absolute Game* fanzine, April 1997.

Scotland also emerged from the tournament with great credit. Their smooth-passing game won them a host of new admirers, and Andy Goram finally nailed the joke about Scottish goalkeepers with his outstanding performances. They were unlucky not to qualify for the quarter-finals and can look forward to the 1998 World Cup in France with optimism.
Prime Minister **John Major** on Euro '96, 1 July 1996.

EUROPE

It was a hard match. People see the score and think it was easy but they scored first and we had to work hard.
Real Madrid's **Ferenc Puskas** on the 1960 European Cup final against Eintracht Frankfurt at Hampden, April 1997.

It was an honour and a privilege to be part of it.
Real's **Alfredo di Stefano** on the 1960 European Cup final, April 1997.

Ronnie [Simpson] looked like an old man, even older without his teeth; Bertie [Auld] walked like a cripple and wee Jimmy [Johnstone] was a midget. We came into the tunnel and the Italians were standing there

wearing a beautiful blue and black strip, cutaway boots, oiled thighs gleaming in the sun and all that. This group of odd allsorts came out opposite them and wee Jimmy is shouting to the defender Facchetti – and this is perfectly true – he's shouting: 'Haw, big man, efter the gemme, swap the jerseys.'
Celtic defender Jim Craig on the 1967 European Cup final, June 1997.

We had the only bus driver in the whole of Portugal who didn't know the way to the national stadium. Suddenly all the players started shouting, 'Hey boss, why is everybody else going the other way?'
Jim Craig on the 1967 European Cup final, June 1997.

One of their players was allegedly struck by a missile from the crowd and came out after half-time with his head swathed in bandages. He looked like Tutankhamun.
Brian McClair, recalling Celtic European Cup-winners Cup tie against Rapid Vienna in November 1984, *Odd Man Out*, 1997.

The best atmosphere I'd ever played in. Anywhere.
Graeme Souness on the September 1987 Rangers v Dynamo Kiev European Cup tie, April 1996.

The worst experience of my career.
Rangers' **Brian Laudrup** on playing in Italy, 1997.

My pillow was like an After Eight mint.
Brian McClair on an Austrian hotel room, *Odd Man Out*, 1997.

All the talking I've done about not giving the ball away, about the importance of possession of the ball in Europe, came home to them. Because if you don't keep possession you are chasing about all night.
Manchester United boss **Alex Ferguson** reflects on the 4–0 November 1994 drubbing by Barcelona in *A Year in The Life – A Manager's Diary*, 1996.

If they play like that in the Champions' League I don't see them winning any of their games.
Anorthosis Famagusta midfielder **Dimitris Assiotis** after losing 1–0 to Rangers in the European Cup, August 1995. He was right. Rangers drew three and lost three.

I don't think we've fallen behind; they've advanced. They looked at the European results of the 70s and 80s and said, 'We are better players, more skilful, how do they keep getting results against us? What have they got?'

Now they work like hell for each other and are more aggressive. Twenty years ago they were all good players but there were always a couple of lazy ones and that was how you overcame them. Now every single one of them works. That's the difference.
Celtic's John Collins on foreign players, March 1996.

When you go abroad you can't be Johnny Foreigner. You've got to be one of them. If they're eating funny things on plates, then you eat funny things on plates.
Former Barcelona striker **Steve Archibald**, April 1996.

I asked for time to think about it – about 0.1 of a second!
Paul Lambert, then with Motherwell, recalling being offered a three-year contract by Borussia Dortmund, August 1996.

They were here for a holiday.
Grasshopper Zurich striker **Kubilay Turkyilmaz** on Rangers after helping his side win 3–0 in the Champions' League, September 1996.

It's not just Rangers. It's not just Scotland. Look at Blackburn. £30m to build a team to win the English League then they go out to Trelleborgs, a team you didn't even know existed.
Former Dundee United boss **Ivan Golac** on British teams in Europe, October 1996.

It got a bit chilly here after Christmas, mind. There was even a bit of frost on the ground at training one day.
John Collins on life with Monaco, June 1997.

People say 'You always get into the Champions' League,' but it's very difficult, you know. In the seasons when English clubs had to prequalify, none of them did so. It's only because they get in automatically now that they get there all the time.
Rangers boss **Walter Smith**, August 1997.

I keep it at home because I think if you put it in a bank you would put the memory away with it.
Borussia Dortmund's **Paul Lambert** on his European Cup-winners' medal, September 1997.

I've been to a few countries where the football would bore you rigid because they don't take any risks.
Kilmarnock boss **Bobby Williamson**, February 1999.

The biggest disappointment of my entire time here was losing to FC Zurich in the UEFA Cup last autumn. We had beaten a better team in the previous round [Portugal's Vitoria Guimaraes] and we knew even from the first leg at home that we were much better than the Swiss . . . I sat there knowing that we were going out of the UEFA Cup to an inferior team.
Celtic managing director Fergus McCann reflects just before leaving Celtic, April 1999.

FAME

You have to remember he was the first football pop star. Nobody had been in that position before so no one knew how to handle it. He was also the guy who used to come in with his legs black and blue after every game and never reported an injury.
Martin Buchan on George Best, April 1996.

Footballers today are bigger than pop stars. Giorgio Armani would never have looked at a footballer in my day.
Graeme Souness, April 1996.

I wasn't addicted to coke. I was addicted to the lifestyle.
Frank McAvennie on his cocaine days.

Go to his house. The gates are locked but there will still be somebody sitting outside waiting for him. No one else I know lives with that kind of attention.
Rangers chairman **David Murray** on Paul Gascoigne, April 1997.

It wasn't just the odd person who called me it, it was absolutely everybody. I got pelters in the dressing-room, away fans would shout it at me, even people in the street would shout it at me.
Morton's **Owen Archdeacon** on his resemblance to TV's Mr Bean, December 1997.

I now know why Rod Stewart and Sean Connery don't stay in Scotland. You can't get any peace. We're sitting ducks.
Andy Goram after withdrawing from Scotland's World Cup squad, May 1998.

He [Rod Stewart] embarrasses me by calling me 'Mr Brown'. 'Can I join in with training, Mr Brown?'
Craig Brown, July 1998.

The majority of [Scottish] supporters understood that when Craig Burley was red-carded against Morocco it was the clumsy challenge of a lad flogging his guts out in a beaten team, but in the south they seem to be obsessed with finding heroes, putting them on a pedestal and then shooting them down in flames at the merest hint they might be getting too big for their boots.
Motherwell's Brian McClair, July 1998.

They'd bring out a big form and it was a case of 'Right son, what's your name and what position do you play?' I'm not being ba' heided, and I know I'm fat and old-looking, but I had hoped that at 34 and having scored nearly 200 goals for league clubs, they might have known a little about me.
Much-travelled striker **Willie Watters**, on meeting junior club secretaries prior to signing for his eleventh senior club, Stenhousemuir, August 1998.

You shouldn't be seen drunk as a football player, it's not on. If you want to get drunk, lock yourself in the house. If you're getting 100 times more than the average wage, it's celebrity status and you're there to be picked on. If you want to be a celebrity, stick yourself on the celebrity pages, but if you want to be a footballer, be a footballer.
Coventry boss **Gordon Strachan**, August 1998.

FAMILY

I believe my greatest success would be to be a good father to my children, a good husband to my wife, a good son to my mother, brother to my sisters, uncle to my nephews and nieces.
Celtic boss **Tommy Burns**, November 1994.

I took a long look at Claire and the girls that night and realised how much I wanted to enjoy my time with them.
Charlie Nicholas recalling the night Davie Cooper collapsed with a brain haemorrhage while filming a coaching video with Nicholas, April 1995.

My mother came to watch me one day when I was about 13 years old. Later she told me, 'Don't try to copy your father. That's the worst thing you can do because I can't stand him on the pitch!'
Rangers' **Brian Laudrup** on father Finn, September 1996.

My brother played for Hearts. All right, he only played one first-team game but he was a good player.
Graeme Souness, April 1996.

My dad's great – he never asked for anything, apart from a house, 740BMW, a boat and a canny wage.
Paul Gascoigne, in TV documentary, *Gazza's Coming Home,* October 1996.

My family comes first and foremost, football a long, long way behind.
Coventry boss **Gordon Strachan,** January 1997.

I won't say I'll definitely pick Gavin until he does something about his room. It's a real tip and it's driving his mum crazy.
Gordon Strachan, preparing to give son Gavin his first start for Coventry, February 1998.

I'm aware of that the TV audience will be against Brazil but it's not important. The only people I will think about watching the game are my parents, my wife and my children. They are the audience who really matter.
Colin Hendry, June 1998.

It was an unbelievable thrill meeting him, especially as I took my wife to see *The Godfather* on our honeymoon.
Arbroath chairman **John Christison,** March 1999, on a visit to the club by Hollywood actor Robert Duvall, who was researching a part.

FANS

I must also pay tribute to the spectators. Most were neutral, but they encouraged us to keep raising the standard of play.
Real Madrid's **Ferenc Puskas** on the 1960 European Cup final, April 1997.

I love people's company. I love talking to people. I enjoy them coming up as long as they are pleasant. Once they come up and start taking liberties, which the Scottish public is apt to do, then you have got to start drawing the line.
Rangers' **Ally McCoist,** June 1994.

I wasn't very popular when I came into the Manchester United team because I wasn't as flamboyant as Alex Forsyth, whom I had replaced. There was an FA Cup tie when we beat Newcastle 7–0 at Old Trafford. It was 3–0 at half-time and I got the fourth soon after. I ran toward the crowd to celebrate and saw this man with his head pushed against the red railings they had then. He was shouting, 'I hate you, Nicholl.' It turned out that he had never forgiven me for scoring an own goal in a Manchester derby.
Raith Rovers boss **Jimmy Nicholl,** March 1995.

The son asked me to come round and see the guy, who was a Celtic fan, and I did. I brought along some pennants and badges, then I went back to Scotland and, I must admit, clean forgot about it, That November I got a letter from the son. His dad had lived much longer than anyone had expected him to, and all he talked about for the last six months of his life was that a Celtic player had been to see him. Not 'Jim Craig', but a Celtic player. It's hard for players: you're fighting with the manager, you're injured, you're carrying an injury, you're coming back from injury, and it's very much a job. You forget that that other side of football is a tremendous thing.
Former Celtic star **Jim Craig** recalls visiting an ill fan in Ulster, quoted in Simon Kuper, *Football Against The Enemy,* 1994.

Q: What's the most trouble you've taken to attend a football match?
A: The last time we beat England at Wembley in 1985 1–0, when John Robertson got the penalty, I flew all the way back from Hong Kong. I got to Wembley an hour before the kick-off.
Rod Stewart in a magazine questionnaire, August 1998.

At birth, God asks you if you want logic or passion. If you want passion then He next allocates you a football team to support.
Hearts' **John Colquhoun,** March 1996.

'One team in Tallinn, there's only one team in Tallinn.'
The indefatigable Tartan Army when Estonia failed to turn up to face Scotland in the World Cup, October 1996.

It is the only slavery I am enchained by.
New Yorker writer, poet and Hearts fan **Alastair Reid** on listening to Scottish football results on the World Service, November 1996.

By now I had decided I had to do something so conspicuous that there was no possibility of my actions being missed or considered accidental by [ref] Mike Reid being in a charitable mood as it was a friendly. As the ball winged across, I rose like a swallow to bat the ball away with my hand. At

last the whistle blew and the ref pointed to the spot. Not everyone had cottoned on. A friend in the crowd told me later that someone sitting next to them turned round and said: 'Do you think he meant to do that?'
Brian McClair on conceding a penalty so Coventry's David Busst could score in his testimonial game, in *Odd Man Out*, 1996.

I was frightened to death by the fans.
Rangers' **Brian Laudrup** recalling life in Italy, 1997.

Q: If you could buy a football team, who would it be?
A: Celtic. I've been a Celtic supporter for 25 years, since I first met Kenny Dalglish, when he was playing for them in 1971. Yes, I remember playing football on *Top of the Pops*. I wanted to make things different from the run-of-the-mill fucking shit that was on the programme then.
Rod Stewart, January 1997.

One of the worst things I've heard in Scottish football.
Rangers boss **Walter Smith** after a section of Aberdeen's travelling support sang a song during a minute's silence for Ibrox legend George Young, who died two days before, January 1997.

I have never been so embarrassed as I was then to be part of Leeds United. It was a grotesque and disgraceful dishonour by a few to one of the men who has done more for football in this country than almost anyone else.
Gary McAllister on Leeds fans ignoring the minute's silence for Sir Matt Busby in January 1994, quoted from *Captain's Log*, 1995.

The sound of 50,000 committed, partisan people is incredibly exciting, a sort of exhilarating cacophony. I love to hear the rise and fall of the fans' chants. I'm continually thinking about it as an inspiration for new music, an opera maybe.
Scottish composer and Celtic fan **James MacMillan**, February 1997.

The essential code of conduct for all Scotland supporters after a humiliating result:
i. Hang around stadium until nearly everyone's buggered off.
ii. Clasp hand firmly to chin and look pissed off.
iii. Do not move until a photographer's got at least half a dozen pictures of you.
The Absolute Game fanzine, April 1997.

Some of the songs are brilliant. I can remember way back when Arsenal had a player called Sammy Nelson who had bared his backside to the fans.

So they were playing Rangers on the Wednesday night. I was at Ibrox with a 70,000 crowd at this annual fixture, 25–30 years ago, and out came Sammy with the Arsenal team and the chant went up – 'Sammy, Sammy show us your arse.' I like the humorous ones, but I don't think you need to abuse folk.
Craig Brown, *The Absolute Game* fanzine, April 1997.

I played for Celtic for 18 months and never got a cheer from their fans like I did that night.
John Colquhoun recalling missing a penalty for Hearts against Celtic in a League Cup shoot-out, September 1997.

Celtic have gone public, many of their fans have stumped up money to buy shares, which in turn has helped to finance their stadium. As a result, I sometimes think their supporters feel greater loyalty to the cause. Rangers fans basically got the stadium for nothing, and some of them have had it too easy for too long.
Rangers chairman **David Murray**, October 1997.

Celtic fans are about as loyal to their team as Philby, Burgess and Maclean were to the British Expire.
Rangers' *Aye Ready* fanzine, 1990s.

You can sing 'Live Forever' and get a good feeling. I don't know whether you can get a good feeling out of 'Follow Follow'.
Creation Records boss (and Rangers fan) **Alan McGee**, February 1998.

The saddest thing about going to Ibrox is when Rangers score a goal and people sing 'The Sash'. It's sad, too, that all the cool people support Celtic, but what can you do?
Alan McGee, February 1998.

It really hit home to me when we went up to Scotland and played a pre-season friendly at Dunfermline and Gary got booed every time he got the ball. What was that about? What right do these people have to do that? What have they ever done for Scottish football? If you put all these people who criticise Gary together – all of them – their patriotism is nowhere near the patriotism that man has for his country.
Coventry boss **Gordon Strachan** on criticism of skipper Gary McAllister, February 1999.

There are people who will try to appeal to the extremist attitude, this hide-bound attitude. One opponent [of my regime] was quoted as saying, 'This

is an Irish–Catholic club' – he hoped to get this headbanger group as his support, then point to our anti-bigotry campaign and say, 'How dare they tell us how to behave. We can sing the songs we want.' But he got a very bad response from the majority of supporters.
Celtic managing director Fergus McCann, February 1999.

Those songs are anti-Scottish. They have no connection with football, no connection with Celtic. This is not a political organisation.
Celtic managing director Fergus McCann, February 1999.

The crowd was blasé. The Liverpool crowd at that time was the quietest of the lot. They were spoilt.
Former Anfield defender Alan Hansen, March 1999.

We had to be careful what we said on the park because the crowd could hear us, they were so quiet.
Aberdeen midfielder Andreas Mayer on playing in Norwegian football, March 1999.

When it comes to the crunch they're brilliant, but their support is a bit like their singing – they chant with enthusiasm for a couple of lines then it fizzles out.
St Johnstone midfielder Kieran McAnespie on the Perth club's fans, April 1999.

They know nothing about football. They probably have to wash the dishes and do the hoovering when they're at home.
Ayr United manager Gordon Dalziel after home fans booed the team during a 2-1 defeat by Falkirk, 24 April 1999.

FERGIE (1)

Plenty of Accies fans shout worse things than Fergie. But he shouts for the whole 90 minutes. It never lets up. It's one and a half hours of vehement verbal abuse.
Hamilton Accies secretary Scott Struthers on Scotland's maddest fan, Ian Russell (aka Fergie), December 1996.

He's harmless. He's not violent or anything; he just shouts all the time. At Accies players. Or ex-Accies guys who are now playing for the opposition.

Or referees, the police, stewards, at everybody, basically. At away games he's usually thrown out after half an hour.
Accies fan Craig Duguid, December 1996.

Fuck off, I paid to get in here with my pension. You're all a bunch of wankers.
Fergie gives a Stenhousemuir steward some of his inimitable invective, Stenhousemuir v Hamilton, December 1996.

I just can't help myself. I don't know why I'm doing it. It's just that every time my team gets beat, I go berserk. I crack up.
Fergie, December 1996.

Q: Favourite moment from the last decade?
A: Fergie offering Graeme Souness a consoling handshake outside Douglas Park amid press reports of the latter's marital problems, then poignantly remarking, 'So ye'll no' be gettin' yer nookie then?'
Donald Anderson, *The Absolute Game* questionnaire, March 1997.

The ban was reimposed then and won't be lifted in the foreseeable future.
The long-suffering **Scott Struthers** on Fergie's latest ban (in March 1994) from Hamilton's home games.

(At the time of writing an uneasy truce appears to have descended on relations between the club and their number-one fan. 'He's as well behaved as ever,' said secretary Scott Struthers in August 1998, a tone of weary resignation in his voice. 'I had him on the phone yesterday, screaming abuse because we wouldn't leave him a complementary ticket for home games. It lasted until his ten pence ran out . . .')

FERGIE (2)

You've got to be firm, but occasionally he needs an arm around him. If he gets the feeling he's not wanted, he'll play havoc.
Maurice Malpas on his former Dundee United team-mate, August 1993.

To go from housing scheme or suburban obscurity to sporting fame and fortune is a transformation that wreaks havoc. Suddenly, they have more money than they can spend. Suddenly, they are fêted and acclaimed.

Suddenly, they seem to have unlimited access to anyone and anything. Suddenly, the door in the pokey is clanging shut behind them.
Journalist **Graham Spiers** on Duncan Ferguson's problems and the nature of fame, *Scotland on Sunday.*

I don't think he's a bad lad at all, it's just that things got on top of him in Scotland. Perhaps he was something of a marked man in Glasgow. I think it might do him good to get away from there. I don't think he's as bad as he's painted – he couldn't be.
Everton boss **Joe Royle** after signing Ferguson, 1994.

He's asked me not to go down there [to England] because he's off drinking and not planning to go out.
Former minder **Stephen Dennehy,** October 1994. Six weeks later Ferguson was stopped by police on Merseyside, admitted drink-driving, and was fined £500.

A lot of people have ridiculed his [Ferguson's] purchase. We paid £3.75m for a 22-year-old we believed would help us to continue playing the way we do with Mark Hateley. What happened was that the moment we bought Duncan, Mark started playing like a £4m player and Ferguson couldn't get into the team.
Rangers chairman **David Murray,** November 1994.

We're not so naïve as to suggest that Duncan has been an angel, but Scotland is a small country and he's been under a fair bit of pressure.
Rangers chairman **David Murray,** November 1994.

He definitely made contact and I have a cut inside my lip to prove it.
Raith Rovers' **John McStay** after being head-butted by Ferguson, Rangers v Raith Rovers, 16 April, 1994.

I stepped forward, misjudged my distance and my head came into contact with Mr McStay. I made slight contact with his forehead and he fell to the ground.
Ferguson, giving evidence after being charged with assault on Raith Rovers' John McStay.

Such behaviour cannot be tolerated. You are in a prominent position and you are looked up to by younger people.
Sheriff Alexander Eccles hands Ferguson the first-ever jail sentence for on-field violence: three months in Barlinnie, 11 October 1996. After an appeal failed, he served 45 days.

I am very disappointed that a young man who has a job and is no danger to society has been sent to prison.
Everton chairman **Peter Johnson**, 1995.

You can look back to that day and think that if ref Kenny Clark had been harsher and red-carded Dunc' none of this would have happened.
Rangers team-mate **Ian Durrant**, *Blue & White Dynamite – The Ian Durrant Story*, 1998.

Anyone who knows him will tell you he's a very pleasant young man and isn't a bad lad at all. He's been guilty sometimes of stupidity but mostly of immaturity. Consider that a young man who is certainly no danger to society is now behind bars with hardened criminals.
Everton boss **Joe Royle** on Ferguson's jail term.

He's a very deep boy, sensitive even. We'd go down to dinner some nights and chat and that would be the only time he'd speak to you for three days.
Rangers (and Everton) team-mate **Ian Durrant**, *Blue & White Dynamite – The Ian Durrant Story*, 1998.

He took part in a move we were rehearsing and, after his first touch, he shouted across to Andy Roxburgh who was the boss at the time: 'Sair tae,' he yelled, and walked off. 'Sair tae' in English translates into 'sore toe', but rather than call the physio on or say to Andy what was happening, he just shouted across and disappeared.
Gary McAllister on Ferguson's first Scotland training session, *Captain's Log*, 1995.

What can you say about him? Where do you want me to start? He's the softest lad I've met in a long tine.
Everton keeper **Neville Southall** on Ferguson, May 1996.

Everything in life is shallow apart from Duncan Ferguson. He is God.
Mansun lead singer **Paul Draper**, November 1996.

A player who makes ten minutes with Alan Shearer feel like an audience with Peter Ustinov.
Bill Borrows, *Goal Magazine*, after a difficult encounter with Ferguson, August 1997.

It's not that he doesn't like the press. It's just that he doesn't like talking to them.
Everton boss **Joe Royle** on Ferguson's refusal to speak to the media.

A boy in a man's body.
Everton goalkeeper Neville Southall.

A career which has stopped and started more often than a Damon Hill racing car has seen Ferguson earn only seven caps in five years. Not only has he not scored in that time, but Scotland themselves have only scored in two of the seven games in question. So much for the 'provider not scorer' theory.
Nigel Grant, *The Absolute Game* fanzine, November 1997.

You don't expect a player to do that. You maybe expect a bit of pushing and shoving but not that. Ferguson's a hard player but there's hard and being silly, isn't there? I wouldn't call what he did football. I don't mind people being hard but there's a limit.
Spurs' Sol Campbell on an encounter with Ferguson which left him with an injured shoulder, January 1998.

I've retired from playing for Scotland. Nothing has changed. It's the status quo. That's it. You can write that in your newspaper.
Ferguson to journalist, April 1999.

FERGIE (3)

A throat lozenge, hard on the outside and soft and runny in the middle.
Brian McClair on Alex Ferguson, *Odd Man Out,* 1997.

Nihil Sine Labor (Nothing Without Work)
Motto from the Govan shipyard which hangs on the wall of Alex Ferguson's Old Trafford office.

It was wrong, as there had to be a two-thirds majority, but they didn't know that.
Alex Ferguson recalling casting the crucial vote to strike while working as an apprentice toolmaker in the Remington Rand typewriter factory in 1961, October 1996.

We played quizzes for nights before, although Fergie had to win every time otherwise we would never have got to our beds. Trivial Pursuit? He was the biggest cheat in the world at that and disputed every answer.
Alex McLeish on Alex Ferguson during Aberdeen's run to the Cup-winners Cup final.

Under Fergie we were strong mentally and had to be as we were up against the Old Firm, the media and the whole shebang. We closed ranks, didn't talk to the press. We were our own wee unit against the world and it worked.
Former Aberdeen striker **Steve Archibald**, April 1996.

He wanted control of everything. At Pittodrie he'd know how many toilet rolls we used in a week.
Former Aberdeen striker **Mark McGhee** on Ferguson, October 1996.

He seemed, even back then, to like mobile full-backs, midfield steel and a wide left player.
Ferguson's former assistant at Aberdeen, **Pat Stanton**, August 1998.

He fined John Hewitt for overtaking him in his car after training . . . I was in Fergie's car and I'm sure he hadn't noticed until we started winding him up about it. He was just humming away to his Frank Sinatra tapes.
Alex McLeish on Ferguson, August 1998.

If Lew Grade made the office by six in the morning at 80 years of age then I can make it at eight.
Ferguson, October 1996.

The FA Cup probably saved my job. It would have been easy to sack me. Nobody would have been surprised and I couldn't have complained – I'd had a good crack at it.
Ferguson on the 1990 Cup win, October 1996.

Why should they be bothered with interviews at 18 years of age? Ask any parent if they would be happy having their boy the focus of newspaper and magazine articles and personal appearances to open shops. They don't want all that.
Alex Ferguson, 1992.

I don't think anyone else in football would have got the sentence Eric got, unless they had killed Bert Millichip's dog.
Alex Ferguson on Eric Cantona's six-month ban, 1995.

I can meet managers and monarchs and my children are not much impressed but when we met Alex Ferguson, they realised there was some point.
Labour leader **Tony Blair**, 1995.

We are playing Nottingham Forest on Thursday and Alex Ferguson objected to that. The game was fixed up four months ago. That sort of stuff – we're bigger than that. We've never resorted to that. I have kept really quiet, but I tell you something, he went down in my estimation after that. And I'll tell him this – we're still fighting for this title. He has to go to Middlesbrough and get something. And I tell you honestly, I will love it if we beat them, love it.

Newcastle boss Kevin Keegan feeling the pressure of going from having a nine-point Premiership lead with a game in hand on 31 January to prospective (and eventually actual) runners-up, May 1996.

Players respond to anger. Players want you to discipline them.

Alex Ferguson, October 1996.

I'm careful which players I lay into. Some can't handle it. Some can't even handle a team talk. There are some I don't look in the eye during a team talk because I know I am putting them under pressure.

Alex Ferguson, October 1996.

The best manager in Britain is Alex Ferguson without doubt and he has been for some time. I've had the privilege of knowing him, he was my room-mate in the youth team and he took me to Mexico. It always intrigues me when people say let Alex Ferguson come in and pick his staff. Well, when he did pick his staff I was fortunate I was on it.

Craig Brown, *The Absolute Game* fanzine, April 1997.

For him, winning is an obsession. I'm not the least bit surprised by what he's achieved but it does surprise me when they talk about him retiring. They'll have to carry him out.

Ex-Scotland boss Andy Roxburgh on his former Falkirk striking partner Ferguson, April 1997.

It's like Alex Ferguson at Man U, I suppose. He's been at it 26 years, it's a drug. It's time to put out a record, I'm up for it big time. It's like strolling back into town, climbing back on a horse.

ABC lead singer Martin Fry on surviving in the record business, April 1997.

In over ten years of playing I've never once heard him criticise one of his own players. He certainly does you down in the dressing-room but never ever publicly; to me that is fantastic.

Former Manchester United captain Steve Bruce on Ferguson, June 1997.

My job is not to criticise my players publicly. When a manager makes a public criticism, he's affecting the emotional stability of a player and that cannot be the professional thing to do.
Alex Ferguson, October 1996.

He wants to be a winner and wants to be associated with winners and if you don't match that then you don't get on. It's as simple as that.
Steve Bruce on Ferguson, June 1997.

I've seen him throw a few but he usually misses. He intentionally misses.
Steve Bruce on Ferguson's famed tea-cup throwing, June 1997.

He is bad-tempered but he doesn't throw things or hit anyone – in fact he hasn't got close to it, and no one has ever hit him. It is a very emotional game and he is an emotional man.
Brian McClair on Alex Ferguson, *Odd Man Out*, 1997.

We'd have a five-a-side at the end of every training session and Alex himself played up front and played to win. He was very proud of his goalscoring record, as he should be, but he did keep reminding us of it every time he put one in the back of the net.
Neil Webb on life with Ferguson at Old Trafford, May 1997.

With the amount of chances we created, I wish I was still a centre-forward.
Alex Ferguson as United, and Andy Cole in particular, missed the chances at West Ham that cost them victory and the 1994–95 title.

For three weeks they thought I was lying. I'd made out he was Hannibal Lecter and he'd been a pussycat. Then we lost at Wimbledon . . .
Gordon Strachan on Ferguson's early days at Old Trafford, May 1997.

His great strength is his single-mindedness – his ability to make decisions and stick to them. He's got real self-belief that what he's doing is right. His record suggests he usually is.
Brian McClair on Ferguson, May 1996.

It was the worst moment of my life. It makes me cringe just thinking about it. I will never forgive Alex Ferguson and from the moment he broke the news to me that I was dropped for the replay we have never spoken a word.
Ex-Manchester United goalkeeper **Jim Leighton** on being dropped following the 1990 FA Cup final, June 1996.

I don't have anything but admiration and respect for him and what he's done, but that's no good, is it? That's not what you want me to say.
Kenny Dalglish on Ferguson, May 1997.

If your father's from Govan you'll be all right.
Alex Ferguson on Labour Party leader Tony Blair, 1996.

Whatever Fergie's done, he's been successful. He had a good team at St Mirren as well. They were really attacking. Winning the European Cup-Winners' Cup cannot be underestimated. For a Scottish team to win in Europe is a great achievement.
Kenny Dalglish after Ferguson had led United to their fourth title in five years, May 1997.

He ruled by fear, make no mistake.
Ross County boss – and former Pittodrie player – **Neale Cooper** on Ferguson, October 1997.

If they act like children, I treat them like children.
Alex Ferguson, explaining why he made four Aberdeen players recite a string of nursery rhymes in public after a landlady reported them for damaging her airing cupboard.

Not the nicest of men. He'll say, 'Alright, Doc' when I'm at Man. United, but we don't really see eye to eye. He bears grudges and I've always disliked that about him.
Tommy Docherty on Ferguson, November 1997.

I was reading Jim Smith's comment that the present-day player can't take a bollocking. He's absolutely right. They are encouraged the American way with pats on the back all the time instead of facing reality. They don't like being told off. They don't like hearing the truth.
Alex Ferguson, December 1997.

He used to come round your house on a Friday night. You seen his car sneaking by on a Friday night, seeing if you were in. What a sad man – on a Friday night sneaking about in his car to see if I was in.
Gordon Strachan on Ferguson, 1998.

He is the best manager I had, and he's the one I respected the most, and I still respect him. And that will be for all my life.
Eric Cantona, 1998.

He's disciplined, he's honest, he's meticulous – he's the lot. I am privileged to have worked under him.
Sheffield United boss **Steve Bruce**, November 1998.

I met Paddy Crerand recently and he gave me a tip. He said: 'Just listen to Alex. All his 'l' sounds are 'w's.' And it's true.
Impressionist **Alistair McGowan** on Alex Ferguson, January 1999.

Some people are naturally energetic. I've got a lot of energy. I'm never tired.
Alex Ferguson, February 1999.

When the Italians tell me it's pasta on the plate I check under the sauce to make sure it is.
Alex Ferguson begins the build-up to the European Cup match with Inter Milan, March 1999.

I know my worth and if it came to a point of principle over the contract, there could be some tough decisions to be taken.
Alex Ferguson amid talks with Manchester United about extending his contract, April 1999.

FITNESS

This is not a man who looks like an athlete.
Some understatement from Rangers team-mate **Ian Durrant** on Andy Goram, in *Blue & White Dynamite – The Ian Durrant Story*, 1998.

In the run-up to European games he'd get dangerously excited. He'd be in the gym doing weights frantically, then 100 sit-ups, and this was 20 minutes before kick-off. Every time I went to calm him down all I got was 'I'm fine, I'm fine.'
Trevor Steven on Paul Gascoigne, November 1997.

Throughout my career, at whichever club, no one's spent more time training than me.
Kilmarnock's **Pat Nevin**, November 1997.

After some of the negative publicity we got – 14 out of 14 pundits said we were going to get relegated – the fans expected to see the players coming out of the tunnel with a fag in one hand, a can of lager in the other and a beer belly.
Clyde general manager **Ronnie MacDonald**, October 1998.

When I first went to Liverpool, they had one machine, an ultrasound machine. If you had a bad Achilles you had five minute ultrasound. Hamstring, five minutes ultrasound. Flu, five minutes ultrasound up your nose. Everything was five minutes ultrasound. They had that machine 25 years.
Former Liverpool defender **Alan Hansen**, March 1999.

I ran alongside Stevie Fulton just to make myself feel a bit better. Then Rob McKinnon came over beside us and there was no room left in the penalty box.
Kilmarnock striker **Ally McCoist**, enjoying the last laugh after getting stick from Hearts fans, April 1999. McCoist equalised in a 2–2 draw.

FOOD

First week I lost about 15 lbs. The second week I ate like mad and put it all back on again. Went to a restaurant every night, ate steak and drank champagne. Well, they wanted me to get my strength back.
Bobby Murdoch on being sent to a health farm to conquer a weight problem while with Celtic, May 1997.

It was my birthday and I invited the players out for lunch – champagne, caviar, smoked salmon, the works. It was the first time the squad had ever been together socially but within 15 minutes they were squabbling and the centre-half punched the goalkeeper. By 5 p.m. we had moved on to a restaurant and the players started a food fight with cous-cous, which was a bit messy. Eventually we all went night-clubbing till four in the morning and the biggest laugh was seeing all these £200,000-a-year French footballers emerging from the club singing 'Angleterre, Angleterre, Angleterre' at the top of their voices.
Former Dundee boss **Simon Stainrod**, February 1995.

I get most of my ideas from Africa. When I was there they were all six-footers, these natives, all muscle and as fit as anything. I'd go in their mud huts and ask them what they ate and it was all rice, beans, peas and fish . . .

I learned lessons from that. At soccer clubs they'd say, 'Have a steak at 12 before the match.' A load of baloney.
Former Hibs keeper John Burridge, August 1995.

They don't have to eat it. They can eat or go hungry.
Coventry's Gordon Strachan after changing the food 'dramatically' at the club's training ground, January 1997.

The food in Scotland is similar to Germany – McDonald's burgers.
Rangers' Jorg Albertz, 1997.

Q: Biggest improvement to have taken place in Scottish football in the last 10 years?
A: The standard of the sweet trolleys at Scotland national team get-togethers. More used by Craig Brown than any of the players, though.
Tranmere's Pat Nevin, *The Absolute Game* questionnaire, March 1997.

If we win the league then maybe we will go out and eat and drink bad things.
Celtic striker Jorge Cadete, April 1997.

Fruit is very good for you. I particularly like Terry's Chocolate Oranges.
Paul Gascoigne, in *Gazza: Daft As a Brush*.

I've been on that peach diet. I eat everything but peaches.
More on Paul Gascoigne's fruit obsession, on Channel 4's *Under the Moon* show, April 1997.

Players eat fish and chips and cheeseburgers then think if they have a bowl of pasta before a game they'll go out and play like Gianfranco Zola. They're more likely to play like Zola Budd.
Hibs boss Jim Duffy, calling in a nutritionist, August 1997.

Scandinavian players are more professional than players in Scotland and England. The culture in Britain is totally different from what it is in Norway. Most towns don't have more than one pub. Here there's one on every corner.
Dundee United's Erik Pedersen November 1997.

If every professional here does what he says, we'd be running out four stones overweight with beer bellies, stinking of kebabs and burgers. He can't have a social life and must spend his nights at home watching *Neighbours* and *High Road*.
Kilmarnock's indignant Dylan Kerr responds to Pedersen's claims, November 1997.

Too much gets made of diet. Different people have different needs. I've gone out the night before training and been able to do anything. Other days I've not been out and I can't run the next day.
Hibs' **Chic Charnley,** January 1998.

I play a lot of golf and make my own chutney.
Denis Law's reply to a magazine interviewer as to what he was doing now, February 1998.

I would never eat haggis, not if you paid me.
Celtic defender **Marc Rieper,** June 1998.

I can barely sit at the breakfast table in the morning and watch the rest of the boys eating eggs, sausages and beans – I couldn't do that. In Holland we only have bread with either chocolate sprinkles, jam or cheese.
Rangers new signing **Arthur Numan,** August 1998.

When we go away to a hotel to prepare for a game I always take a bag of biscuits with me. Well, when you get into those hotel rooms there's always only two silly wee shortbread biscuits. That's not going to keep anyone going, is it?
St Johnstone's **Allan 'Biscuits' Preston,** November 1998. His fondness for Penguin biscuits had inspired an Internet website, 'Biscuits For Scotland'.

FOREIGN

Why should we be surprised by the Turks? At Stoke we've had Canadians turning up for trials and Germans from so far down their league that I've never heard of them and they are miles ahead of our players in technique, understanding of the game, even in terms of physical fitness. It's frightening.
Stoke boss **Lou Macari** after Manchester United's 3–3 draw with Galatasaray, October 1993.

When Brian [Laudrup] was at Milan he was put in the same flat that Mark Hateley had lived in. There was a sense of being on a conveyor belt.
Rangers chairman **David Murray,** November 1994.

We call him Superman. He's got the looks, he's really well educated and has everything going for him. We all hate him.
West Ham boss **Harry Redknapp** on Marc Rieper, 1995.

Some people said that he wasn't scoring enough goals but that was all keech.
Pierre van Hooijdonk leaps to the defence of team-mate Andreas Thom,
January 1996.

I've got a reputation for having my own opinion and they don't like that
in Great Britain.
Former Aberdeen striker **Hans Gillhaus**, quoted in Simon Kuper, *Football
Against the Enemy*, 1994.

It's like any other league in the world. Only three or four teams can win it
and the rest are there to upset them.
Galatasaray boss **Graeme Souness** on Turkish football, April 1996.

What impresses me is that every Dutch player has a wee appreciation of
every other position on the park. They spend time practising and try out
the other positions so that they get to see the game from their team-mates'
perspective.
Scotland captain **Gary McAllister**, April 1996.

John Spencer I can just about understand if he speaks slowly but Dennis
Wise is impossible. What is this Cockney that he's always speaking?
Chelsea's **Gianluca Vialli**, August 1996.

Where is ball?
Aberdeen's new Bulgarian midfielder **Ilian Kiriakov**, to a member of the club
coaching staff at half-time on his hectic début against Celtic, 10 August 1996.

Dynamo were under the control of the Stasi. You were always aware of that
when you played for them. Everywhere we played we were booed. Other
team's fans hated us. They reckoned we were actual members of the Stasi.
We weren't, of course. We were only footballers.
Celtic's **Andreas Thom** on his time with Dynamo Berlin, September 1996.

It was a Wartburg, the one my father wanted. He worked hard as a
mechanic but he had to wait. I was 19 and felt bad about being able to
march straight to the front of the queue. I was terrified about what he
would say as I drove it home but he was fine.
Celtic's **Andreas Thom**, whose father had been on a twelve-year waiting list
for a car, September 1996.

If you went to get past a Scots defender you first have to massacre his
whole family.
Pierre van Hooijdonk tells a Dutch journalist about life in Scotland, 1996.

It was harder to miss than to score. I was as surprised as anyone when the ball went over but I can forget. I doubt if anyone else will, though.
Rangers' **Peter van Vossen** after missing an open goal against Celtic, November 1996.

Peter Van Vossen did his Marty Feldman impersonation.
Ally McCoist on the same incident.

I used to work out a lot at Celtic but I got a real shock when these guys took off their shirts. I couldn't believe how well-built they all were.
Monaco's **John Collins**, February 1997.

They don't waste their time trying to play on muddy pitches in winter. If the weather is that bad, they take us for a run in the woods and then some ball-work indoors.
Borussia Dortmund's **Paul Lambert**, February 1997.

To begin with, I couldn't tell which players were the defenders because everyone out there was so comfortable on the ball. We think that foreign players are more gifted, but really it's just that they work at it.
Monaco's **John Collins**, February 1997.

I ran up and spat on him. I got him in the face. I don't see what the fuss is about. People who complain about this sort of thing have obviously not played in Europe where it happens all the time.
St Johnstone's **Attila Sekerlioglu** after being accused of spitting on Airdrie's John Davies, February 1997.

If it wasn't played like that we may as well all spend the afternoon at the bingo.
Airdrie boss **Alex MacDonald** after the same game, February 1997.

They play the American national anthem before every game. I would teach Richard the words if I knew them myself.
Kansas City Wizards' **Steve Pittman**, an American international, preparing to welcome Richard Gough to the MLS club, February 1997.

I studied English at school for three years but it's not the English they speak in Scotland, I had to learn a different language and even now Ian Durrant is still too difficult for me.
Rangers' **Jorg Albertz**, February 1997.

I was impressed that the first time I ever met him he tried to use his broken French to communicate with me – although he was greatly relieved when I said, 'It's OK, we can speak English.'
Prince Albert of Monaco on John Collins, February 1997.

He'd come in, list the 11 names, bang bang bang, and out again. You'd look around and think, 'Oh, I'll be dropped then.' His argument was that at Milan he'd found out if he was in the team at 2 p.m. on match day same as everyone else.
Chelsea's **Steve Clarke** on Ruud Gullit's management style, March 1997.

If I were Tommy McLean and I could go and get Scandinavian players like he's got, I'd go and get them.
Craig Brown, The Absolute Game fanzine, April 1997.

I now speak Scottish with a little bit of English.
Celtic's **Jorge Cadete**, April 1997.

They're nothing like the Scots. When I crack a joke I have to hold up a sign that says 'Laugh'.
Former Scotland boss **Andy Roxburgh** on life in Switzerland as UEFA technical director, April 1997.

When I grew up in Yugoslavia I never saw any high balls. At home, football was always played on the ground, always, always, always. I come to Scotland, to Kilmarnock, and what is this I am suddenly seeing?
Kilmarnock goalkeeper **Dragoje Lekovic** on cultural differences, May 1997.

Very lazy and, usually, very tall.
Kilmarnock goalkeeper **Dragoje Lekovic** on Montenegrans (Lekovic considers himself Montenegran although he was born in Serbia), May 1997.

Maybe there is a question of stress and it may result from the fact that he realises the kind of behaviour he has demonstrated towards the Celtic supporters, his team-mates and a club which gave him the opportunity to get back on a big stage from the AC Milan subs bench.
Celtic general manager **Jock Brown** on Paolo di Canio's refusal to play for the team, July 1997.

The kudu (African antelope) are the most dangerous because they are crazy animals who jump at cars. They have long pointed horns and if they

jump on top of the car their horns come right through the window and kill the driver or passenger. That is very common on the roads.
Motherwell's Namibian international Eliphas Shivute on hitch-hiking to play for his former club Eleven Arrows, September 1997.

At the beginning I thought I could adapt to any situation. Instead it was always raining and I was doing some incredible things with my car.
Marco Negri on life at Ibrox, November 1997.

Years ago we used to laugh at Iceland and Norway – now these people have passed us by in terms of bringing on young players and maintaining continuity.
Newcastle coach Tommy Burns, October 1997.

When I went to Norway and Iceland I could not believe how good their kids' technique was. These countries are in darkness half the year so they've put money into building good indoor facilities.
Dunfermline boss Bert Paton agrees, 5 July 1998.

The most disgraceful thing that happened there was the signing of Cadete, di Canio and van Hooijdonk. They had no interest in Celtic Football Club. They were mercenaries – only interested in grabbing the money and heading off. The way they treated Tommy Burns – especially van Hooijdonk – was terrible, no respect whatsoever. Mind you, I do think Tommy was far too soft on them.
Tommy Docherty, November 1997.

I've thought about bringing in a batch of foreigners but at the end of the day they would only be here to pick up a wage. I want guys who know what Kilmarnock is about and know what Kilmarnock means to the people who work here.
Killie boss Bobby Williamson, August 1998.

The gap between attitudes of foreign and British players has narrowed. I am noticing more foreign players who have bad habits. A lot of foreigners smoke, and no one can tell me that is going to benefit a footballer.
Rangers defender Colin Hendry, February 1999.

FURY

The bad blood has been there for as long as I can remember. There were always heaps of sendings-off when the two teams played and it has become a fixture in which players and fans get carried away.
Former Aberdeen midfielder Neil Simpson on games between Rangers and Aberdeen.

He is asked to do a photograph with the supporters, with whom he is a big favourite, and he says, 'No, I'm not going.' We tell him who it is for and he says, 'I don't care, I'm not going.' Then twice he refuses to warm up. How long can you put up with someone's arrogance?
Celtic boss Tommy Burns on problems with Pierre van Hooijdonk, September 1996.

The boss then went on to say I was an arrogant arse.
van Hooijdonk on Burns, September 1996.

Ferguson speak to me and say 'F***** B******'. For what? You won, you maybe even won season. You speak to me these words, for what? It's normal, my reaction.
Celtic's Paolo di Canio on a bust-up with Rangers' Ian Ferguson at the end of a tousy Old Firm game, March 1997.

When a reporter called me for a reaction to what di Canio had claimed I'd said to him I was absolutely furious. It was a downright lie. I know it. Di Canio knows it. I'll tell him that to his face, anytime, anywhere . . . I rang Parkhead and spoke to Tommy Burns for ten minutes. I think he knew I was serious when I told him, 'Tommy, I swear on my daughters' lives I didn't call di Canio that.'
Ian Ferguson responds, August 1997.

I am a man. Ferguson is not a man.
Paolo di Canio on the same incident, March 1997.

He went on about being a man. I offered him the opportunity to have it out man-to-man after the game and he didn't want to know.
Ian Ferguson, August 1997.

The comet will be coming round again by the time my ban is finished.
Former Scotland striker **David Speedie**, quitting non-league Guiseley after
being sent off twice in his first three games, March 1997. Comet Hale-Bopp was
visible in the skies at the time. (Astronomy fans will know it isn't due back in
Earth's skies until 4367.)

I know it sounds crazy but Aberdeen's seventh was definitely offside and I
got carried away in the heat of the moment.
Raith Rovers' **Paul Browne** on the booking for dissent in a 7–0 reserve game
defeat which ruled him out of a first-team comeback against Celtic, April 1997.

You have decided to give your opinions on the game now and your mouth
is as big as your head.
Dundee United boss **Tommy McLean** lashes out on air at TV pundit Charlie
Nicholas, 17 August 1997. Nicholas had criticised United's Maurice Malpas,
who'd been sent off in a live TV match against Hibs.

Look at the David Beckham affair, for example. All right, the boy was
stupid – there was no provocation for him to act as he did and he deserved
to be sent off – but the over-reaction has been incredible. What's he really
done, for heaven's sake? He hasn't killed anybody or committed a capital
crime, yet we have the Archbishop of Canterbury and the Prime Minister
intervening to request the nation's forgiveness.
Motherwell's **Brian McClair** on his former Old Trafford team-mate's World
Cup trauma, July 1998.

I don't recall one season as a professional when I didn't witness a fight at
training.
Former Hearts striker **John Colquhoun**, January 1999.

What annoys me is when a policewoman tells me to sit down, as happened
at Everton, or a steward, or a linesman who should be watching the game,
a referee, likewise. The only person who should be saying anything is the
fourth official.
Coventry boss **Gordon Strachan**, February 1999.

FUTURE

If they [Rangers] had continued to limp along, then Celtic probably would have too. The potential at Ibrox is frightening. There is a chance that they could just run away with the championship for years ahead. Football is unpredictable and we will certainly compete, but you have to recognise the standard of player they are buying. Rangers are littered with established internationals – people with 30 or 40 caps. It's bound to bring down your failure rate. They are signing people for £1.5m while Celtic have to operate in the £600,000 range.

A prescient **Tommy Burns**, then a Celtic player, July 1989, quoted in Tom Campbell and Pat Woods', *Dreams, and Songs to Sing*, 1996. Rangers won the title for the next eight seasons.

It will take ten years for the work of the commission [The Commission of Enquiry into the decline of the Scottish game] to bear fruit, but these will be the most important ten years in the history of Scottish football.
Ernie Walker, 16 August 1995.

I don't ever see myself playing in Scotland again.
Scotland skipper **Gary McAllister**, September 1995.

Unlike their parents, these kids will be brought up playing Sevens on grass pitches, not being ostracised from their team-mates and the ball, able to make decisions for themselves and able to encourage adults to shout nice things to them rather than scaring the hell out of them by bawling when they make a mistake. These are the players of the future.
SFA community development programme co-ordinator **Jim Fleeting**, May 1996.

The purist view of football is over, it is history. When I supported Ayr United as a boy, it was pure blood, sweat and liniment. But football has moved on to a different planet and Scottish football has got to go with it.
Rangers chairman **David Murray**, January 1997.

I would like the bigger clubs to be allowed to have a nursery team. Celtic maybe have Clydebank, Rangers maybe have Stenhousemuir. Let them put the players there and let them play.
Craig Brown, *The Absolute Game* fanzine, April 1997.

Not having a manager is very much a continental principle and, far from dying out, it is the way forward for the game.
Clydebank chairman **Jack Steedman**, whose club have never had a manager, April 1997.

It's not so much that the English approach is wonderful, it's just that the Scottish one is so awful.
Sports industry consultant **Alex Fynn** on the SFA's slow-moving Think Tank, May 1997.

We cannot finance 40 clubs in Scotland in my view. I'm not suggesting you need to close them down or whatever, but why do they have to be professional, or even semi-professional? Why can they not be amateur? All along everyone has been defending players directly or indirectly who don't stand a hope of making the grade.
Agent **Bill McMurdo**, The Absolute Game fanzine, May 1997.

I have a very impressive medal from that evening. Later in life, when everyone has forgotten what that competition actually was, I will embellish its significance.
Brian McClair, on scoring the only goal in Manchester United's November 1991 European Super Cup win over Red Star Belgrade, Odd Man Out, 1997. McClair admitted United were 'comprehensively hammered by a terrific Red Star team.'

Players will just be players in future, not amateurs or professionals. There should be no reason why Ally McCoist shouldn't be able to play for his local village team when his professional career is over but, at the moment, some guy who once received a few quid for playing with Tarff Rovers is not allowed to play amateur football. That is absurd.
Think Tank chairman **Ernie Walker**, January 1998.

I will be happy when the day comes that one of our women coaches is invited to coach the men. The best managers are housewives on low incomes who have to juggle with finances to look after the family. There are teams here with problems. They could bring in women to solve them.
Scottish Women's FA secretary **Maureen McGonigle**, January 1998.

I've got to delegate and, let's be honest, Rangers probably needed a new face. Bob is a better day-to-day business manager than me. I don't have the patience.
Rangers chairman **David Murray** on the June 1998 appointment of Bob Brannan as Chief Executive, August 1998.

I'm not Nostradamus, mate.
Croatia Zagreb's Australian striker **Marko Viduka**, after being asked about his side's hopes of overcoming a one-goal European Cup deficit against Celtic, 12 August 1998.

THE GAME

Kai Johansen, the former Glasgow Rangers player, was our manager. He and I decided to defy the law and field a black man, and we'd see if the sky fell down.
Saul Sacks, chairman of Arcadia Shepherds, who broke South Africa's all-white rule by fielding Vincent 'Tanti' Julius in February 1977, quoted in Simon Kuper, *Football Against The Enemy*, 1994.

It is difficult to stay in an unhealthy house without catching some of the disease.
Jock Stein on the poor standards it Scotland in the early '70s, quoted in Bill Murray, *The Old Firm in The New Age*, 1998.

Joe Jordan takes his teeth out and is a nasty bastard on the park. But, off the park, if you were in a pub you'd find him sitting in a corner drinking half a lager and lime, quiet as a lamb. He goes to his work and does his job.
Former Scotland defender **Kenny Burns**, quoted in Mike Wilson, *Don't Cry for Me Argentina*, 1998.

There is something wrong with the way we look at football in Scotland. If there is someone in the team who can get his foot in and win the ball then it doesn't matter if he is incapable of creating a goal. A player who is the exact opposite of that, though, can expect to get a lot of criticism.
Hibs' **Michael O'Neill**, November 1994.

There are those now going to games in Scotland who have never watched what I would consider to be good football. We have players in this country who are regarded as heroes but who cannot, in my opinion, play football at all.
Think Tank chairman **Ernie Walker**, 16 August 1995.

He [Cantona] came in at me with two feet – late – though fortunately I saw it coming and managed to avoid the worst of it. He still caught me a bit, though, and the incident was highlighted over and over again on television. Maybe it could all have been even worse. But I picked myself up quickly and also helped Eric to his feet which possibly diluted the affair a bit . . . I'm not Mother Teresa but there's no way I would deliberately get a fellow professional sent off. Eric, it seems, can do that for himself.
Gary McAllister, *Captain's Log,* 1995.

It was enthralling. I'd been to rugger matches but never seen Association Football live. One just had no idea of the speed these men operate at.
Countess of Elgin on her first match, Celtic v Motherwell, 1995.

I don't go along with the theory that footballers should play on a Saturday then get away from it. If you love the game like I do you should want to watch two or three games a week. I never get tired of football.
Scotland skipper **Gary McAllister,** September 1995.

I love Newcastle. I love that raw passion. I remember being in Newcastle once and hearing newspaper vendors shouting: 'Sensation! Cole Toe injury!' Sensation? Most vendors use the word for 'Major Resigns' or 'AIDS Spreading Over Country'. It's unbelievable. Glasgow's like that.
Manchester United boss **Alex Ferguson,** 1995.

The biggest difference I've noticed since coming to Scotland eight years ago is how little football players discuss the game over here. Footballers in Scotland seem to regard it as just a normal job. But a professional footballer's job is unlike any other. It's a wonderful way to earn a living and players need to think about it more than they do.
Motherwell defender **Miodrag Krivokapic,** April 1996.

I once described football as 'working class theatre'. Nowadays it's becoming more like middle-class cabaret.
Novelist **William McIlvanney,** June 1996.

The last two under-21 teams have been in European semi-finals. In 1992 we were third in Europe, in 1996 we were fourth. I've been in a World Cup final with the under-16 team. We were sixth in the world with the under-19 team in Chile in 1987. Our record at youth level and under-21 level is excellent, Every country in Europe is desperate to qualify for the Olympics – we qualified twice but we didn't go. We've just beaten the England under-16 team 5–1. The senior team had to qualify for Euro '96 from a tricky group and you can see how tricky it is because Russia and Greece are top

of their sections in the World Cup. We're still top of our qualifying group. So I don't think it necessarily needs to be depression all the time.
Craig Brown, *The Absolute Game* fanzine, April 1997.

My analogy is that lamp up there. If it blew and you want an electrician I'm not going to tell you who to pick. But if you are going to fix it you wouldn't just go outside and take someone off the street, you'd get yourself a qualified electrician. And if they're willing to do that in places like Germany and Italy, why can't we?
Former Scotland boss **Andy Roxburgh** on his ambition that all club coaches should have to hold a UEFA coaching diploma, April 1997.

We were disappointed at being so excited.
Coventry boss **Gordon Strachan** on celebrating avoiding relegation, October 1997.

If I went on TV to talk about reforming committees, some guy sitting in Carfin eating his tea would say: 'Celtic got beat yesterday. What the hell's he talking about?'
Think Tank chairman **Ernie Walker,** January 1998.

What we are great at in Scotland is winning the ball. The problem is that the players don't keep the ball long enough – we just give it back to them then have to tackle for it again.
Scotland boss **Craig Brown,** February 1998.

Why not use the money that's being wasted on that [the redevelopment of Hampden Park] on some kind of gate equalisation to help the Kilmarnocks and the Dundees and the Particks and the Motherwells? Maybe then your clubs would be able to stop doing goofy and dishonest things just to survive. Apart from Glasgow, every team is suffering. People are scared to let 100 years of history go into the toilet, chairmen come and go like the changing of the guard, and the rules are so archaic there has to be jiggery-pokery to stay afloat.
Former Dundee chairman **Ron Dixon** sums things up, February 1998.

We must never lose the day when Rangers go to Ayr United on a wet September night and are in danger of losing. That is what football is about. It is part of our heritage. The tie probably lit up Ayrshire yesterday. If you take that away you lose the spirit of the game.
Rangers chairman **David Murray,** amid talk of a European league, September 1998. Rangers had won 2–0 at Ayr the day before.

There were some good things in the game but I can't remember what they were.
Motherwell manager Harri Kampman after a dreary 0–0 draw with Kilmarnock, September 1998.

I don't see why the government shouldn't be doing more for football. They do in other countries.
Kilmarnock boss Bobby Williamson, February 1999.

He told me, quite openly, that he was under pressure from the board to play Petr Katchouro, the Belarussian striker, so that Petr could play the required number of games and therefore wouldn't have to apply for a new work permit. That's modern-day football for you!
Former Sheffield United striker Andy Walker recalls a novel problem with boss Howard Kendall, February 1999.

I hear people saying 'the way the game should be played'. Rubbish. That's the worst saying in football. You win the game, then worry about the way it should be played.
Former Liverpool defender Alan Hansen, March 1999.

Nothing in football today is done for the good of the game. It's all for the money.
Alan Hansen, March 1999.

It's a terrible game at times, this. He's a terrific type of lad, doesn't drink or smoke, a very good player, but he's just not quite good enough to play for us.
Manchester United boss Alex Ferguson on selling Irish youngster Philip Mulryne to Norwich, April 1999.

GAZZA

He could be a right little devil, but he was never nasty, there was no malice in him. You see all these negative things about him in the press, but they're not writing about the person I know.
Geoff Wilson, Gascoigne's former football teacher at Joseph Swan School, Gateshead, 1998.

Even then he was off his head, completely crackers. He would put sweets down his socks and then give them to teachers to eat.
Nottingham Forest's **Steve Stone** on his former schoolmate, 1995.

I can promise everyone in Scotland that I will be a better player next year now that I know what to expect up here with respect to the pitches, opponents, the banter with supporters, which grounds have trains going past ten feet away, and which grounds are overlooked by houses with people sitting in their windows drinking cups of tea.
Paul Gascoigne, 30 April 1995, on being named Scotland's Footballer of the Year, two days after winning the Players' Player of the Year award.

I couldn't be like him and he couldn't be like me. I can enjoy a Gazza joke but sometimes I'm glad I'm not married to him, because he's talking all the time.
Team-mate **Brian Laudrup**, September 1996.

You get your other good professionals, your Goughies, your Gary Mabbutts, your Linekers and your Platts . . . can't think of any more. They're your goody-goody two shoes.
Paul Gascoigne in TV documentary *Gazza's Coming Home*, October 1996.

He's done well in Scotland and he turns games for Rangers week in, week out. It may be a rung down the ladder from England say, or Spain, but he seems happy there, he's very popular with the fans and he's earning a lot of money, so maybe he should stay put.
Barcelona boss **Bobby Robson** on Gascoigne, amid reports he should return to England, February 1997.

Some people become blind when they get close to the goal. Gascoigne doesn't. See the goal he scored against Scotland in Euro '96. If you were watching the match from the outside that seemed the obvious, the only thing to do. Things are different when you're in there. And that's where you see the outstanding player – calm and cold-blooded at decisive moments.
Middlesbrough's **Juninho** on Gascoigne, February 1997.

For someone like Paul Gascoigne, life has always seemed insecure, full of ambiguity and uncertainties. In football, however, it's more black and white, you know what the rules are. If Gascoigne feels they [referees] aren't properly enforcing the black-and-white rules, then he's cast back into this world of ambiguity he's trying to get away from.
Steven Smith of the British Association of Psychologists, February 1997.

I can't really see him being a coach or a manager when he gives up playing. And I don't know if you could trust him in the media – he'll say what he thinks whether he's got an audience of two in the room or £17m watching on TV.
Bobby Robson on Gascoigne, February 1997.

He's plainly nuts, isn't he? But I've never seen that side of him myself. All I know is that he's a friend and we get on fantastic. I respect him. He goes up to journalists and says, 'F*** off'. It's something I've always wanted to do but never had the guts.
Broadcaster and mate **Danny Baker**, 1997.

When you crack the same gag five times over it soon wears thin, yet it only makes characters like Gascoigne try harder.
Human behaviour expert **Desmond Morris**, 1996.

He's an intelligent boy who likes to let people think he's stupid. He doesn't have a bad bone in his body but he does some stupid, ridiculous things. That's what makes him so interesting.
Rangers striker **Ally McCoist**, 1996.

Gazza is going, 'Oh Jesus, I can't be seen here. It looks like we're on the town.' And God knows there are a few times when we've been out for a few beers. But on those photos, if you have a look, they're all Highland Spring water bottles because Gazza said, 'Walter Smith cannot see this, no drink at the table.'
Danny Baker, June 1998.

There is a limit to anyone's patience.
The ever-patient **Walter Smith** finally snaps, 1996.

It's a disgrace. I took my domestic problems on to the pitch and let everyone down.
Paul Gascoigne apologises for his behaviour after being sent off against Ajax in the Champions' League after revelations about his domestic problems, October 1996.

Out of all the things I regret, the biggest is that I took all my problems out on Sheryl. I have to live with that. Then I never told the gaffer and played against Ajax and got sent off because all I could think about was what I'd done to Sheryl.
Paul Gascoigne after details of his wife-beating become public, October 1996.

He's a national hero and a role model for youngsters. If it's true that Gazza beat up his wife, then sending him to represent England overseas can only give the impression that wife-beating is acceptable in the UK.
Sandra Horley of women's rights group Refuge.

I would love to see women who are at matches turn their backs on him or boo him. Perhaps some of the men would join in to let him know the contempt we feel towards him.
Tory MP **Teresa Gorman** on Gascoigne's domestic violence.

The failure of our referees almost totally to apply the laws of the game to Paul Gascoigne is a lasting disgrace and an indication of dereliction of duty.
Bob Crampsey, *The Absolute Game*, questionnaire, March 1997.

When I signed him I was 100 per cent clear about my judgment, but the percentage drops with every incident that happens. And so does the level of backing at this club.
Rangers' **Walter Smith**, 21 April 1997.

I believe he is one of the biggest talents the English game has ever produced. Yet what he has done is not healthy for him or the club. I just hope he opens his eyes and sees what he's about to destroy. The players here love him – he's a fantastic player when he's not drunk.
Brian Laudrup, May 1997.

His ability far outweighs the hassle.
Walter Smith, August 1997.

If we lose he will come in after the game shouting, 'It's my fault, it's my fault', and you can't help laughing because his chops go all red and he starts shaking, shouting and yelling. He takes every defeat very personally.
Rangers' **Andy Goram**, 1997.

Gazza gains and loses weight quicker than anyone I've ever known.
Walter Smith, 1997.

You can always tell when he's right. He's on his toes. When he's not dancing you know he's not right.
Walter Smith, 1997.

When he's off form they say he's in a Mickey Mouse league but when England need a big performance he's touted as their saviour.
Rangers chairman **David Murray** on Gascoigne, October 1997.

Gazza said he was taking his wallet out on the pitch with him. I didn't understand what he was talking about until he showed me the newspaper.
Rangers team-mate Marco Negri, 1997, on a report quoting his mother as saying her son would have been a thief if he hadn't been a footballer.

I don't know why people think he has to move from Rangers to enhance his career.
Kevin Keegan on reports linking Gascoigne with a return to England, October 1997.

I keep on reading that playing up here is bad for him in an international sense. If that's the case, why has he been an automatic choice for England in the two years he's been here? If it was that bad up here, surely he wouldn't be in their team?
Walter Smith, amid talk of Gascoigne returning to England, October 1997.

Gazza reminds me of Marilyn Monroe. She wasn't the greatest actress in the world, but she was a star so you didn't mind if she was late.
Actor **Michael Caine**, October 1997.

I hadn't been playing well and the gaffer didn't play me for one of the games. He said I hadn't been performing. This time last year I'd scored eight goals. Walter said: 'Maybe the problem is that you've kept out of trouble. Why don't you give Chris Evans a ring and get yourself into a bit of bother?'
Paul Gascoigne, October 1997.

I have to accept that in taking on Gascoigne the player, I've taken on a few other aspects as well.
Walter Smith, 1997.

I understand why you stay at Rangers. It's a great club. Walter Smith said to me: 'There are two stars in Glasgow – Glasgow Rangers Football Club and Paul Gascoigne.'
Broadcaster and mate **Chris Evans,** October 1997.

He'd have no place in my team. What he gets up to is a disgrace, a disgrace. He's 30 going on 6. At Rangers, in general, I'm amazed at the stuff players get away with now. Scot Symon would have had people like Gascoigne out the door in two minutes. They are encouraging clowns to misbehave.
Tommy Docherty, November 1997.

He's the perfect house guest. He folds his blanket in the morning, washes up his own cereal bowl. When he first started coming round he was still having the odd cigarette but he always went out on to the patio to smoke.
Broadcaster and mate **Danny Baker**, 1997.

He's one of the most organised guys I know. He lives through a Filofax.
Rangers team-mate **Trevor Steven** on Paul Gascoigne, November 1997.

The most generous person I have seen in my life. He gives tramps every penny in his pocket and gets the bus home on a night out.
Rangers team-mate **Ian Durrant,** in *Blue & White Dynamite – The Ian Durrant Story,* 1998.

What Gazza needs first and foremost is to take the advice of Robert Burns and see himself as others see him. At the moment he tends to blurt things out and act on impulse rather than thinking beforehand. In listening to his emotions first, and running them past the brain once in a while, the valuable gift of reflection is possible.
Graham Watts, a therapist at Glasgow's Harvest Clinic, speaking on Gascoigne, February 1998.

To be honest, I wouldn't go near him. He's like a runaway horse. I think it's way too late to rescue him because he has probably lost all credibility in the public eye. He doesn't listen to anyone, he's totally impulsive, he's got no humility – which goes a long way in this country – and for me it would be a waste of time and effort to take him on as a client.
PR guru **Max Clifford** on Gascoigne, February 1998.

Reporter: I'm from *The Sun.*
Gascoigne: I'm from the earth.
Exchange between journalist **Jim Black** and **Paul Gascoigne**, March 1998.

With Paul Gascoigne, what you get is chaos.
Radio Five DJ **Danny Baker**, 12 February 1997.

There are people who just say there isn't a problem. The SFA were very disappointing. We had this thing with Gascoigne playing a flute. This is the last thing you want to be doing, and Rangers should be doing something. They took no action whatsoever; not even a reprimand.
Celtic managing director **Fergus McCann**, February 1999, after Gascoigne had mimed playing the flute at the January 1998 Old Firm game.

Gazza obviously thought it was some kind of joke. But he must be just about the only person in the world who did.
Former Rangers defender Tom Cowan, on Gascoigne's mimicked flute-playing, quoted in book, *On the Edge,* 1998.

GIRLS GIRLS GIRLS

They should be in the kitchen. I'm serious. That's where they should be.
Rangers defender John Brown on women's football, 7 November 1994.

Take them seriously? We might if they didn't look like the bouncers from Victoria's.
More from John Brown, probably not a new man, 7 November 1994.

If it was a straight choice between having sex and scoring a goal, I'd go for the goal every time. I've got all my life to have sex.
Former Scotland striker Andy Gray on TV show, *Danny Baker After All,* 1995.

A magazine wanted to team me up with Playboy's Playmate of the Month, who came from Vancouver. She had been paid $100,000. I had been fined for showing mine. I was up for being pictured alongside her, but the wife wasn't keen so I didn't do it in the end.
Willie Johnston recalls playing for Vancouver Whitecaps, May 1996. He'd been fined $2,000 for mooning at Bruce Rioch, then with Seattle Sounders.

After a game Italian footballers like to relax with a few glasses of wine. Scottish players prefer to go looking for a bevvy and a shag.
Hibs manager Jim Duffy on the differing cultural philosophies of the two countries, March 1997.

My chat-up line used to be, 'I know a lot of Page Three birds, so I know a lot about boobs – show me your boobs and I'll see how they compare.'
Frank McAvennie, August 1997.

A woman would be able to nag a wall back ten yards.
TV pundit Chick Young on woman referees, November 1997.

We couldn't do any worse than some of the men who are currently refereeing the Scottish game.
Female ref Helena McGilveray, November 1997.

Women are more perceptive and observant, they notice things more. As for fears that women officials won't be able to stamp their authority on the game, whoever said that can't be married to one.
Manchester United's **Brian McClair** on women referees, *Odd Man Out*, 1997.

If I turn the telly on at 7.30 on a Sunday morning there's some bird with long blonde hair telling me how I should run my team.
Coventry boss **Gordon Strachan**, January 1998. The 'blonde bird' was Soccer AM's Helen Chamberlain.

The shock-horror element is that it will be a woman who takes the seat and she won't be making the tea.
Scottish Women's FA secretary **Maureen McGonigle** on moves for a woman representative on the SFA Council, January 1998.

I think we have reached the stage where man are not as confrontational anymore.
Scottish Women's FA secretary **Maureen McGonigle**, January 1998.

I thought she was outstanding. Lovely girl. When she came on she was wearing no jewellery at all. No earrings, no necklace, no rings whatsoever. And I thought, 'That's class.'
Scotland boss **Craig Brown** on meeting Kylie Minogue on Ally McCoist's TV chat show, February 1998.

We asked Maurice Johnston who his ideal room-mate on a Scotland trip would be and his sheet came back with 'a big blonde' written on it.
Craig Brown on the behind-the-scenes arrangements in the Scotland camp, May 1998.

It's like George Best once said to me: 'When you've had the last three Miss Worlds, then you can start talking.'
Maurice Johnston on footballers' hell-raising tales, quoted in *The Lad Done Bad: Sex, Sleaze and Scandal in English Football*, 1996.

I was a bit upset to see the one with the big knockers leave the band. You'll never replace her unless a girl with even bigger knockers comes along.
Ayr United's **Glynn Hurst** gets involved in the Geri Halliwell debate, August 1998.

GLUG GLUG GLUG

It was a big surprise to me in Ipswich to see how much the players would drink. If you arrive with red eyes, smelling or without sleep in training at Kiev, no one will talk to you because they feel you've let them down.
Former St Johnstone defender **Sergei Baltacha**, December 1995.

I can't dream up worse people to be in rehab together than Durrant, McCoist and big Norman Whiteside. It's like sending Oliver Reed and Dean Martin to the Betty Ford clinic together.
Rangers' **Ally McCoist**, in *Blue & White Dynamite – The Ian Durrant Story*, 1998.

It is usually the legendary drinkers at a club who are the best trainers. Okay, they go out and get into an unathletic state but, come the next training day, they put in more effort than the non-drinkers because they feel they have to.
Former Hearts striker **John Colquhoun**, 1996.

The men really seem to have a good time in there. You can hear them cheering each other and giving directions.
Female patron at Paramount Bar, Aberdeen, where gents' toilets urinals are on top of video screens showing football – punters can relieve themselves on to their favourites, May 1996.

The man with the safest hands in football, especially when there happens to be a white wine and soda clasped in them.
Rangers' **Ally McCoist** on Andy Goram, June 1996.

On last season's pre-season tour, my room-mate returned blind drunk. Mistaking my bed for the toilet, he relieved himself all over it with me inside.
Tranmere's **Pat Nevin** on the delights of pre-season training, August 1996.

The night before a game I'd a couple of beers or something and he [Walter Smith] asked me if I'd had a drink and I owned up to it. I said, 'Yeah'. He said, 'Well, I ain't playin' you' . . . and he dropped me and didn't speak to me for about ten days.
Paul Gascoigne in TV documentary, *Gazza's Coming Home*, October 1996. The match concerned was against Falkirk in November 1995.

I respect people who like beer and I want people to respect that I only drink Coca-Cola.
Teetotal Celtic striker Jorge Cadete, April 1997.

I managed to get him on the roof of the bus, which was a one-off.
Goalkeeper Andy Goram recalls helping Brian Laudrup celebrate Rangers' 1996 Coca-Cola Cup with over Hearts, 1997.

It's a miracle I have as many wines as this because Andy Goram came for a week last summer and he insisted on sleeping down here.
Rangers' Brian Laudrup on the wine cellar at his home in Denmark, 1997.

In America, once you're famous they adore you for the rest of your life. Plus the pina coladas are great.
Paul Gascoigne, suggesting he would go to the US rather than England if he left Rangers, 1997.

My hero's Bryan Robson. He's the only player I've ever known who could drink 16 pints and still play football the next day.
Rangers' Paul Gascoigne, 1997, long before joining Robson's Middlesbrough.

This reputation as a boozer bewilders me because he can't drink. Try taking him to TGI Friday's for cocktails and you're on a winner. It's a cheap night.
Rangers team-mate Ian Durrant on Paul Gascoigne, in Blue & White Dynamite – The Ian Durrant Story, 1998.

Amongst other things I told them that they all had to give up drinking and that they'd be called in for extra training on Sundays. When they realised it was all a wind-up, I've never seen grown men looking so relieved.
Alan Hansen after pretending he was taking over as Liverpool boss from Kenny Dalglish, October 1997.

I walked into the Celtic directors' lounge with my Rangers strip on. I went to the bar and had a double whisky ten minutes before the game.
Paul Gascoigne on his first Old Firm game, October 1997.

In the Coca Cola-Cup final against Hearts . . . I wasn't having the best of games, Archie [Knox] asked: 'Are you all right?' I said, 'No, the last time I felt like this I had a double whisky.' So I had one and scored two goals in the second-half. It relaxes you.
Paul Gascoigne on the Coca-Cola Cup final, October 1997.

When I came to England ten years ago it wasn't a surprise to go out for a pint on a Tuesday night. It would be now.
Blackburn's **Colin Hendry**, January 1998.

If you come in smelling of drink on a Thursday, you're not playing on a Saturday. I'll not fine you, but I'll say, 'You can explain it to the press why you're not playing, explain to the fans, these people who give you all that money, how you've been disrespectful to the people you play with.'
Coventry boss **Gordon Strachan**, August 1998.

We turned up at a party in a pub 20 minutes before it was due to close and downed 25 Blue Label vodkas in that time. Soon afterwards we both hit a brick wall and ended up crying for our mothers.
Kilmarnock's **Gary Holt** recalls high jinks from his teenage army days, August 1998. He is, strangely enough, now teetotal.

If you get the bad ones, who take kids out drinking, are up late at night, eat the wrong things, come in scruffy, then the kids look up to them and think that's the way to be. That's what happened to me at Dundee. I was brought up in that environment, and didn't know any better until I went to Aberdeen. Everybody else went drinking on Thursday night so I did.
Coventry boss **Gordon Strachan**, February 1999.

I'm not denying there were drugs involved. I'm denying I took any.
Clydebank player–manager **Ian McCall** after he'd been taken to hospital suffering from an accelerated heartbeat, March 1999. McCall suggested his drink had been spiked on a night-out.

When I heard that I thought, 'Jesus, does every manager in the Premier League think I'm this nutcase who drinks every night?'
Everton striker **Don Hutchison**, April 1999, recalling being rejected by Blackburn boss Ray Harford while at West Ham.

GOALIES

One of the old trainers, John Latimer, said to me, 'Goalkeepers have got to be crackers and daft. You, son, have got the qualities of an international.' I took it as a compliment.
Former Hibs keeper **John Burridge**, recalling coming into the game as a 15-year-old.

Howard [Wilkinson] rang me to say he needed a keeper. I told him he had one. 'Nah, I've had a look at Goram in training and I'm not impressed,' Howard said. So I told him to take the Pompey keeper, Alan Knight, it'd put a few thousand on the gate. It was a blessing in disguise.

Scotland goalkeeping coach Alan Hodgkinson on England's decision not to pick Andy Goram for an under-21 game against Greece in 1983.

I remember looking at the Hamilton goalkeeper that day, Dave McKellar, and thinking, 'This guy is not going to be beaten.'

Former Rangers goalkeeper Chris Woods after his old club were drawn against Hamilton in the 1998 Scottish Cup. Accies beat Rangers 1–0 in the competition in 1987.

Suddenly everyone was afraid of me. I remember Mark McGhee at Reading rang nine people to check on my frame of mind to join them on loan. You'd have thought I was signing for nine years, not going on loan for a month. It took another 21 months to get away from United and in that time I played in just 7 reserve games.

Scotland goalkeeper Jim Leighton, June 1996.

To this day I have never watched it [the 1990 FA Cup final] on TV. I remember the goals well enough and accept that I was probably at fault for the first and the third. People still ask me if I expected to get dropped for the replay. I didn't. It was the final straw as far as I was concerned. But the worst thing about it was the way everyone was made out to be so caring. Ferguson told the press that Les Sealey had offered to give me his medal. What he didn't tell them was that I was entitled to a medal anyway as I had played in the first game. But I didn't want it. I sent the medal back to the FA.

Jim Leighton remembers the end of his Manchester United career bitterly, June 1996.

The nicest part of it is when my kids come back from school and say, 'The teacher said you had another good game last night, Daddy.'

Jim Leighton, December 1995.

He cried on the bus all the way back to the hotel then all that night and all the way home on the plane the day after. It was awful. There was nothing you could say to him.

Jason McAteer on Celtic's Pat Bonner, after his mistake had gifted Holland's Wim Jonk a goal and sent Ireland to defeat in the 1994 World Cup.

I've had so many stitches that if I shaved my hair off my head would look like a knitted balaclava.

Airdrie keeper John Martin, October 1994.

It wasn't much fun letting in four, five or six goals every week. That's basically what it was. I can't stand there and take stick for that week in, week out. Enough is enough.

Albion Rovers keeper Marc Osborne on why he failed to turn up for a match against Queen's Park, November 1995. Rovers, who'd lost 15 goals in their previous four games, played a striker in goal and lost 4–1.

When I pass away you can put it on my tombstone – Andy Goram broke his heart.

Celtic boss Tommy Burns after Goram's performance had defied his team in a 1996 Old Firm game.

I'd be the ruination of the game if I got my way. All I want to see is goalies keeping clean sheets. That's not what the fans want, is it?

Scotland goalkeeping coach Alan Hodgkinson 1996.

I've played with Peter for years, watched him develop into one of the world's best. But Andy comes close; as strong one-on-one, perhaps on the goalline he's even better. The only way they differ is Andy is quieter on the pitch than Peter . . . and much louder off it.

Rangers' Brian Laudrup on Goram and Schmeichel, June 1996.

He's a character but where the game is concerned he's 100 per cent serious.

Alan Hodgkinson on Andy Goram, June 1996.

In goal we have the remarkable David Wylie, probably the only keeper in the history of football to concede seven goals in a game and still be named Man of the Match.

Philip Patrick, *The Absolute Game,* March 1997. (A heroic defensive performance inspired by Wylie had Morton leading Aberdeen 3–2 until the closing minutes of a Coca-Cola Cup third round tie in September 1996. Aberdeen equalised then scored four times in extra time to win 7–3.)

In my second match for Kilmarnock, I had to shout, 'Please stop all the talking!'

Kilmarnock goalkeeper Dragoje Lekovic, May 1997.

[Sylvester] Stallone had so many minders and bodyguards around him. When you got him on his own he was alright. Did I crack a few by him? Yeah, he was hopeless in goal but he was a trier.
Former Ipswich midfielder John Wark on acting in the film Escape to Victory with Stallone and Michael Caine, May 1999.

GOALS

I've seldom felt so depressed. After 19 years of giving everything to score goals, I'd finally scored one which I almost wish I hadn't.
Denis Law on scoring the Manchester City goal which relegated Manchester United, 27 April 1974. It was Law's last league goal. (Technically speaking, the goal didn't relegate United at all. Wins for Birmingham and Southampton the same day meant they'd have gone down even if they'd won.)

All the Scotland posters in my room had been ripped down after the games against Peru and Iran. After that goal [Archie Gemmill's against Holland] they went back up.
Scotland skipper Gary McAllister's memories of 1978, September 1995.

A complete fluke.
Rangers' Mark Walters on his goal direct from a corner-kick in the Old Firm game, 2 January 1991. Rangers won 2–0.

I remember the game because I managed to do something very few players can claim – I set up an international goal for Brian McClair!
Ally McCoist on the 1992 European Championship match against the CIS, quoted in match programme for his 50th cap against Australia, March 1996.

The game's never over till the fat striker scores.
Hearts' John Robertson after his last-minute equaliser earned Hearts a point in the Edinburgh derby, 1 October 1995. It was his 22nd derby goal and his 184th for Hearts – one ahead of Tynecastle legend Willie Bauld.

You do things that are strange when you score. Once against Celtic I ran behind the goal and jumped into the arms of a superintendent who was wearing ribbons on his cap. As I'm jumping on him I'm thinking, 'What the fuck am I doing?'
Rangers goalkeeper Andy Goram, June 1996.

There are two reasons why I claimed the goal from Gazza. First, I was in the box at the time. Second, it nearly hit me.
Ally McCoist on scoring the goal against Hibs that broke Gordon Wallace's record of 264 league goals, 8 December 1996.

I'm not really interested in playing good football. I just want to score goals.
Ally McCoist, January 1997.

I haven't kept count. I'm not that sad a person.
Brian McClair after being asked how many goals he'd scored for Manchester United, April 1997.

I'm just lucky in that I've always been able to score goals. Over the years I've discovered that managers and supporters quite like that.
Stenhousemuir's **Willie Watters**, scorer of over 180 goals at 11 senior clubs, August 1998.

My role is simply to score.
Stephane Guivarc'h defending his form with Rangers, for whom he'd scored 7 goals in 12 games without impressing, February 1999.

GROUNDS

Jock Stein: What's your park like tonight?
Andy Russell: Good enough for what's going on it.
Exchange between the Celtic boss and the Motherwell groundsman, early '70s. Quoted in *Craig Brown: The Autobiography*, 1997.

I could have signed for Rangers or Celtic but Tottenham were after me. I've always been a sucker for a good ground and White Hart Lane just impressed me.
Graeme Souness, April 1996.

Compared to the facilities at Rugby Park – and Kilmarnock, remember, was not a wealthy club – the dressing-rooms and training ground were a disgrace for a club of Celtic's stature, and the showers were unbelievably antiquated.
Former Celtic winger **Davie Provan**, quoted in Tom Campbell and Pat Woods, *Dreams, and Songs to Sing*, 1996.

I know the big clubs need more money to make their grounds into superstadia but smaller clubs like us need money just to keep going.
Donald MacKay, manager of [then] Second Division Blackburn Rovers, 1991.

Hampden is a testimonial to someone's ego. Can someone explain how you can spend £10m building a stadium that's going to be used 22 days out of 365 and sit in the rain and rot the rest of the time? It's crazy.
Former Dundee chairman **Ron Dixon**, February 1992.

I've noted quite a difference at Fir Park since Motherwell built their new stand. We used to go there and get results all the time but the new stand has added to the atmosphere and the place is more intimidating than it used to be.
Hearts' **Craig Levein**, March 1994.

In the last six years we've spent £52m on players and stadium improvements – with £20m going on players. In the next six years we're not going to spend another £32m on the stadium. We might have to spend £3m or £4m to finish off the corners. We'll go for a 50,000 capacity, and put in giant screens for the big nights in Europe.
Rangers chairman **David Murray**, November 1994.

I would hope to do many things after Hampden has been completely re-built, but it is doubtful if anything will give me greater satisfaction than that project.
SFA Chief Executive **Jim Farry**, January 1995.

If Cantona had jumped into our crowd he'd never have come out alive.
Millwall midfielder **Alex Rae**, 1995.

The dressing-room at Ibrox is very ornate, austere, salubrious. There are a lot of windows, so when the sun shines, the dressing-room can be filled with light . . . it's very much a church-like atmosphere.
Terry Butcher, March 1996.

Five clubs in England obtained relaxation from [the] Taylor Report for the season, yet we got none from the Scottish Football Association, even though Taylor is not law in Scotland.
Celtic Chief Executive **Fergus McCann**, June 1996.

The lads are used to playing in front of cowsheds in Wales at places like Ton Pentre. Some of the pitches are like ploughed fields. You actually see cows walking past sometimes. This is a little bit different.
Barry Town player-coach Gary Barnett at Pittodrie before the UEFA Cup first-round tie, September 1996.

Millions of people who don't know me probably believe I'm a dour Scot who refuses to sit down during matches. I always stood up at Liverpool because I couldn't see. The dugout was low.
Kenny Dalglish, *Dalglish – My Autobiography*, 1996.

I don't think Jesus Christ himself could have put nice passing movements together on that pitch.
Celtic manager Tommy Burns after a 1–1 draw at Stark's Park, 8 April 1997.

When I started working for the radio I'd to ask people how to get to every ground except Ibrox and Rugby Park, because when I'd been playing I'd get on the bus, never look out of the window, play cards or talk. Then we'd get to the ground and get off. I'd never had to get to grounds myself.
Pundit Gordon Smith, Radio Scotland, 4 October 1997.

To ensure the shamrocks would grow when the sod was replanted on the field.
The *Derry People and Donegal News* explains why the first piece of the new Parkhead pitch was kept watered after being cut in Mullaghduff, Donegal, before being transported to Glasgow, April 1995. Quoted in Tom Campbell and Pat Woods, *Dreams, and Songs to Sing*, 1996.

HEALTH

I wake up after an operation so relieved to see the legs are still there.
Morton manager Allan McGraw, who's had six knee replacement operations, May 1996.

One stupid little injury, when I was probably feeling as sharp and as quick and as fit and as confident as I had ever done in my life . . . well, it's hard to explain, really hard to explain. It's not as if occasions like that crop up

every year. That was it. My chance had gone. I was inconsolable, absolutely devastated, and I still think about it now. Of what might have been.
Gordon McQueen on the injury which kept him out of the Argentina '78 World Cup, quoted in Mike Wilson, *Don't Cry For Me Argentina*, 1998.

When I saw the Raith goalie save the last penalty my life flashed before my eyes. I felt like throwing myself in the River Forth but chose pills instead. It was a silly thing to do but I can't think of a worse afternoon in my life. The hospital kept me in for two days because I had done such a good job on myself.
Celtic fan **Peter Marshall**, who required his stomach pumped after downing a bottle of sleeping pills after Celtic's Coca-Cola Cup defeat by Raith Rovers, November 1994.

He's a vain bastard. I thought he was going to tell me he was having another nose job.
Liverpool assistant manager **Phil Boersma** recalls hearing of manager Graeme Souness's triple heart by-pass, quoted *in The Lad Done Bad – Sex, Sleaze & Scandal in English Football*, 1996.

It was like someone saying, 'You're dying, but it's not as bad as it sounds.'
Aberdeen defender **Brian Irvine**, on being told he'd multiple sclerosis in June 1995.

I'm the fittest man in the game. Alan Shearer? I'd run him into the ground.
Former Hibs keeper **John Burridge**, August 1995.

I've got a job I love at a club I love. If you're going to have a heart attack, you might as well have it at a game. At least all the medics are there already.
Morton manager **Allan McGraw**, May 1996.

I was out in Toulon for the under-21 tournament when Maradona was banned for having traces of cocaine, and one of the medical staff out there who works for a big pharmaceutical company said Maradona would have needed to have come off the pitch once every five minutes to have a line of cocaine to make it enhance his game.
Chelsea striker **John Spencer**, May 1996.

I don't think a player ever plays 100 per cent fit now. Never.
Scotland captain **Gary McAllister**, November 1997.

Doctors are like aeroplanes: sometimes there are mistakes.
Profound words from Rangers' striker **Sebastian Rozental** after being told
he required a second knee operation, February 1998.

My father lost his leg and yet he played in goal for his team. That was my
driving force.
Former Scotland manager **Ally MacLeod**, April 1998.

I've never met this woman and I never will.
Sceptic Scotland skipper **Gary McAllister** after England faith healer Eileen
Drewery offered to help him over the knee injury which ruled him out of
France '98, June 1998.

I gave Tina a card and a box of chocs as I was leaving. That's the least I could
do for someone who has to stand and watch me trying to pee into a bottle.
Former Rangers defender **Tom Cowan** on a nurse in the Bradford clinic
where he was recovering from a cruciate operation, quoted in book *On The
Edge*, 1998.

HO HO HO

I don't know whether to line the park or just put kerbstones down the
sides.
Rangers groundsman **Davie McLeod** on hearing wingers Willie Henderson
and Bobby Hume both wore contact lenses. Quoted in *Craig Brown: The
Autobiography*, 1997.

Andy Roxburgh: My touch has gone. I'll need to take a couple of weeks
to get it back.
Player: It'll need to be a couple of weeks in Lourdes.
Exchange between Scotland boss and player, mid-'80s.

You couldn't give him a brass neck with a blowtorch.
Rangers' **Ally McCoist** on a member of Scotland's backroom staff, 1993.

Policeman: Do you have a police record, Mr McCoist?
Ian Durrant: Aye, *Walking On The Moon*.
Exchange in East Kilbride police station, 1986, quoted by Ally McCoist in *Blue
& White Dynamite – The Ian Durrant Story*, 1998.

People say I am the presenter with the biggest tits on television. That's true. They're called Chick Young and Rob Maclean.
BBC's **Hazel Irvine** at celebrity team Dukla Pumpherston's charity dinner, April 1994.

He came out for a cross ball like a drunk man chasing a balloon.
Premier Division manager on opposition goalkeeper, April 1994.

I wouldn't say 'you should take six off the Faroes', I'd say 'from the Faroes'.
Scotland boss and semantics expert **Craig Brown**, October 1994.

He's so small we didn't have to pay VAT on his playing kit.
Falkirk chairman George Fulston on 5' 2" in new signing **Jamie Patterson**, December 1994.

I don't know if he'll improve the team but he'll improve the team picture.
Hearts' **John Colquhoun** on Premier Division rivals signing a handsome new player, (Aberdeen's John Inglis, since you ask) 1995.

The last time Thistle were in Europe the stewardess didn't come round with earphones, she came round with goggles.
Partick Thistle boss **John Lambie** as the club embarked on an InterToto Cup run, 1995.

I tell the players they have made a happy man very old.
Raith Rovers boss **Jimmy Nicholl**, April 1995.

They've nicknamed me Ena Sharples because my head was never out of the net.
Keith goalkeeper **Ian Thain** after losing ten goals to Rangers, Scottish Cup, January 1996.

Don't worry about making mistakes. If we didn't make mistakes I'd be manager of AC Milan and you'd be playing for me.
Livingston boss **Jim Leishman** pre-match talk, Livingston v Queen's Park, 10 January 1996.

I like coming here [to Ibrox] with Gerry. He gets even more stick than I do.
Scottish Television pundit **Charlie Nicholas** on commentator Gerry McNee, Rangers v Aberdeen, 28 April 1996.

The only man in the Scotland squad who could walk on to the back of a horse.
Ally McCoist on goalkeeper Jim Leighton, June 1996.

His epitaph will read: Here lies Stuart McCall, a groundsman's nightmare. He made it into the Guinness Book of Records for the world's longest slide tackle – he dispossessed a guy playing on another park.
Ally McCoist on Stuart McCall, June 1996.

'Is it a life ban, Kenny?'
'Depends how long you live, Matt.'
Exchange between Liverpool boss **Kenny Dalglish** and **Matt D'Arcy** of the *Daily Star*, quoted in *Dalglish: My Autobiography*, 1996.

Our Ibrox five-a-sides in training are the front page against the back page.
Member of Rangers' coaching staff, September 1996. At the time, the doings of McCoist, Goram, Brown (driving offences), Miller (assault), Dodds and Van Vossen (marital problems) had all been eagerly scrutinised by newspapers.

Hear about the two cows in the field? One of them says to the other, 'Hear you've got that Paul Gascoigne disease.'
Paul Gascoigne, in TV documentary, *Gazza's Coming Home*, October 1996.

If I meant it I should be playing in Serie A.
Kilmarnock defender **Kevin McGowne** after being penalised for a miskicked clearance construed as a passback, November 1996. Motherwell scored from the resultant free-kick.

Archie Knox: You don't know what the pressure of this job is like. You don't know what it's like to be in our shoes.
Willie Young: Archie, if I was in your shoes your IQ would treble.
Trackside exchange between Rangers assistant boss **Knox** and fourth official **Young** during the New Year Old Firm match, 2 January 1997.

The story had sufficient credence for BBC Scotland to seek the authoritative view of Chick Young. 'What'll this new team be called?' enquired Chick, bringing his usual gravitas to the subject. 'Timbledon?'
Gary Oliver, *The Absolute Game* fanzine, April 1997. A proposed Celtic takeover of Wimbledon was the topic under discussion.

[Jorge] Cadete reminds me of Hans Eskilsson. But only in the hair.
Hearts' **John Colquhoun**, BBC TV, after Cadete scored his 28th goal of the season against Hearts, 1 March 1997. Swede Eskilsson, a former team-mate of Colquhoun's at Tynecastle, was not so prolific.

I went into a shop in Manchester where the star of a children's show was trying to use his celebrity status to extort free goods from the assistants. He asked me what I'd had free as a footballer and I told him, 'Verbal abuse!'
Brian McClair, *Odd Man Out*, 1997.

No. 6: Johann Cruyff. We had a lot in common. The same initials.
John Colquhoun, picking his top ten players of all time, October 1997.

He looked like a pint of Guinness.
Rangers' **Paul Gascoigne** after Paul Ince played for England against Italy with a bandaged head, 11 October 1997.

It stands for Most Bandy Ever.
Team-mate **Billy Dodds'** unkind observation on the MBE awarded to Aberdeen's Jim Leighton, 3 January 1998.

He should have had a part in *The Full Monty*. You can see why he's nicknamed 'Tripod'.
Clydebank player-boss **Ian McCall** on defender Paul Lovering, January 1998.

The black players at [Nottingham] Forest always had the last laugh when we got into the showers. Chris Fairclough was nicknamed 'Mamba'. I'll leave the rest to your imagination.
Dundee's **Jim McInally**, March 1998.

We've 53 caps between us.
Craig Brown on his and Glenn Hoddle's varying international careers, February 1998. Hoddle has 53 caps, Brown, none.

I've never played against Marc Rieper. But I don't fear him.
Blue Öyster Cult reference from **Ally McCoist** on the eve of the Old Firm game, 3 April 1998.

The players are calling me Robert Van Vossen but the park was bumpy, the ball bobbled, the sun was in my eyes, my hair was in my eyes and the crowd were trying to put me off.
Queen of the South's **Robert Connor** convincingly explains away a miss against Forfar, 18 April 1998.

They want to use me as a centre-forward because I'd be the biggest player in the country.

5' 9" **Ian Durrant** considers an offer from Japanese J–League side Hiroshima SanFrecce, May 1998.

Our first league game is against Airdrie at their new stadium. Hopefully they won't mind playing seven-a-sides across it.

Clydebank manager **Ian McCall**, 23 July 1998. Cash-strapped Bankies had only 7 signed players 16 days before their opening league game.

I had a bad game and the boss fined me £80,000.

Former Dundee United defender **Paul Hegarty** on his Tannadice testimonial which earned him £70,000, March 1999.

It would take a mad axeman running amok in the dressing-room for me to get back into the team.

Frozen-out Spurs defender **Colin Calderwood**, March 1999. He signed for Aston Villa soon afterwards.

He would feel at home wearing our strip because it's red, white and blue like the French national side's. We might manage to throw in a penthouse flat in Portpatrick as well.

Stranraer manager **Campbell Money** on prospects of signing World Player of the Year Zinedine Zidane, whose wife wants him to move to a club on the coast, April 1999.

Grant [Johnson] has a university degree in European Studies and completes a trio of graduates in the Town dressing-room. The Three Degrees, we call them.

Former Rangers defender **Tom Cowan**, then with Huddersfield, quoted in book, *On The Edge*, 1998.

Pontefract Collieries 1 Huddersfield Town 5. It doesn't sound much but it meant a hell of a lot to be back in a Town starting line-up, even if it was basically a reserve team. The manager gave me 75 minutes. Almost the full Ponty.

Former Rangers defender **Tom Cowan**, quoted in book, *On the Edge*, 1998.

I got my wee mastiff puppy when I was still at Rangers. It was pissing and shitting all over the flat so I kept on having to run off after training to let it out. After a couple of weeks one of the coaches there pulled me over and said, 'What's up – you aren't eating with the rest of the lads after training. They want you to eat with them, they want you to stick around.' I suddenly realised that playing football isn't just about being fit and skilled. It's about team spirit and knowing each other.
Chelsea's John Spencer, May 1996.

I don't want to offend any woman, but not many players could say they can go back home and really talk about football like they do with another man.
Rangers' Brian Laudrup on wife Mette, September 1996.

I've got a local pub I go to on a Saturday night about half past nine and everybody there knows absolutely zero about football. So whether you win 7–0 or lose 7–0 you go and talk about who's been doing what in the village.
Coventry boss Gordon Strachan, August 1998.

Remote? It's not remote enough for me.
Former Scotland goalkeeper David Harvey, now a pig farmer on the Orkney island of Sanday (population 548), September 1995.

My political life has also brought me friendship with Yasser Arafat, Gerry Adams, Saddam Hussein and his son Uday. I am general sales agent for Yugoslavia for Iraqi Airways and visited His Excellency last year in Baghdad.
Prospective Dundee investor Giovanni Di Stefano fails to build a winning case for his defence amid claims of an alleged friendship with Serbian war crimes suspect Zelkjo Raznatovic, 17 March 1999.

It is better that I am here. If I was in Scotland I would be worried sick.
Motherwell coach Miodrag Krivokapic on being trapped in Belgrade during the NATO bombing offensive, April 1999. Krivokapic had returned to visit his family three days before the bombing began.

It's incredible. It really does sound as if there is a train going through the room. Even if you stuff a pillow over your ears there's no escape. It's a wonder he doesn't keep the whole hotel awake.
Wimbledon's Neil Ardley on team-mate Neil Sullivan's snoring, April 1999.

INTERNATIONALS

We looked like liquorice allsorts.
Midfielder Willie Fernie on Scotland's 1954 World Cup squad, whose players trained in their own kit.

The competition was treated almost as an end-of-season tour.
Scotland's Neil Mochan on the 1954 World Cup.

Scotland's number four, the captain, shouted at me a couple of times during the match, 'Nigger, hey nigger!' He spat at me too, and he spat in Mana's face. Scotland's number four is a wild animal.
Zaire's Mulamba Ndaie on playing Scotland in the 1974 World Cup, quoted in Simon Kuper, *Football Against The Enemy*, 1974. Number four was Billy Bremner.

Q: What is your most treasured material possession?
A: The Scottish cap given to me by Denis Law in 1974 when Scotland qualified for the World Cup finals in West Germany.
Rod Stewart, magazine questionnaire, January 1997.

The whole trip was a shambles, a joke. Peru had us watched five or six times. Ally MacLeod never got the chance to watch them. We were just handed a strip and told to go out and play for Scotland.
Willie Johnston on Argentina '78, May 1996.

I actually came of age that day . . . I always remember their manager, this guy Borras. He'd said before that match, 'No matter what, we will not resort to roughhouse tactics.' And of course they assassinated us for the best part of that game and got through. So I got hold of Borras after that and said, 'What was the deal?' He said, 'My friend, you have to remember this is a game for men, not women.' It is difficult to get up from that and I thought, 'You dirty bastard.'
Scottish Television's Jim White on Scotland v Uruguay in the 1986 World Cup, March 1996.

They were unavailable to us the last time, we're unavailable to them this time. Their ability has nothing to do with this.
Scotland boss **Andy Roxburgh** explaining why Liverpool's Steve Nicol and Gary Gillespie had been left out of the squad for a game against Argentina, March 1990.

It was as big a travesty of a result as I have ever been involved with.
Gary McAllister on Scotland's defeat by Germany in the 1992 European Championships, *Captain's Log*, 1995.

Scotland is not an international team – it's a mix of sheep shaggers.
Paul Gascoigne in Channel 4 documentary, *Gazza's Coming Home*, 1996.

It's a big regret for me, not playing for Scotland, but I look at some of the people who have been capped and you realise if they give out caps that cheaply, maybe I'm better off without one.
Rangers' **John Brown**, *Blue Grit*, 1995.

I saw a lecture by Carlos Alberta Parreira – Brazil's manager – and in this lecture he says that Brazil have the best players in the world – always have done. So why didn't they win the World Cup for 22 years? It was because they weren't organised and disciplined, especially when the other team had the ball. Criticising Aime Jacquet is horrendous because France have gone something like 24 games without defeat – it's not flamboyant but it's very good and safe. That's what we've tried to do with Scotland – make us hard to beat first.
Craig Brown, *The Absolute Game* fanzine, April 1997.

After nearly 100 senior international games on the bench in some capacity I still consider it a privilege to be able to sit at the side of the dug-out and watch Scotland as a supporter.
Craig Brown, *The Absolute Game* fanzine, April 1997.

It was a tricky situation. It was a very, very close game, a horrible pitch, not a great place. It was nice to see it hit the back of the net.
Scotland captain **Gary McAllister** on his match-winning penalty in Belarus, June 1997. It was his first penalty since missing at Wembley at Euro '96.

He chose to retire, I was retired.
Chelsea's **Steve Clarke** on his final appearance for Scotland – against Holland in May 1994 – which was also Ruud Gullit's last international, April 1997.

Darren Jackson: I'll be picked for Scotland before you are.
Ally McCoist: You could be right.
Exchange between the Scotland strikers before the Scotland v Belarus World Cup tie, 4 September 1997. Jackson had had a brain operation two days before. McCoist had said he wouldn't play in the game if it coincided with the funeral of Diana, Princess of Wales.

Nobody knew much about Jari Litmanen, the Ajax striker and Finnish playmaker, so we taped his domestic games and edited together every touch he had. Turned out he used the same trick over and over. We showed this edited version to Alan McLaren, who was going to do a man-to-man on him. Litmanen did nothing and we won.
Scotland boss **Craig Brown** on video coaching, June 1998.

The man has made his decision and I respect it.
Craig Brown on Andy Goram's retiral from the international scene on the eve of the World Cup, June 1998.

Once you retire, you retire.
Motherwell goalkeeper **Andy Goram** on refusing to change his mind about playing for Scotland, 12 January 1999.

Some people want me to return to the Scotland squad but it will never happen.
Andy Goram, 3 February 1999.

There was never any thought in my mind that I did not want to play for Scotland ever again.
Andy Goram, 4 February 1999.

I always said if they had any problems I would consider it.
Andy Goram, 5 February 1999.

When NATO say no, they mean no.
Bosnian FA head of international affairs **Velid Imamovic**, 25 March 1999, after the cancellation of his country's European Championship match in Scotland because of the war in the Balkans.

The game, whether the public likes it or not, needs a bureaucracy.
SFA Chief Executive Jim Farry, January 1995.

There is a journalistic predisposition towards equating anything that has
to do with the game's establishment with reward.
SFA Chief Executive Jim Farry, January 1995.

I consider myself one of the best administrators in Europe but there has
been criticism directed towards me which has abused the platform that
journalists have for comment.
Jim Farry, January 1995.

All I ever read is criticism of Jim Farry. For some reason the fact that he
was a market gardener is held against him. He joined my staff at the SFA
when he was 16 years old so I don't know when he fitted in the gardening.
But is there something wrong with gardening?
Former SFA secretary Ernie Walker, August 1995.

Myths have grown [around me] that I was a landscape gardener and that
rugby was my first love. Being a landscaper would have been job
promotion. I drove the dumper truck and shovelled soil. I was labouring
but that's character-forming. I played football before I did rugby and only
switched when I realised there was more chance of getting a regular game
in a 15-man side than one of 11.
Jim Farry, November 1996.

Players and managers . . . many of them wouldn't know what you mean
by the laws of football. They wouldn't know the colour of the book they
are contained in. And yet they are supposedly 'professional' while our
referees are meant to be the 'amateurs'.
Jim Farry, March 1996.

I'm a gregarious guy and I can tell and take a joke.
Jim Farry, November 1996.

We [secretaries of the SFA] do our best to ensure that when we come into
contact with people they leave saying, 'Hey, you're not like the guy I read

about.' Now all I need to do is meet another 4,900,000 people and the job's easy.
Jim Farry, reflecting on his job, August 1997.

If other people, clubs or public or the greater football audience don't like it, sometimes that is a testimony you are doing it quite well. If they liked you it could be a problem.
Jim Farry, August 1997.

When new people get involved in clubs we ask them to pop down and have a chat. They are amazed that we do not have three heads and actually look like them. Sometimes.
Jim Farry, August 1997.

Given the job I have, you can't be laugh-a-minute Jim or the Karaoke King of the SFA.
Jim Farry, August 1997.

I have never ducked a question in my life. All I do is answer questions, not make pronouncements.
Jim Farry, August 1997.

It is interesting to me to read that I growl or roar or fume. I don't. I just speak.
Jim Farry, August 1997.

I know myself, and my close peer group know me. So do the people I come into contact with. And I would like to think that if you conducted a poll among them you would find that the majority of these folk don't recognise that picture of me.
Jim Farry on his media image, August 1997.

Colin Hendry's out of the game and big Donald might be a valuable addition to the back four.
Jim Farry's ill-advised joke at Scottish Secretary Donald Dewar's calls for the Scotland v Belarus game to be moved because it coincided with the day of Diana, Princess of Wales's funeral, 2 September 1997.

We know stores will open at 1 p.m. or 2 p.m. on Saturday. We agree with that. It is a mark of sensitivity. We will open at 3 p.m.
Jim Farry refuses to change the Scotland v Belarus game from the day of the funeral.

It seems obvious to me there has been an awful lot of cant and hypocrisy about this matter. Worse, there has been deliberate massaging of reports and clever juxtapositions of truths which has raised media 'spin' to an art form.

Jim Farry on the storm surrounding the Scotland v Belarus match, 5 September 1997.

I don't feel any inclination to apologise. I may feel an inclination to review it with the benefit of hindsight but I don't think an apology would be an appropriate response at this time.

Jim Farry after the SFA bow to mounting pressure and change the Belarus game to Sunday 7 September.

There was absolutely no reason why Scotland should not have played Belarus hours after the service at Westminster Abbey – not because of any significance attached to that particular match or to football in general, but because the imposition of grieving by decree was itself insulting. As the few commentators who dared dissent from the prevailing orthodoxy pointed out, a full sporting card took place immediately following the state funeral of Winston Churchill; it would be a peculiar argument which asserted that Britain owed greater reverence to Princess Diana.

Gary Oliver, *The Absolute Game* fanzine, November 1997.

Let us examine, for instance, the possible motives of Ally McCoist and his blue-shirted chums who, displaying a praiseworthy fragility which had not been previously evident in their character, claimed that their emotional distress was so great as to prevent them giving their best if the game were to go ahead as planned. Even if this were true, one wonders whatever happened to the idea that players are professionals, expected to produce of their best unaffected by their personal circumstances. One was at least grateful that the death of Mother Teresa did not spark an exodus of Celtic players from the squad.

Ed Horton, *The Absolute Game* fanzine November 1997. McCoist and Rangers team-mates Gordon Durie and Andy Goram had expressed unhappiness at playing the Scotland game the same day as the funeral.

I don't mind Jim Farry because he's not the disease, he's just the symptom of it. The mindset is the problem, not the man.

Former Dundee chairman **Ron Dixon** on Jim Farry, February 1998.

I have never intentionally delayed anything in 26 years of administration.

Jim Farry, 5 March 1999, amid claims that he delayed Jorge Cadete's registration with Celtic three years previously.

The implication is that everything that happens at the SFA is personally handled by Jim Farry. This is correct only inasmuch as every story which appears in a newspaper is personally written by the editor.
Jim Farry, 5 March 1999.

The decision has been taken to dismiss Mr Farry for gross misconduct.
SFA statement firing Farry, 8 March 1999.

We all talk about showing loyalty but the first time something like this happens Jim has been persecuted. I'm certain this was more about personalities than anything else.
Stirling Albion director **John Smith** after Farry's sacking, 8 March 1999.

The view of my family is that I should just get the hell out. The last thing they would want is for me to become an obsessive old man with long fingernails worrying my life away about the outcome of a long drawn-out court case.
Jim Farry on taking legal advice over his sacking, 9 March 1999.

What kind of person do we need? I would say Superman.
SFA president **Jack McGinn** names the ideal choice as Farry's successor, 11 March 1999.

KENNY

That wee fat boy won't make a footballer.
Alex Ferguson's early verdict on Kenny Dalglish, quoted in *Dalglish – My Autobiography*, 1996. Ferguson and Dalglish played against one another when Dalglish was a Celtic reserve and Ferguson at Rangers.

Kenny Dalglish was a genius footballer, but he became a genius through hard graft. When we all played in the Celtic reserve team that became known as the Quality Street Kids, there was no way anyone would have thought Dalglish would go on to become such a fabulous player. He just couldn't score goals. He'd balloon balls away over the bar and into the terracings. With players in the team like Danny McGrain, Davie Hay, George Connelly and Vic Davidson, he just didn't stand out. But Kenny came back in the afternoons and grafted like mad to improve.
Former team-mate **Lou Macari**, 1994.

One of my weaknesses as a footballer was a shortage of self-belief. If I had had more self-confidence, I would have been a better player, and maybe a better manager as well.
Kenny Dalglish, *Dalglish: My Autobiography*, 1996.

Kenny Dalglish has as much personality as a tennis racket.
Mick Channon.

I just made the runs knowing the ball would come to me.
Liverpool striker **Ian Rush** on his striking partnership with Dalglish, 1983.

He is on a par with di Stefano. And that is the best compliment I can pay him.
George Best.

For the benefit of Anglo-Saxon viewers, I wonder if the TV sports presenters would consider using subtitles when interviewing Kenny Dalglish.
Letter, *Evening Standard*, 1986.

We were seeing an additional dimension to the man. It was a glimpse into the inner chamber that showed he was more than just a footballer. His shyness was cracked open by the tragedy. The man was clearly emotional in a way we had not imagined possible.
Rogan Taylor, Football Supporters' Association, after Hillsborough.

To sit and see people make mistakes will drive him nuts.
George Best, 1990.

The pressure is incredible. I can cope during the week but on match days I feel like my head is exploding.
Dalglish offering his resignation to Liverpool, 1991.

Kenny's such a football nut that you could mention any player in England and he'd know who you were talking about.
Alan Hansen, 1993.

He uses psychology, when you're injured he won't even speak to you. I think it comes from Bill Shankly: 'You're no use to me if you're injured.' Not even with Alan Shearer, at least not in front of the other players.
Blackburn's **Graeme Le Saux**, 1994.

If I was a punter I'd rather have Kenny Dalglish too.
Craig Brown amid criticism that a bigger name should have been appointed
Scotland manager, 1994.

He scored his few goals and when he did, he shared his enjoyment with
everybody. He had a better smile than Clark Gable. Beautiful teeth, arms
wide . . . he wasn't that big but he had a huge arse and that's where he got
his strength from.
Brian Clough on Dalglish, 1995.

He knew how to distribute his weight because there were far bigger players
than him trying to get the ball off him.
Graeme Souness, April 1995.

We won 2–1 and I was made up afterwards. Then the door opens and
Kenny Dalglish is standing there. 'Are you the groundsman? I've got some
advice for you – save up and buy a bloody mower!' I said, 'Mr Dalglish,
when I'm working for Liverpool I'll prepare pitches for Liverpool to play
on, but while I'm working here I'll prepare them for Crewe.' Christ! He
slammed the door so hard it nearly came off its hinges. I don't suppose I'll
get a job at Ewood Park now.
Crewe groundsman **John Huxley**, recalling a pre-season friendly, 1995.

In an ideal world I'd like to be Kenny Dalglish: go straight into
management with a successful team, win three Championships then leave
and return to management with another team whose chairman has bags of
money and win the Championship there.
Scotland skipper **Gary McAllister**, September 1995.

What has Dalglish done? He decides he doesn't want to stand in the tunnel
any more with his overcoat on. He wants to sit up there with the directors.
That's certainly not a crime but I'll tell you what: it's an abdication of his
managerial responsibilities.
Brian Clough, 1995.

After a few hiccups, Dalglish spent his way to the title then got out of the
hot seat rather than tackle obvious problems.
Former Celtic director **Michael Kelly**, August 1996.

Kenny has associates, colleagues, but only a few true friends. There's
nothing wrong with that because, at the end of the day, you only need six
people to carry your coffin.
Alex Ferguson on Dalglish, quoted in *Dalglish – My Autobiography*, 1996.

Q: Who's the greatest player you ever played with?
A: Kenny. Well, apart from Zico.
Graeme Souness, magazine questionnaire, April 1996.

I never fancied going abroad simply because I was afraid.
Kenny Dalglish, *Dalglish – My Autobiography*, 1996.

He's a lot of fun. You don't win many arguments but you have a lot of laughs.
Pal **Alan Hansen**, 15 January 1997.

He has marketed the dour image to protect himself.
Graeme Le Saux on Dalglish, May 1997.

My public image as a dour Scotsman doesn't worry me. Joe Fagan used to say he had a great relationship with me: 'I can't understand him and he can't understand me!'
Kenny Dalglish, in *Dalglish – My Autobiography*. 1996.

He is Liverpool to me, Kenny Dalglish. I just wanted to play for Liverpool like him, I just wanted to be like him.
Jason McAteer, June 1997.

Dalglish suffers from constipation of the emotions . . . In his belief, the world is divided into two groups: a select minority who know as much about football as Kenny Dalglish does, and the rest of us who know nothing, particularly his critics.
Michael Parkinson, February 1998.

Kenny was one of the dirtiest players I've ever seen. Not in a bad sense. But he had this way of shimmying and drawing players into fouls. It was totally deliberate and amazing to watch.
Frank McAvennie on Dalglish, February 1998.

He was everything, the best footballer I have ever played with or against. He's up there with Best, Beckenbauer and Maradona,
Former Liverpool striker **David Johnson** on Dalglish, April 1999.

MANAGERS

I have come to the conclusion that nice men do not make the best football managers.
Graeme Souness, in *No Half Measures*, 1985.

I don't like being a manager. I like being a coach.
Coventry boss **Gordon Strachan**, August 1998.

At half-time he [Jock Stein] came into the dressing-room at Cappielow and told our goalkeeper that he should have come for one of the crosses. The goalkeeper had the nerve to answer back: 'It's not my fault, it's their fault.' Jock responded by walking over and shutting each of the small windows so that nobody outside could hear. Then he went off his trolley, pouring verbal abuse on the keeper and us. Everyone knew there and then exactly where they stood. Answer back at your peril.
Kenny Dalglish recalls a Celtic reserve match, *Dalglish – My Autobiography*, 1996.

A marvellous man who maybe didn't have the luck, didn't get the support he should have got from the club.
Alex Ferguson on former Rangers boss Scot Symon, May 1997.

I played for Tommy Doc at Chelsea and the main thing I remember about him was that he was always throwing things. Anything from olives to pork pies. He'd just pick things up and throw them at people. Hit me with a fucking pastie once, right on the back of my head. I said, 'What d'you do that for?' He said, 'You weren't paying attention.' Fair enough, I suppose.
Ron Harris on Tommy Docherty, July 1995.

I worked under the Doc at Derby. I fancied a new contract for myself so I said to him, 'Get the fucking chairman in here.' So the chairman comes in. This bloke called George Hardy. I said, 'Listen, you cunt, get the fucking minute book out 'cause I'm having a new contract.' He went out and Tommy Doc says, 'You shouldn't call the chairman a cunt, you know.' I said, 'Listen Tommy, if I want to call him a cunt, I'll call him a cunt. And if I want to call you a cunt, I'll call you a cunt. All right?' He said, 'Fair point, Charlie, but you're asking for more money than Martin Buchan at Manchester United.' I said, 'Well, yeah, but Martin Buchan's not fit to wipe my arse.' After that he was as sweet as a nut. He couldn't

do enough for me. All you had to do with Tommy was put him right on a few points.
Negotiations expert Charlie George on Docherty, July 1995.

It was a dressing-room of old pros and shit-stirrers.
Tommy Docherty on the Manchester United team he inherited, April 1996.

My name is Ally MacLeod and I am a winner.
Ally introduces himself to the Scotland squad after taking over as manager, quoted in *Ally MacLeod – The Story*.

It was different. Some days he couldn't do enough for you, others he'd just ignore you.
Asa Hartford on his 63-day spell as a Nottingham Forest player under Brian Clough, quoted in *His Way*, 1993.

At two o'clock Joe Fagan sends the waiter away, saying, 'This is secret', then he gets up and says, 'Now lads, this team we're playing tonight are obviously a good team, because they won the Italian League and they're in the final of the European Cup, but they're not as good as us. Now I don't want to see any of you until five. Get to your rooms and get some sleep.' The kick-off was at seven. At twenty-five to, Alan Hansen is still telling jokes in the dressing-room and Joe comes in and points to his watch and says, 'Eh, lads, there's a game on tonight.'
Graeme Souness recalls Liverpool's preparations for the 1984 European Cup final against Roma in Rome. Liverpool won on penalties.

I had talks with Ron Atkinson when he was the manager at Old Trafford but he spent more time talking about himself than Manchester United and that put me off.
Charlie Nicholas, April 1995.

Graeme [Souness] was crucial for Rangers. People looked on Rangers as a tired club. He was the catalyst for change. Graeme made it possible for big names to want to come to Ibrox. David Murray and Walter Smith have been important but not as important as Graeme in the beginning. The ship was on the rocks and he turned it around.
Rangers chairman **David Murray**, November 1994.

What you needed was a manager who had the balls to say, 'Stuff everyone else, I'm going to do my own thing.' I don't think [Andy] Roxburgh was that man.
Rangers' **John Brown** on the former Scotland coach, in *Blue Grit*, 1995.

That Roxburgh, he looks like a BB captain. What you need are a bunch of corner-boys.

'60s photographer **Harry Benson** on Scotland coach Andy Roxburgh, October 1993.

Managing a club the size of Celtic or Rangers requires 24-hours-a-day commitment. You don't leave the problems behind you when you walk out the front door, and you don't look forward to a quiet night with your feet up in front of the television.

Tommy Burns, still a player at that point, on management, March 1989, quoted in Tom Campbell & Pat Woods, *Dreams, and Songs to Sing*, 1996.

He [Clough] had a real go at the young lad. It made me distinctly embarrassed and it looked, and sounded, dreadful. There was absolutely no need for the row.

Gary McAllister, *Captain's Log*, on the breakdown of his transfer from Leicester to Nottingham Forest. The 'young lad' was a waiter who'd angered Clough by noisily piling spoons into a tray nearby.

He [Macari] was not giving tactical instruction, was not around for training, would arrive at the last minute before the match and would give no team talk or preparation. They felt he had a very low opinion of the players.

Celtic managing director Fergus McCann at Lou Macari's claim for unfair dismissal at the Court of Session in Edinburgh, February 1997. Paul McStay, Pat Bonner, Charlie Nicholas and Peter Grant had visited McCann shortly after he took over in March 1994 to voice concerns about Macari's management style.

There were occasions when the players had no idea of the formation of the team even 15 or 20 minutes before kick-off. It was an intolerable situation and one that obviously affected the performance of the team . . . Basically, Lou was hardly ever there. When you wanted to speak to him, you were told he was down south.

Celtic's Peter Grant on life under Lou Macari, July 1994, quoted in Tom Campbell & Pat Woods, *Dreams, and Songs to Sing*, 1996.

I can remember worrying midway through lung-bursting, gut-busting running sessions about whether I would be able to recognise a ball again in the unlikely event of ever seeing one.

Garry Nelson recalls training under Lou Macari at Swindon.

He is a strange organiser of football tactics, and he never took people's emotions or personalities into account.
Former Celtic goalkeeper Allen McKnight on Macari, January 1995, quoted in Tom Campbell & Pat Woods, *Dreams, and Songs to Sing*, 1996.

Jim Duffy's a fine man and if the SFA have any sense they'll make him Scotland team coach.
Dundee chairman Ron Dixon, April 1994.

In 19 years involved in sport I have never come across a more capable person.
Dundee chairman Ron Dixon on manager Jim Duffy, May 1994.

Thick skin, a knowledge of every cliché ever invented, no sense of humour whatsoever, no personality and absolutely no money to spend. Then you have a fighting chance.
Dundee boss Jim Duffy on what's needed to be a good manager.

I must have been cuckoo to take the job.
Falkirk boss John Lambie after quitting, 22 March 1996. His troubled seven months in charge had seen them slump to the bottom of the Premier Division, prompting one fan to attempt to run his car off the road.

I can sleep at night, speak to the kids and I can smile. I can't remember being able to do that when I managed Kilmarnock.
SFA community development programme co-ordinator Jim Fleeting, May 1996.

If things go well here [Bristol City], if we progress together, the opportunity will arise again.
Joe Jordan on hopes of managing Scotland, June 1996.

I wish this man was Scottish.
Rod Stewart after being presented with a magazine award by Chelsea's Ruud Gullit, November 1996.

I quit as a manager because of the attitude of players and the involvement of agents.
Jim McLean after 25 years at Tannadice, December 1996.

It looks like another Merry Christmas in the Totten house.
Alex Totten after being sacked by Kilmarnock, 3 December 1996. He had been sacked by St Johnstone on 14 December 1992.

With guys like Kenny Dalglish and Graeme Souness it doesn't matter if they're playing tiddly-winks, they want to win. They've got to be involved in football. I've never had any regrets. I don't know if I've got the passion. I loved playing but I can take it or leave it now. I only need football five days a week, these people need it seven days a week – and a bit more.
TV pundit **Alan Hansen,** April 1997.

The best manager and the most knowledgeable man in football that I ever met was Willie McLean. It doesn't surprise me that Jim and Tommy do well because Willie helped them a lot. When I was assistant to Willie at Motherwell, Jim and Tommy would be on the phone for advice. He's the sharpest and most imaginative football brain.
Craig Brown, The Absolute Game fanzine, April 1997.

All a manager would do would be to put the club out of business.
Clydebank chairman **Jack Steedman** on why his club will never have a manager, April 1997.

He once made history by going almost a minute without mentioning Bill Shankly, or the fact that he was once signed for Liverpool.
Ally McCoist on Falkirk manager Alex Totten, May 1997.

If anyone is looking for an ugly wee man who shouts more than anyone else in Scottish football then I'm there for them.
Frank Connor offers his CV after quitting as Celtic reserve team boss, May 1997.

Wim [Jansen] didn't even ask how much Burley was costing nor does he know what any of the players earn.
Celtic general manager **Jock Brown** on coach Jansen, July 1997.

[Jock] Brown's immediate priority was to ensure the acquisition of a big-name coach and Celtic had clearly set their corporate heart on Bobby Robson, amidst heavy hints from Brown that the appointee would be 'of proven ability and able to walk into any of the top clubs in world football'. Instead, the new coach turns out to be Wim Jansen, who could no doubt walk into any major club, provided he paid at the turnstile like the rest of us.
Alastair McSporran, The Absolute Game fanzine, August 1997.

The best advice I had from people like Fergie and Bert Paton was that I wasn't there to please the players, they were there to please me.
Ross County boss **Neale Cooper,** October 1997.

If the team are crap, then that makes me a crap manager. Simple.
Wolves boss Mark McGhee, October 1997.

He sold keeper Paul Jones to Stockport for £60,000 and he is now valued at £1m. I am not impressed.
Wolves owner Sir Jack Heyward on McGhee, October 1997.

I underachieved as a player and I'm not going to underachieve as a manager.
Clydebank player-boss Ian McCall, January 1998.

I might not be a typical boss, but the most successful manager in Scotland goes to Bon Jovi concerts and rocks and he's got grey hair. So what's typical?
Clydebank player-boss Ian McCall, January 1998.

Whoever the next guy is, I'd advise him to live at least forty miles outside Glasgow.
Benfica manager Graeme Souness's advice to the new Rangers manager, January 1998.

I used to be a raving lunatic as a manager.
Craig Brown, February 1998.

Son of a bitch! The guy's the best coach in Scotland – and the best guy as well.
Former Dundee chairman Ron Dixon reacts with typical bluntness on hearing his former Dens boss Jim Duffy had been sacked as manager of Hibs, February 1998.

He's told me about the other teams interested and I've been talking him off them. As you do.
Raith boss Jimmy Nicholl on attempts to sign Ally McCoist, July 1998. McCoist eventually signed for Kilmarnock.

I didn't like him and he didn't like me.
Stenhousemuir striker Willie Watters explains the simple facts behind his fall-out with Stirling boss Kevin Drinkell, August 1998.

I had a call the other day from an agent who wanted to sell me a Cameroonian centre-forward. I told him, no. He said, 'But you don't even know his name.' I told him, 'I've got two forwards who made the England squad this season. I've got [Viorel] Moldovan at the World Cup with

Romania. And I've got two lads I can't even give a game to. I don't need to know his name.'
Coventry manager **Gordon Strachan**, August 1998.

We just become ex-football managers or ex-players in the end.
Tommy Burns, October 1997.

Dick's got that look that sometimes says, 'Whoever you are you're not going to mess with me, pal.' In Scotland we have this great tradition of the wayward Scot. I dread to think what he would make of it.
Former Scotland coach **Andy Roxburgh** on new Rangers coach Dick Advocaat, February 1998.

I would probably have eaten him alive as a centre-forward but the body language off the pitch, what with that Scottish mask of his, definitely said, 'I'm the boss. Be careful.'
Arsenal's **Tony Adams** on George Graham, September 1998.

Some of the money that has been lashed out by clubs like Clyde has been ridiculous and, without naming names, some managers should be sued for negligence.
Clyde general manager **Ronnie MacDonald**, October 1998.

I had one player come to me and apologise for playing badly the other day. That's incredible, isn't it?
Coventry boss **Gordon Strachan**, February 1999.

A great man and a great coach.
Motherwell striker **John Spencer** on his former Chelsea boss Glenn Hoddle, February 1999, the week after Hoddle was sacked by England.

At 2.15 on a Saturday I used to go back and forth to the toilet 45 times. So I knew management wasn't for me.
Former Liverpool defender **Alan Hansen**, March 1999.

As a manager you become streetwise quicker than normal. I am not as naïve as I used to be.
Stand-in Aberdeen boss **Paul Hegarty**, March 1999.

Because of the levels at which our ambitions lie, it's really quite difficult to improve our squad.
Manchester United boss **Alex Ferguson**, April 1999.

I've read of people refusing the coach's job here who haven't even been spoken to, far less made an offer. There's a pattern there: a guy punts a story saying he's been approached when he's not. I can speak of Gerard Houllier, because he was the one who broke our confidentiality agreement and put this into the public domain. We simply made an enquiry of Houllier about his possible availability, as we did with several people . . . let me say this emphatically, Houllier was never made an offer by us.
Celtic managing director **Fergus McCann**, April 1999.

He is a real gentleman, with intelligence, culture and integrity. He is a very different style from what you normally come across in football management.
Celtic managing director **Fergus McCann** on coach Jozef Venglos, April 1999.

Managers are just former players trying to hang on to something they no longer have.
Former Celtic and Hibs defender **Jackie McNamara**, April 1999.

I remember signing on the Friday and then he resigned on the Sunday. I thought to myself, 'Bloody hell, what have I let myself in for here?'
Manchester City striker **Paul Dickov** recalls the abrupt 1996 exit of manager Alan Ball, April 1999.

MARK

I am pleased to announce that the Department of Employment has today verbally confirmed that a work permit will be made available to Marko Viduka. We are now making arrangements for Marko to come to Scotland for a medical.
Celtic managing director **Fergus McCann**, 30 November 1998.

It was only after I arrived in Glasgow last week that I started to realise how much I had been affected by everything in Zagreb over the last few months.
Marko Viduka explains his disappearance on 6 December 1998.

Yesterday, Marko was visited by Eric Riley, Jozef Venglos, Eric Black and Dr Jack Mulhearn. He was offered medical counselling and he was offered his parents to be flown from Australia to Glasgow. He was offered a change

of hotel, a furnished apartment, a car and a driver, an extended Christmas break, a member of the Celtic staff to be with him at all times. These offers were all rejected.
Fergus McCann after Viduka's walk-out, 6 December 1998.

There are question marks surrounding that fee and who is getting it.
Fergus McCann gives the first hint of problems regarding the Viduka £3m fee, 6 December 1998.

At the time of the medical he had no problems whatsoever and yet within 36 hours of that he claimed it was impossible for him to carry on. Based on the player's behaviour and what he has been telling us in the past two days, we don't expect to see him back.
Fergus McCann, 6 December 1998.

It is all very peculiar.
Fergus McCann, 6 December 1998.

Once you get on the bad list of our fans it is almost impossible to win back their support. Our supporters are cruel. They don't think about people's emotions, only their own.
Croatia Zagreb's **Goran Bradic** on Viduka's problems there, 14 December 1998.

Celtic's patience with IMG is running low, as they continue to perpetuate this tedious and unacceptable behaviour. IMG is not acting in the best interests of Mark Viduka, and certainly not Celtic Football Club. If they had been, this situation could have been resolved some time ago.
Fergus McCann, 12 January 1999, as IMG attempt to get Viduka on the plane to Celtic's mid-season break in Spain.

We are appalled by the lack of professionalism being displayed by IMG and their cynical use of Mark Viduka in this stunt.
Fergus McCann on the same incident.

It is unfortunate that Mark Viduka's and IMG's good intentions have been misinterpreted.
IMG's statement in response, 12 January 1999.

We will act to ensure every party receives what they are due from the deal.
Fergus McCann, 22 January 1999.

The Celtic supporters are very nice people and they don't deserve people in charge of the club who don't know how to deal in business.
Croatia Zagreb executive director **Damir Vrbanovic**, 29 January 1999, as it emerges that Celtic had paid only £900,000 of the £3m transfer fee.

You can go from hero to zero in a minute.
St Johnstone midfielder – and former Croatia Zagreb reserve – **Nick Dasovic** on the problems facing players at Viduka's former club, April 1999.

Some people I know say he's a very nice man once you get to know him. Everyone is entitled to their own opinion, I suppose.
Mark Viduka manages to hold back tears on the day of Fergus McCann's departure from Celtic, 3 April 1999.

MOJO

I think there was a bit of devilment in Graeme's decision to sign Maurice.
Rangers chairman **David Murray**, November 1994.

I just said to him, 'Can you handle it?' His response was, 'Yes, I can.' I then asked, 'Why do you think you can handle it?' His answer was, 'Because I'm a professional'.
Agent **Bill McMurdo** on Maurice Johnston joining Rangers, *The Absolute Game* fanzine, May 1997.

I said to him, 'What about the religion thing?' and he replied, 'Look, I'm not asking to go to church with them.'
McMurdo on Johnston signing for Rangers, *The Absolute Game* fanzine, May 1997.

I've never seen jaws fall so quickly in my life as when Johnston walked into the room with us.
Rangers chairman **David Murray** on the events of 10 July 1989, February 1997.

The remarkable thing was that at the end of the day Maurice didn't cost Rangers a penny. When he left for Everton, we got slightly more for Maurice than we'd paid for him.
Rangers chairman **David Murray**, November 1994.

Despite his somewhat chequered history, I haven't seen many players work harder. He trained like a beast and was a smashing player for Scotland. I

hope that's never forgotten when people look at his international career. That sometimes happens when a player has been a bit, how shall I put it, controversial.
Gary McAllister on Johnston, *Captain's Log*, 1995.

MONEY

Football professionalism as it is known in England could never exist in Scotland. I do not believe there are two clubs in the country which could afford to pay men a weekly wage of even 25/- [£1.25] or 30/- [£1.50] for playing football.
Rangers president **Tom Vallance**, October 1887, quoted in Tom Campbell and Pat Woods, *Dreams, and Songs to Sing*, 1996.

There's always room for an exceptional youngster, but I think the Old Firm will be fielding cheque-book teams more and more in the future.
Tommy Burns, then a Celtic player, July 1989, quoted in Tom Campbell and Pat Woods, *Dreams, and Songs to Sing*, 1996.

I felt something wasn't right. I felt Robert, a striker, had only played to about 10 per cent of his ability, and Burruchaga to about half of his. So when everything eventually came out into the open, well . . . let's say I wasn't totally shocked.
Dundee goalkeeper **Michel Pageaud** on the Marseilles bribes scandal. Pageaud played for Valenciennes in the May 1993 fixture which led to Christophe Robert and Jorge Burruchaga being given prison sentences.

If I was to try to do a swap deal with any English club, the first thing their chairman would ask is: 'How much is your lad on?' When I tell them they would say, 'Bloody hell. I can't afford that.'
Celtic manager **Lou Macari**, October 1993, quoted in Allan Caldwell, *Sack The Board!*, 1994.

I like honesty out on the park. The good days are gone in terms of the quality of players that I was fortunate enough to play with. I can't expect lesser players to go out and do what Jimmy Johnstone did but I want them to go out and earn their money. In the present climate of recession and unemployment it's the least they can do.
Celtic manager **Lou Macari**, 1994.

He was completely money mad. He'd be in the office [at Bournemouth] every day asking for a pay rise. In one year he had over six separate pay rises . . . he was the most difficult player I've ever had to deal with.
John Bond on striker Ted McDougall, May 1996.

I left Celtic because of money – a fiver to be exact. Jock [Stein] wouldn't give me the rise I'd asked for, so Liverpool and Manchester United made me an offer and I went to Old Trafford. If it wasn't for that fiver I'd have stayed at Celtic.
Lou Macari, 1994.

I was on £70 a week . . . my wages would rise to £300 if I was in the first-team, with £100 appearance cash and £120 win bonus. The best of weeks meant £520 and I couldn't believe money like that – my entire family weren't making that at the time.
Rangers' **Ian Durrant** on early cash at Ibrox, *Blue & White Dynamite – The Ian Durrant Story*, 1998.

I'd hang myself but we can't afford the rope.
Hamilton boss **Iain Munro**, 1995.

If you look at last year's accounts, only 46p of every £1 Rangers earned came through the gate.
Rangers chairman **David Murray**, November 1994.

If you had taken £150,000 out of the club in consultancy fees and a further £100,000 in expenses over a twelve-mouth period you would want back into the game, wouldn't you?
Hearts chairman **Chris Robinson**, responding to suggestions that former chairman Wallace Mercer wanted back into football, January 1995.

I was on a drip in a hospital bed and this player came to see me. I thought he was enquiring about my health. He never even asked how I was. All he was interested in was how he stood regarding his contract. He'd even brought his agent in.
Former St Johnstone boss **John McClelland**, 1995.

We play with Mitre Deltas but look how many clubs train with the cheaper Deltas. If you ask why, they tell you it's because the Deltas cost 60 quid a ball. It's complete amateurism.
Celtic's **John Collins**, March 1996.

He's had a very eventful life.
Burnley manager **Adrian Heath** on former Rangers winger Ted McMinn, after the player fled to Australia amid allegations the Child Support Agency were on his tail, April 1996.

When I was at Sampdoria I was summoned to a breakfast meeting with Robert Maxwell who wanted me to be the player-manager of Oxford. I outlined what I would require to bring me back from Italy and that seemed a bit much, even for Robert Maxwell.
Graeme Souness, April 1996.

When Ray [Wilkins] told me recently he had £1m to spend I started laughing. I told him he could buy one of my bad players.
Stoke boss **Lou Macari**, April 1996.

Gordon and I have both bet Gazza that Gordon will score more goals than him. I was merely protecting my investment.
Rangers' **Ally McCoist** on why he let Gordon Durie score from a penalty against Raith Rovers, 30 April 1996. Durie finished the season with 20 goals, Gascoigne 19.

It took me nine months to put together the money I had to pay FIFA. I can't sit back and watch someone act in an unauthorised manner when I know that person hasn't put up so much as the price of a fish supper.
Edinburgh agent **Jake Duncan**, explaining why he raised the transfer of Alan Stubbs from Bolton to Celtic – done using an unlicensed agent – with FIFA, August 1996. Celtic were fined £42,000 and Stubbs £28,000.

Gordon Durie was feeling tired and the Gaffer said, 'Coisty, get yourself ready, you're going on.' Quickly, quickly, Coisty's got himself ready and I knew what he's thinkin', he's like, '12 and a half grand'. He's gettin' excited. He's ready to go on and there's about a minute left but he's still goin' to get his 12 and a half. He's givin' it to the linesman, 'Check my boots, check my boots.' He's dyin' to get on. Then Ian Durrant went down, done his calf in, so it's like, 'No, hold on, hold on.' Durranty's comin' off and I'm givin' it like, 'Well done, pal, well done'. Coisty's givin' it, 'You bastard, you bastard, you've done me. I want half of your money.'
Paul Gascoigne on a late substitution switch in the August 1995 European Cup match between Anorthosis Famagusta and Rangers, quoted in TV documentary, *Gazza's Coming Home*, October 1996. McCoist stayed on the bench when Durrant came off. Neil Murray went on and got it instead.

Someone on the committee had £50 on us but the bookie started to get suspicious when he saw the club ties and wouldn't take any more than a tenner a head.

Whitehill Welfare skipper Davie Millar on cleaning out the local bookies in Fraserburgh, who had offered 4/1 against the Edinburgh side in the Scottish Cup second round replay, January 1996. Whitehill won 2–1.

In Fergus's world there have to be two columns in the ledger – profit and loss. In mine the column headings read hopes and dreams.

Celtic boss Tommy Burns on managing director Fergus McCann before the 1995 Scottish Cup Final.

My concern is that he [Fergus McCann] is consumed by his five-year business plan and has lost his sense of what Celtic stand for and where they have come from.

Former Celtic director Brian Dempsey, March 1997.

If I wasn't a Celtic supporter I would be 3,000 miles away right now. There are easier and more hassle-free ways to make money than investing in a football club, especially one that was massively in debt.

Celtic managing director Fergus McCann, March 1997.

If I lose this case I'll be selling the *Big Issue* the next day.

Stoke boss Lou Macari after announcing he was quitting the job because of the pressure of his court case with Celtic, April 1997.

To spend millions on a 30-year-old player is not good value for the club, and means that money that could be used in other areas is wasted. That applies to Colin Hendry or Kennet Andersson. We did sign Mark Hateley, but that was basically £300,000 for one game and it did the trick.

David Murray, April 1997. The 'one game' was the vital league clash with Celtic, which Rangers won 1–0 – and in which Hateley was sent off. Rangers signed Hendry – then 32 – for £4m in August 1998.

The offer was an insult.

Millwall boss Jimmy Nicholl on the £350,000 offer from Hibs for Stevie Crawford, April 1997. Hibs signed Crawford for £400,000 three months later.

You'll not get movie fans saying 'No I'm not going to see Robert Redford because he got two million pounds for his last picture.' They just have to accept that that's the going rate.

Agent Bill McMurdo justifying large salaries, *The Absolute Game* fanzine, May 1997.

I don't know who put it in Jorge Cadete's head that he paid his own transfer fee. There were no ifs and buts and this £400,000 has only appeared recently – somehow it fell through the cracks. What happened, did he just check his bank account and realise it was missing?
Celtic managing director Fergus McCann on Jorge Cadete's contract wrangles, May 1997.

If fans think I can bring in Jonas Thern on a salary of £1m a year and give them the Champions' League for £6 a head in return, they are wrong.
Rangers chairman David Murray, August 1997.

[Gareth] Southgate [along with Pearce and Waddle] contaminated a pure moment of shared emotion with a money-grabbing lark. This was the most shocking abuse of the lived experience and memory of fans I can ever remember. Yet there was no protest, no outcry. Can you imagine McAllister exploiting his and our nemesis for a quick buck and a slice of mouldy pizza? Can you imagine Hendry selling himself and us in a comic replay of *that* goal?
David Hayes, *The Absolute Game* fanzine, August 1997.

In my village there was great poverty, no electricity, and often we had trouble getting water. The only telephone was in the church and if you wanted to make a call you had to make an appointment and hope to be connected.
Motherwell striker Eliphas Shivute, on growing up in the village of Olukonda in Namibia, September 1997.

My ultimate dream is to buy Glasgow Rangers but that's never going to happen. Oasis could sell 30 million records but I'll still never be able to do that.
Alan McGee head of Creation Records, September 1997.

I felt that with the Bosman ruling they wouldn't be able to get any transfer fee when my contract was up so if they could get some sort of money now they could go out and buy a replacement. But I went out to see the chairman and he said he wanted to have me around for another season. I was amazed by that. A number of clubs in Europe would've said, 'Let's get the money, he's out of here, we can buy a replacement.' But that wasn't the case. Amazing.
Brian Laudrup recalls being talked into seeing out the remaining year of his Ibrox contract, 1997.

I did the right thing with Laudrup at the time but, I tell you, I'll never do that again. That cost Rangers £6m and it hurt us very badly. But he'd just carried us to the title and when he's sitting in your house in Jersey and the conversation is 'Will you reconsider?', 'Yes', 'Will you please stay?', 'Yes', then what do you do?
Rangers chairman David Murray, August 1998.

[Commercial manager] Bill Wilson will be hanging from a tree.
Craig Brown after Scotland were drawn in a financially unrewarding section containing Lithuania, Bosnia, Estonia, the Faroes and the Czech Republic for the 2000 European Championships, 18 January 1998.

I used to have an argument with Walter Smith at Rangers about whether it would be possible to have a socialist background but, once you start earning good money, stay loyal to your principles.
Clydebank player-boss Ian McCall, January 1998.

I dropped $10m in my time in Scotland. I don't begrudge that because I can afford it.
Former Dundee chairman Ron Dixon reminisces, February 1998.

There were many, many times when Jimmy could have screwed me for money because I was in Canada or Russia or someplace. But he never once took me for a farthing. I love the kid.
Former Dundee chairman Ron Dixon on ex-Dens boss Jim Duffy, February 1998.

Anyone who looks me in the eye and suggests I'm washing my hands of my responsibilities will get a punch in the mouth.
Falkirk chairman George Fulston on the club's financial crisis, 5 March 1998.

You want to buy a 23-year-old Dutch international midfielder? You have to spend £5m. Otherwise you end up with a second-rater for £2m.
Rangers chairman David Murray, August 1998.

For years they've been clamouring on about getting the same money as Italians or Spaniards. Now they've got it they should behave like them. You cannot go and drink on a Tuesday and Wednesday but stay in on a Friday. That's no good. You have to stay in all week now.
Coventry boss Gordon Strachan, August 1998.

In football there are some clubs who can be blackmailed but we are not one of them. These players really do need to get a reality check.
Celtic managing director Fergus McCann after donating £50,000 to the Royal Hospital for Sick Children at Yorkhill in response to Celtic's players wrangling over bonuses for Champions' League qualification the day before the qualifying tie against Croatia Zagreb, 11 August 1998.

We do not want the money, or what is left of it. It is a matter of principle. But equally, we would like to see the club remain true to its charitable roots and hand the other £230,000 over.
Celtic captain Tom Boyd's reponse.

I'm very impressed by the players' gesture. The matter is now resolved.
McCann on donating the rest of the money to Yorkhill, 11 August 1998.

I've no idea what guys like Ally McCoist and Ian Durrant are paid. Why should I? What do I know about money?
Kilmarnock boss Bobby Williamson, August 1998.

He can abide by the rules the same as any other player. If he doesn't then he can go to whoever wants him. The game has gone bonkers. It's been led by money and greed.
Celtic's Tommy Burns on Pierre van Hooijdonk, 1996.

He's hurting himself and he's hurting us. He's had a lot of bad publicity. He's been condemned in many quarters. He's been slaughtered in a lot of ways. Now a lot of managers will look and think, 'Do I want him playing for me? No, because he could be trouble.' I'm sure a lot of people wouldn't touch him with a bargepole. Even when I bought him nearly everybody advised me against it. 'He's a handful, he's not the right type.'
Nottingham Forest boss Dave Bassett, after Pierre van Hooijdonk's walkout on the club, August 1998.

I would love to see the FA, PFA and all the Premiership clubs get together and pay Forest the £4m they spent on van Hooijdonk. Then we would tell Forest, 'Use that money and leave van Hooijdonk to rot.' It would be good for the whole of football because we would be making an example of this man.
Coventry boss Gordon Strachan on van Hooijdonk, August 1998.

A disgrace to his nation.
Feyenoord coach Leo Beenhakker on van Hooijdonk, August 1998.

He wasn't particularly well-liked by the players anyway.
Dave Bassett, October 1998.

I was a team-mate of Pierre van Hooijdonk for a couple of seasons at Celtic and, despite the suppressed sniggers, I can say sincerely that it was a real pleasure. It was great to be around a player who was so professional with regard to his football.
Former Celtic striker **Andy Walker**, February 1999.

We talk about clubs going to the wall but it never seems to happen.
Alloa boss **Terry Christie**, February 1999.

Top players can now earn in a week what I earned in a year when I was first at Blackburn.
Rangers' **Colin Hendry**, February 1999.

The latest results are disappointing, but £6m isn't even a player these days, is it?
Rangers chairman **David Murray** announcing club losses of £6.3m, April 1999.

There was one guy earning a twenty-fifth of the company's entire turnover.
Celtic managing director **Fergus McCann** recalls investigating club finances soon after taking over five years before, April 1999. The player concerned was probably Paul McStay.

Too many football people are driven by their ego. Clubs rely on sugar daddies, successful businessmen who see the game as a vehicle for them to bask in the glory of it all. Clubs such as Hearts are buying players they can't afford in a sad attempt to keep up with the rest. Where is it all going to end? The bubble is bound to burst some day. You simply cannot justify paying certain players £35,000 a week, especially when a nurse is only on £150.
Former Celtic and Hibs defender **Jackie McNamara**, April 1999.

In support of his request for more money he said: 'I could be 100 per cent more supportive of you if I had a better deal.' I stopped in my tracks. I could not believe that I had heard correctly. Our relationship never recovered from that exchange.
Former Celtic general manager **Jock Brown** on former assistant coach Murdo MacLeod, in book, *Celtic-Minded*, 1999.

It was in all the way. I'm surprised Andy Goram even had the gall to move for it.
Keith's Mark Garden after scoring against Rangers in the Scottish Cup, January 1996. Rangers won 10–1.

He got a 17-match ban for his ninth red card. He just can't keep his mouth shut. Maybe we should get him a sponsorship deal with Sellotape.
Kirkintilloch **Rob Roy** committee member on wayward striker Scott Smith, 1996.

Moaning about the physical side of junior football is a bit like moaning about getting wet when swimming.
Duncan Mackay, *The Absolute Game* fanzine, August 1997.

They came down out of the hills with knives and bottles. It was like a scene from *Braveheart*.
Manager of Saltcoats Mermaid Amateurs, on a cup-tie against Telford United played in Edinburgh's tough Muirhouse housing scheme, 1997. He required emergency surgery after being stabbed in a post-match riot, initiated by a last-minute Mermaid equaliser.

I had to sign a team rapidly, but Clyde couldn't afford to buy anybody and the ones who were around in senior football weren't worth buying anyway.
Clyde general manager **Ronnie MacDonald** on signing 14 players from junior football, October 1998.

OFF!

They've got half-a-dozen Argentinians in their pool and the manager's one, so that means a riot for a start.
Celtic boss **Jock Stein**, apparently joking, on hearing of drawing Atletico Madrid in the European Cup semi-final, quoted in Tom Campbell and Pat Woods, *Dreams, and Songs to Sing*, 1996.

I watched – transfixed in a cocktail of fascination and disbelief – as Atletico set about a game plan that seemed to combine the manners of a whorehouse cat-fight with the fanaticism of a particularly keen kamikaze squadron. They sneered, they snarled, they spat. They kicked, they punched, they gouged. They argued, they acted, they agitated. They got sent off.
Danny Kelly in his book, *The Cult of the Manager*, on the notorious European Cup semi-final first leg between Celtic and Atletico Madrid in April 1974. Atletico had seven players booked and three sent off.

Okay, so I was sent off 20 times, but I played for 22 seasons. So it was under one a season. That's not too bad.
Willie Johnston, May 1996.

When I was at Rangers I knew I was home and dry when I got sent off against Celtic. You're distressed about getting sent off but the reaction from the team was great. If there's togetherness you've got a chance.
Southampton boss **Graeme Souness**, May 1997.

I hope Frank Bruno has a better chin than Robbie Winters.
Dundee player-manager **Jim Duffy** after Chic Charnley was sent off – for the fourteenth time in his career – after an incident with the Dundee United striker, 16 March 1996. Bruno was fighting Mike Tyson the following day.

I could see it in Paolo's eyes. He was a crazy man and I knew he wasn't going to leave the field quietly.
Hearts' **Pasquale Bruno** on countryman Paolo di Canio. He was responsible for the impressive – and possibly unique – achievement of scoring from a penalty then being immediately sent off for scuffling with an opponent, 30 November 1996. Di Canio was the tenth Celtic player of the season to be sent off.

Di Canio was stupid. That's all it was – sheer stupidity.
Tommy Burns on the same incident, 30 November 1996.

OLD FIRM

The ultimate experience.
Monaco's **John Collins** on Old Firm games, March 1997.

You're exhilarated and nauseated all in one.
Reading boss **Tommy Burns** on Old Firm games, April 1998.

The worst club match in the world, without a doubt.
Former Celtic defender Jim Craig, quoted in Simon Kuper, *Football Against The Enemy*, 1994.

Sometimes I went through the whole game without doing anything constructive and got praised at the end.
Jim Craig on Old Firm games, quoted in Simon Kuper, *Football Against The Enemy*, 1994.

Both clubs soon saw the financial advantages in playing each other in games where the ethnic edge was clear cut, and it was this commercialism, which the amateur sports writers of the day found repellent, that led to the two clubs being branded 'The Old Firm' in a *Scottish Referee* cartoon of 1904.
Bill Murray, *The Old Firm in The New Age*, 1998.

I remember playing in a Reserve League Cup section with Rangers in it. By the last section game we had to beat Partick Thistle by eight goals to qualify and put Rangers out. Big Jock came into the dressing-room and offered us £20 a head if we did it. That was some money for a reserve team bonus and we were all peeing with excitement before we went out to play. I remember Kenny [Dalglish] making a bee-line for the toilet and shouting 'Come on, we've got to f****** win this!' By full-time we'd won 12–1 and big Jock paid out. I think that was when we first realised how good we were.
Lou Macari, 1995.

I couldn't wait to get out on the pitch, so I'd have a couple of cigarettes – though we weren't allowed to smoke in the dressing-room – and get changed at the last minute.
Willie Johnston recalls pre-Old Firm game nerves, March 1996.

I red-carded another of their players, Tony Shepherd . . . only to bring him back on. I had booked him for a foul when I felt a blow on the back of my head. I thought I had seen his hand come up and hit me. But then, as Shepherd made his way to the tunnel protesting his innocence, I saw a 50-pence piece on the ground and realised what had happened. So I went over to my linesman and said: 'You just saw me getting hit on the head with a 50p piece.' He hadn't, but replied, 'Anything you say, Davie.' So that got me off the hook and Shepherd back on the park.
Ref Davie Syme on the 1986 League Cup final between Rangers and Celtic, May 1994.

A tirade of abuse ended with him [Jock Stein] calling me 'A big f******
poof' – exactly the words I was to have hurled at me by Graeme Souness
ten years later. So at least the Old Firm view of me from the two sides of
the fence was consistent.
Former ref Davie Syme, May 1994. The Stein encounter occurred after the
League Cup final in March 1978.

It was like Goldilocks and the Three Bears.
Frank McAvennie on his October 1987 Old Firm bust-up with Chris Woods,
Terry Butcher and Graham Roberts which landed the four of them in court,
March 1998.

If somebody from Rangers says something it is believed. If somebody from
Celtic says something it is not believed . . . I don't care about Rangers. I
don't think about Rangers. I don't, like a lot of people, have an obsession
about Rangers.
Celtic Chief Executive Terry Cassidy, December 1991.

The most attack-minded Celtic team I've ever seen here.
Rangers' Richard Gough on the opposition at Ibrox, 2 January 1993. Despite
a line-up featuring Joe Miller, Andy Payton, Gerry Creaney and Stuart Slater,
Celtic lost 1–0 and went ten points behind despite having played two games
more.

We're not ready to stick our heads in the oven.
Celtic boss Tommy Burns after losing 3–1 at home to Rangers, October
1994.

After five years of Rangers victories in the league, Celtic fans would have
seen the club sold to the Ayatollah Khomeini if it gave a glimmer of hope
of success on the park.
Former Celtic director Michael Kelly, *Paradise Lost*, 1994.

Of course I regretted banning your average, good, well-behaved Celtic
supporter after the damage to Ibrox. But look at how it all came to a head.
If you examine the people in charge at Celtic now, you can see
businessmen coming in under Fergus McCann to run the club.
Rangers chairman David Murray, November 1994.

Rangers will stand still until this nine-in-a-row thing disappears. It's like a
monkey on our backs.
Rangers chairman David Murray, 1996.

There's nothing worse than sitting in the dressing-room at Celtic Park after a defeat, not a word being said, listening to them next door going mental.
Rangers' **Ally McCoist**, 1996.

Celtic need a competitive league. People might think we would be happy with a league we dominate with Rangers. Not so. We played a match recently. We had to keep 1800 seats for visiting fans and only 285 turned up.
Celtic managing director **Fergus McCann**, June 1996.

I'm surprised that it's taken so long for a mainstream station in Scotland to conceive of it or to allow a show to exist that hates the Old Firm. It's so obviously a good thing to put on the radio, I can't think what's taken so long.
Stuart Cosgrove, host of Radio Scotland's *Off The Ball*, January 1997.

I still don't know if I was meant to have made a handball or been offside. The decision was a bad one.
Celtic's **Jorge Cadete** on his disallowed goal in the New Year Old Firm game, April 1997.

I like everything in Scotland except the refereeing. What I don't like is how 90 per cent of refs in Scotland are Protestant and I am playing for a Catholic club. They are shameless.
Celtic's **Paolo Di Canio** after a controversial Old Firm game, January 1997.

We won an Old Firm match two weeks ago with dignity. We didn't try to rub it in and we'll lose with dignity. It's always important to win with class and lose with class.
Celtic boss **Tommy Burns**, after losing 1–0 to Rangers and going eight points behind in league race, March 1997.

When we won at Ibrox on January 2, the following day brought stories of a conspiracy against Celtic by referees and their assistants because a goal had been disallowed. Now we are being told that Rangers players were to blame for incidents during Sunday's match. But when Rangers lost to Celtic in the Cup, they had the pleasure of reading that I thought they had fully deserved their victory. It seems that when Celtic lose all we hear about is what went wrong against them. I ask you, whose is the more dignified approach?
Walter Smith, March 1997.

In the first [game] we had a player sent off for a very, very minor infringement and were denied what in many people's eyes was a penalty. The other night we had a player assaulted. I've always felt that when that happens a player is sent off but there was only a booking given. Then we score a goal and it doesn't stand. Maybe that's why Celtic fans think something is going on.
The view from Celtic boss **Tommy Burns**, March 1997.

Rangers had one player stamped on. Another one was punched and another was punched after the game was over. I don't see how it is possible to point a finger at Rangers for a lack of discipline.
Rangers boss **Walter Smith** responds, concerning the Old Firm game of 16 March 1997 which saw nine booked and two sent off.

When my players performed their huddle at Celtic Park, it was not meant to be a disrespectful or undignified act. If Celtic can do it, why can't Rangers? Why does it cause offence?
Walter Smith, March 1997.

You are trying to prove to the fans that you are capable of playing for the jersey as well as the Ian Durrants and Peter Grants. It becomes harder to stay detached and even Graeme Souness, who had ice in his veins, became totally caught up in the Old Firm atmosphere.
Former Rangers captain **Terry Butcher** on Old Firm games, March 1997.

Nothing had prepared me for what it would be like. It was the best game I've ever played in.
Rangers' **Jorg Albertz**, on Old Firm games, April 1997.

OK they [the fans] hate each other but that has nothing to do with me. I'm not interested in all that. I'm a German and I'm here to play football.
Rangers' **Jorg Albertz**, on Old Firm games, April 1997.

If I was picking a Great Britain side, I couldn't include one Old Firm player in it. I'd love to but I couldn't.
Tommy Docherty, November 1997.

It's like people reporting to a headmaster. I find it pathetic.
Rangers chairman **David Murray** after Celtic complained to the SFA about Paul Gascoigne when he mimed playing a flute in the Old Firm game of 2 January 1998.

You need the balls of a rhinoceros to play in an Old Firm game.
Rangers' **Ian Durrant**, *Blue & White Dynamite – The Ian Durrant Story*, 1998.

It defines living for me in terms of a pure football experience.
Reading boss **Tommy Burns** on Old Firm games, April 1998.

There is an élite in England just as in Scotland, only it comprises about six teams compared to our two. Rangers and Celtic would be among that six if they played in the Premiership. Their impact wouldn't be immediate but they would have bigger crowds than anyone else, increased commercial income and they would easily compete in the top six. Easily.
Everton boss **Walter Smith**, January 1999.

There are a few people who just don't like it, but that's just too bad. We still have the issue of Protestants and Catholics, and this sort of divide, which is so unproductive and not business-like. Sponsors and so forth – it doesn't help Celtic, doesn't help Rangers.
Celtic managing director **Fergus McCann**, February 1999.

I know what it's like to be called an Orange bastard or a Fenian bastard, even though I've never been religious. There is real hate in these people's eyes. I don't like going to Old Firm games because of it. They turn my stomach.
Former Celtic and Hibs defender **Jackie McNamara**, April 1999.

There were moments that weren't the way to do things, but I don't want to talk about that.
Rangers coach **Dick Advocaat** after the stormy Old Firm match of 2 May 1999 which saw ten booked, three sent off, four pitch invaders and ref Hugh Dallas struck by a coin.

At Celtic if you wear the name, you wear the reputation.
Celtic chief executive **Allan MacDonald** announcing disciplinary action against supporters who invaded the pitch and players Stephane Mahe and Vidar Riseth who were both sent off in the Old Firm match of 2 May 1999.

In my opinion we did nothing wrong. Of course, I'm a foreigner so maybe I don't understand it.
Rangers' coach **Dick Advocaat** on his team's infamous post-match huddle at Parkhead after winning the title, 2 May 1999.

The huddle is not Celtic's property. Everyone can do the huddle if they want to. The German national team do it at every game. But it was right that the huddle was criticised. It was a stupid thing to do.
Rangers' Jorg Albertz after Rangers' huddle at Parkhead on the day they won the title had been criticised as inflammatory, May 1999.

I jumped to my feet after the foul and said, 'Yellow card for him, yellow card for him', but my English is very poor and I don't know if Mr Dallas misunderstood me.
Celtic's Stephane Mahe on his ordering-off at the 2 May 1999 Old Firm game.

I am sorry, but Mr Dallas was not very good.
Stephane Mahe's summing up of the same incident, May 1999.

The hardest game I've ever had to handle.
Referee **Hugh Dallas** on the Old Firm match of 2 May 1999. Dallas needed four stitches after being struck by a coin and four spectators tried to invade the pitch to reach him.

Most problems aren't caused by the guys involved in the original incident. It's the Henry Kissingers who run 50 yards to get involved in something, thinking they can sort it out, who give me most trouble. They should leave me to deal with the offenders.
Referee **Hugh Dallas**, May 1999.

I'd only had three-and-a-half pints and I didn't do anything wrong. All I did was go for a pie.
Celtic fan **Alex Rafferty**, who was seen on TV waving his arms and singing as he was stretchered away after falling from the upper tier at the Old Firm match of 2 May 1999. He claimed he'd over-balanced as he went for a half-time pie. Celtic banned him from Parkhead for life.

OTHER SPORTS

Some dads pay a fortune to buy a Rangers or Celtic season ticket. I put my money into my son. What is wrong with that?
Former Motherwell defender **Alan Mackin,** whose son, Alan junior, is a promising tennis player, May 1997.

The difficulty in playing Ruud [Gullit] is that he insists on playing by what he calls Dutch rules. Like he'll talk about an ancient Dutch rule that allows you to move your ball from behind any tree greater than 160ft in height. It doesn't matter though. 'Cos I thrash him anyway.
Alan Hansen on his golfing partner, October 1997.

Q: What sporting event would you pay most to watch?
A: Someone absolutely mashing Prince Naseem Hamed.
Leeds' midfielder **David Hopkin**, clearly not a fan, in newspaper questionnaire, November 1997.

I will give any player £100 if he can even touch the ball. You want to have a go?
Rangers defender **Gordan Petric** on his basketball prowess, August 1998.

Once I turned 30, if I played 18 holes on a Wednesday, I always knew it in training on a Thursday.
Former Liverpool defender **Alan Hansen**, March 1999.

What a card player. The rest of us paid for his house. I must have written off half his mortgage myself.
Former Liverpool striker **David Johnson** on Alan Hansen, April 1999.

OUCH! (KICKINGS, PHYSICAL AND OTHERWISE)

There were a few players at the club that wouldn't have got a game for Aberdeen reserves, and they were playing regular first-team football for Manchester United.
Martin Buchan on the United team he joined, April 1996.

He couldn't play anyway. I only wanted him for the reserves.
Bill Shankly, on learning that Lou Macari had joined Manchester United rather than Liverpool, January 1973.

One of them's got a dicky knee, one's too old and the other's a drunkard.
Bill Shankly in team talks before Liverpool played Manchester United. The players concerned were Denis Law, Bobby Charlton and George Best.

One of the few players as nasty off the field as on it.
Brian Clough on Archie Gemmill, quoted in *His Way*, 1993.

He looks like a pissed vampire.
Chris Donald, editor of *Viz* magazine, on Alan Hansen, 1994.

I remember trying to light this thing in the bloody room to keep insects away but I think Robbo got bitten all over his arse. Right enough, it was some size of an arse.
Kenny Burns on Scotland team-mate John Robertson at the Argentina '78 World Cup, quoted in Mike Wilson, *Don't Cry For Me Argentina*, 1998.

You can't head the ball, you can't tackle and you can't chase back.
Brian Clough's assessment on **Gary McAllister** while in talks to sign the then–Leicester player, quoted in *Captain's Log*, 1995. McAllister, oddly enough, turned down the move.

The only players I am interested in are potential Scotland internationals or future opponents. Gough does not come into either category.
Scotland boss **Craig Brown** on Rangers' Richard Gough, September 1993.

The late Hibs chairman, Tom Hart, used to say the Scottish Professional Footballers' Association was the only union where the members deliberately kicked each other. We are dedicated to the SFA's Fair Play campaign and the association will continue to fund that from the fines we impose on those who have not yet got the message.
SFA Chief Executive **Jim Farry**, January 1995.

I've seen harder tackles in the pie queue at half-time than the ones punished in games.
Falkirk chairman **George Fulston** after his side were warned for a crime count of seven red cards and 47 bookings, January 1995.

These lads seem to be footballers so they can go out at the weekend and tell whatever bird they're chatting up they're a professional footballer. I can only suggest they're wanting to get done by the fraud office because they're kidding themselves on.
Ayr United boss **Simon Stainrod** after a 4–1 home defeat by Berwick, 2 September 1995. He quit three days later.

I left him out because after his performances earlier in the season you're waiting for a calamity to happen.
Ayr United boss **Simon Stainrod** on Kevin Biggart after 4–1 home defeat by Berwick, 2 September 1995. He quit three days later.

He looked as if he'd never played football before.
Ayr United boss **Simon Stainrod** on defender Neil McKilligan after a 4–1 home defeat by Berwick, 2 September 1995. He quit three days later.

He's forever knocking on my door asking when he'll get his chance. I would suggest after this he won't get another one.
Ayr United boss **Simon Stainrod** on Colin McFarlane after a 4–1 home defeat by Berwick, 2 September 1995. He quit three days later.

He wants to know what his long-term future is here so he can sort out a career. After a performance like that, he won't build a career playing football.
Ayr United boss **Simon Stainrod** on Ross Tannock after a 4–1 home defeat by Berwick, 2 September 1995. He quit three days later.

The penalty he gave away showed a complete lack of professionalism. If an amateur side did that you would be absolutely mortified. For a professional footballer to do that is just wholly unacceptable.
Ayr United boss **Simon Stainrod**, a man who says his piece, on Vinnie Moore after a 4–1 home defeat by Berwick, 2 September 1995. He quit three days later. Moore was appointed manager of Albion Rovers four months later.

He's walking about with a lip you could hang your coat on.
Premier Division manager on an unhappy player, 1996.

It had ceased to be a club where you were proud to wear the shirt and had become a place where the players were thinking about their next testimonial.
Graeme Souness on Liverpool, April 1996.

Dick Dastardly had a miserable time in the USA but we suspect he was missing Muttley.
Rangers' **Ally McCoist** on international team-mate Darren Jackson, June 1996. Scotland were touring the USA at the time.

They caused a moment of panic when one of them went down in training with a spot.
Ally McCoist on Aberdeen and Scotland team-mates Eoin Jess and Scott Booth, June 1996.

It doesn't matter if you cost £15m and earn £37,000 per week, the human body can only take so much. Suffering during pre-season training is unavoidable.
Pat Nevin, August 1996.

The poor bloke can't play the game. Couldn't trap a dead rat.
Former QPR striker **Stan Bowles** on Mark Hateley.

Chic's suspended, as usual.
Dundee boss **Jim Duffy** on midfielder Chic Charnley, speaking on Radio Scotland before his team's game against Airdrie, 9 November 1996.

I was quite upset. Everyone knows Jock is bald and ugly.
Scotland boss **Craig Brown** on being mistaken for his TV commentator brother, November 1996.

Because he didn't like being called a fat bastard, that's why.
Former Scotland striker **David Speedie** explaining why ex-Ranger Terry Hurlock threw a pint tumbler at him while the pair were at Southampton, December 1996.

If you dropped these FIFA people in an ocean they couldn't decide whether it was wet.
Scots agent **Jake Duncan** after FIFA delayed ruling on Celtic's appeal over being fined £42,000 for using an unlicensed agent to sign Alan Stubbs, December 1996.

I've wasted more than you're worth in phone calls trying to sell you.
Premier Division manager to player, January 1997.

He [John Greig] said I couldn't blame him this time because he never kicked anybody that high.
Billy McNeill recounting Old Firm adversary John Greig's reaction to the news that McNeill needed heart surgery, February 1997.

When we look back in years to come and remember Brian Laudrup scored the winner with a header from a cross by Charlie Miller's left foot, we still won't believe it happened.
Ally McCoist on the goal that clinched Rangers' ninth title in a row against Dundee United, May 1997.

Even if Rangers were to offer me a new contract and a guaranteed place in the team I would still want to leave. I hate the place.

Erik Bo Andersen preparing to leave Rangers for Danes Aalborg, October 1997. The move fell through and he had to return to Scotland before finally moving some weeks later.

Any more questions before I go away and hang myself?

Dunfermline boss **Bert Paton** at the after-match press conference after losing 7–0 at Ibrox, 18 October 1997.

The girls in our office at the SFA have nicknames for us all. Frank Coulston's Old Spice and Ross Mathie's Grey Spice because of his hair. I hate to admit this but I'm Constipated Spice. At my age I spend more time in the loo than the rest. I tell them it's because I'm the only one who washes his hands.

Scotland boss **Craig Brown**, October 1997.

His record playing for Hearts has been unbelievable, especially for a little fat bloke who can't run and whose boots would look better hanging on a car mirror.

Former Hearts striker **John Colquhoun** on John Robertson, October 1997.

Take Colin Hendry. A good centre-half, a winner, but not world class. Gallacher up front? A nippy little player and a good goalscorer. Probably as good as we've got – but not world class.

Tommy Docherty, November 1997.

That keeper Leighton, personally speaking, I think he's a joke – always have done. Down here [at Manchester United] he was a disaster . . . but unfortunately he would have to be in the team because Goram, who's the best keeper in Scotland, is a liability. He'd be my number one choice, but only if he grew up and started behaving himself. But not with his present attitude. He shouldn't be at Rangers anymore.

Tommy Docherty, November 1997.

The last time I saw something like that it was crawling out of Sigourney Weaver's stomach.

Ally McCoist on Dundee United's David Bowman, November 1997.

We should call him Baloo from *The Jungle Book* because of his big bear's backside.

Leicester goalkeeper **Kasey Keller** on defender Matt Elliott, January 1998.

I formed the impression of a rather devious individual. I had the clear impression of an uncompromising and somewhat arrogant employer who expected unquestioning compliance with his instructions and unfailing deference to his views.

High Court Judge Lady Cosgrove on Fergus McCann, in her ruling on Celtic's cash battle with former boss Lou Macari, 19 February 1998. Macari claimed £430,000 damages for unfair dismissal, but she threw out his claim and left him facing a £250,000 legal bill.

All the time I was there [Glasgow] I seldom had a full night's sleep because of blinding headaches. They were so bad I would lie awake counting off the hours before I could take more painkillers.

Graeme Souness on his heart problems, February 1997.

I don't think he'll be going home to his girlfriend for a while yet.

East Fife goalkeeper Lindsay Hamilton after defender George Johnstone stopped one of Rangers' Jorg Albertz's thundering free kicks in a very tender place, February 1997.

If the incident is shown on television I think the censors will have a fit.

George Johnstone on the same incident.

I think they sent the forms by pigeon and it obviously flew past us.

Nottingham Forest manager Dave Bassett after the non-arrival of registration forms from Celtic prevented on-loan Brian O'Neil playing against Liverpool, March 1997.

Bunion isn't afraid to put his head in where it hurts. And by the looks of him he's proved that over and over again in his career.

Ally McCoist on Kilmarnock's Paul Wright, May 1997.

I was really impressed he [Kilmarnock's John Henry] scored a hat-trick against Morton in the fifth round, until I realised Brian Reid had been playing for Morton.

The ever-cutting **Ally McCoist's** pre-Cup final verdict, May 1997. Reid had been a team-mate at Ibrox.

He was furious when Lorenzo Amoruso was signed because he's better-looking and his tan is real.

Rangers' Ian Durrant on team-mate Derek McInnes, in book, *Blue & White Dynamite – The Ian Durrant Story*, 1998.

Have you noticed how big Pat Nevin's bald patch is these days?
Author **Hunter Davies**, June 1998.

Rugby with a round ball.
Pierre van Hooijdonk on Scottish football, quoted in Bill Murray's *The Old Firm in The New Age*, 1998.

I've been at United eleven months and he has yet to utter one word of sense.
Dundee United's **Iain Jenkins** on team-mate Andy McLaren, Celtic v Dundee United match programme, 27 February 1999.

Surly and largely uncommunicative.
Former Celtic general manager **Jock Brown** on former coach Wim Jansen, in book, *Celtic-Minded*, 1999.

[His] industry and integrity, in my opinion, did not appear to match his ambition.
Former Celtic general manager **Jock Brown** on former assistant coach Murdo MacLeod, in book, *Celtic-Minded*, 1999.

THE PAST

My grandad ran the Carmyle Rangers supporters' club and I'd go to the games and watch the team that had Millar, Brand and Wilson playing. Jimmy Millar was my favourite player at the time.
Rangers boss **Walter Smith**, 1994.

It was a newish drug then. Now they say nobody should have more than three injections in a lifetime. I had 25 that season alone.
Morton manager **Allan McGraw** on having cortisone injections in his knees in 1964, May 1996.

He [Bobby Collins] was the hardest little player I've ever seen. He'd break your leg as soon as look at you. He had boots specially made, three-and-a-half on one foot and four on the other. Hunched shoulders, pug face. He made more of an impression on me than anyone.
Tranmere manager **Johnny King**, April 1996.

When I played in the 1960s we were doing handstands when we drew a Scandinavian team in Europe because we knew it would be an easy game. Now it's the other way about.
Dunfermline boss **Bert Paton**, July 1998.

I still don't think it was a penalty. I was determined he wasn't going to turn past me and I thought, 'If I bump into him, the referee isn't going to give a penalty, not at this stage of the game.' How wrong I was.
Celtic defender **Jim Craig** on conceding the seventh-minute penalty in the 1967 European Cup final, quoted in Simon Kuper, *Football Against The Enemy*, 1994.

Once Inter scored, John Clark and I could have gone and sat in the stand.
Celtic captain **Billy McNeill** on the 1967 European Cup final against Inter Milan, quoted in Tom Campbell and Pat Woods, *Dreams, and Songs to Sing*, 1996.

It was brilliant winning [the 1972 Cup-Winners' Cup] in Barcelona, but that wasn't the best Rangers side I ever played in. In 1967 we also reached the Cup-Winners' Cup final and were beaten 1–0 by Bayern in extra time. Celtic had won the European Cup the week before and nobody realised just how good a side we were then. It was just that Celtic were better.
Rangers' **Willie Johnston**, May 1996.

The Celtic team which won the European Cup and nine Championships in a row achieved something no British team will achieve again, yet none of them are financially comfortable. They were driven by hunger.
Stoke boss **Lou Macari**, April 1996.

I just kept my head down. There was so much shit flying around.
Graeme Souness on Argentina '78, April 1996.

I don't get up or down about it because I didn't do anything wrong.
Willie Johnston on Argentina '78, May 1996.

They were awake when they should have been asleep and asleep when they should have been awake. If I have one regret it's that we didn't go out there a week or two earlier to acclimatise.
Scotland boss **Ally MacLeod** on Argentina '78, April 1998.

I was a horrible person when I was a footballer.
Born-again Christian **Don Masson**, quoted in Mike Wilson, *Don't Cry For Me Argentina*, 1998.

I always doubted if I had the right personality to be a manager. I didn't know if I had the knowledge or the ability to spot players. When I first came to Celtic Park I began to feel a little scared of what I'd taken on. The directors had given me a copy of the video celebrating the club's centenary in 1988. As I watched what had gone before me I got even more scared.
Liam Brady after taking over as Celtic manager.

I had a meeting this morning over one player's contract and there were four different factions there plus an interpreter. I used to sit here with Goughie and sort things out. Same with Coisty. Me and Jukie [Gordon Durie] did it in an hour last week. It's sad. Maybe that's why we were one happy family.
Rangers chairman **David Murray** reflects on changing times, August 1998.

I didn't touch the ball for the first 18 minutes, but people don't remember that. They remember that I hit the post twice.
Former Ipswich midfielder **John Wark** remembers the 1978 FA Cup final, May 1999.

PHILOSOPHIES

You need four men at the back who can tackle, four in mid-field who can pass the ball, and two up front who have pace and can shoot. Then, as long as the balance is right between right-sided and left-sided players, you've got a team.
Jock Stein on building a team.

I like to take time off to stop and smell the flowers. That's my way.
Dundee United boss **Ivan Golac** after reaching the 1994 Scottish Cup final.

What I learned [in Seattle] were the Americans' positive attitudes – making people feel bright every day. I have tried to use that at all my clubs. If you ask people how they are, 95 per cent of them will say: 'Not bad'. Well, no one says 'not bad' at Bolton. The response at this club is, 'Brilliant'. If people feel bad I don't want to know. I didn't get up in the morning to hear their problems.
Bolton boss **Bruce Rioch**, 1994.

I'm not the type who is looking for plaudits. You'll never see me when the club win anything. I don't think it's my place to appear on television in

those circumstances. But if there's a crisis or there's a problem, then that's my time to step in and put a firm hand on the tiller.
Rangers chairman David Murray, November 1994.

I love to listen to the football results and the lulling roll-call of team names – Sheffield Wednesday, West Bromwich Albion, Partick Thistle, Queen of the South. What glory there is in those names . . . I genuinely believe that one of the reasons Britain is such a steady and gracious place is the calming influence of the football results.
American humorist Bill Bryson, *Notes From A Small Island*, 1995.

My father gave me standards yet I stepped out of them when I played. You could say it was the spirit of the time, the law of the jungle, but then you look at Bobby Charlton and realise that was no excuse. It was down to your own temperament and the guidance you were given by managers and coaches. That's why I wouldn't countenance, from my players, some of the things I did.
Bruce Rioch, 1995.

I tend to buy family men. With a married player you generally know he is at home in the evening watching *Coronation Street* . . . The only single man I bought at Bolton was Alan Thompson and he was 19 at the time. We put him into digs and worked on finding him a girlfriend – which we did.
Arsenal boss Bruce Rioch, 1995.

I quite like my players to be married. They're young and good-looking and you hope they're going to meet a nice girl and settle down.
Aberdeen boss Alex Ferguson, 1984.

Some supporters believed my motives were self-serving because I wanted to see a new manager brought in who would keep me on at the club. But they were wrong. I did what I did because I was shocked by the way Celtic were losing their soul. I didn't even buy shares when they became available to everyone. That's not what being a Celtic fan means to me. I bought three season tickets instead and gave them to friends.
Charlie Nicholas on Celtic's takeover battles, April 1995.

When I had my misfortune in the drawn Cup final against Palace in the FA Cup six years ago I had to leave immediately after the replay to join the Scotland squad for a pre-World Cup friendly against Malta. It was the best thing that could have happened to me. Players don't want sympathy from

their peers at a time like this. They want to be the butt of the squad's jokes because, believe it or not, it helps.
Jim Leighton gives some advice to Gary McAllister, who played for Scotland against Australia three days after his Leeds side lost 3–0 to Aston Villa in the Coca-Cola Cup final, 26 March 1996.

As a player I got into a few scraps because of remarks that were made to me but people on a pitch will pick on the first thing they see, whether it's a big nose, ginger hair or whatever. I know that the colour of your skin is a different matter but I could still understand comments being made in the heat of the game.
Montrose's **Dave Smith**, Scotland's first black manager, March 1996.

Q: What's the best part of your job?
A: Every minute of it and footballers should be thankful people look up to them. If they are not happy with that, they are mental.
Hearts' **Pasquale Bruno**, newspaper questionnaire, April 1996.

It's only since I've come to Scotland that I've started taking my boots home and cleaning them myself because otherwise they lie wet and dirty from Saturday to Monday. In Yugoslavia, that is done for you. These are small things. But small things matter.
Raith Rovers defender **Miodrag Krivokapic**, April 1996.

This is a working area and my opinion is that they want hard-working players. No crap, no prima donnas.
Stoke boss **Lou Macari**, April 1996.

See the boy Rudyard Kipling who said it's the taking part, not the winning that counts? Well that's a load of shite.
Andy Goram, June 1996.

I didn't really give a shit about managers, directors or chairmen. I didn't take football very seriously. To me it was just fun. As soon as they started paying me all the fun went out of it. The supporters enjoyed the time I was at Shrewsbury. That's the bottom line.
Vic Kasule, October 1996.

There is no point in wondering about the colour of the curtains if the rain is coming in through the roof.
Think Tank chairman **Ernie Walker**, announcing plans for a major shake-up in the way the game is run, January 1998.

I can't speak highly enough about the BB: it taught me that discipline and behaviour are important, and that being a decent human being is a far greater priority than being a good footballer. Some of the best people I've ever met have been involved with this organisation.
Derby and Scotland defender **Christian Dailly**, June 1998.

PLAYERS

He threw away a magnificent career and he has gone from bad to worse since.
Tommy Docherty on George Best, June 1996.

Q: Why did you leave Manchester United?
A: Tommy Docherty. If he says 'Good morning' to you, you'd better check the weather outside.
George Best, August 1996.

When we got off the plane at Córdoba and on to the bus for our hotel, one of the players said, 'I'm bored.' I clearly remember him saying it – I'd rather not say who it was – but it just showed that when it comes to picking players for a long trip it's vital to think about their personalities as well as their football abilities.
Martin Buchan on Argentina '78, quoted in Mike Wilson, *Don't Cry For Me Argentina*, 1998.

If you were a kid and somebody told you, 'You will play in the World Cup but you'll have to sleep in a rough room', what would you do? Would you care a shit about it? People get above themselves.
Kenny Burns on Argentina '78, quoted in Mike Wilson, *Don't Cry For Me Argentina*, 1998

It was disgusting. They were acting like toe-rags.
Stuart Kennedy on his Scotland team-mates at Argentina '78 as bonus money wrangles arose, quoted in Mike Wilson, *Don't Cry For Me Argentina*, 1998.

It was a squad of cliques.
Stuart Kennedy quoted in Mike Wilson, *Don't Cry For Me Argentina*, 1998.

He was fatter than I was. But he used to treat a football better than most people treat a woman.
Brian Clough on Scotland winger John Robertson, December 1995.

You don't put in what he has. God gives him that.
Scotland coach **Andy Roxburgh** on Pat Nevin, October 1986.

My reasoning behind changing captains was that, first and foremost, Alan is a very lucky person as well as being a talented and respected footballer. If Al is sitting at 17 playing pontoon, he will get a four.
Kenny Dalglish explaining why he made Hansen Liverpool captain, in *Dalglish – My Autobiography*, 1996.

The most naturally gifted player I have ever worked with.
Scotland coach **Andy Roxburgh** recalling Charlie Nicholas to the international squad, 30 January 1989.

A strong man of a different kind. Good game or bad, the bottom line was that he always wanted the ball. Exactly the mental courage I appreciate. In fact, I demand it.
Alex Ferguson on Gordon Strachan.

He didn't get the credit he deserved with Scotland because you've got to play Brian McClair all the time to get his trust.
Manchester United's **Alex Ferguson** on Brian McClair, April 1994.

Looking back on it, I think he was not really a bench player – he isn't the type of player who's going to come on and ignite a game. His effectiveness is over a full 90 minutes and it took me some time to realise that.
Former Scotland coach **Andy Roxburgh** on Brian McClair, April 1994. 10 of McClair's 30 caps came as substitute.

In 26 years of refereeing matches in Scotland and around the world, [Alan] McLaren is probably the most difficult player I have ever had to deal with . . . he is undoubtedly the most consistently troublesome player I have had to deal with. In comparison, Willie Miller and Roy Aitken were angels.
Former ref **Davie Syme**, May 1994.

Like Alan McLaren, [Richard] Gough seems to believe he has never committed a foul. There is a look of disbelief on his face when he is pulled up – even for the most blatant, illegal tackles.
Former ref **Davie Syme**, May 1994.

He's so hard he's got tattoos on his teeth.
Raith boss **Jimmy Nicholl** on defender Davie Sinclair, 1995.

As a tall player, I was never going to look as busy as the 5' 7" ginger dynamo who was running everywhere around me.
Scotland skipper **Gary McAllister** on Gordon Strachan, September 1995.

I should have gone to Liverpool but Joe Fagan, their manager, had Ian Rush and Kenny Dalglish and I could foresee only a long time spent waiting for my first-team chance at Anfield.
Charlie Nicholas, April 1995.

When I was down there I was surprised at how much bigger the players were. I'm not kidding – they were all about six inches bigger and the ball seemed to be banged into the box earlier.
Jim Leighton on playing in England, February 1996.

When I am asked who my favourite player is, I can honestly answer Stuart Pearce. He is exceptionally talented, of course, but he is as honest a player as I have ever known.
Pat Nevin, April 1996.

After Pele, Vic [Davidson] was my favourite number ten.
Scotland skipper **Gary McAllister** on the former Motherwell midfielder, April 1996.

I don't think I have played with a better all-round player in my life. He had skill, vision, strength, he never gave the ball away, he scored plenty and, of course, he could give and take tackles.
Pat Nevin on Norman Whiteside, April 1996.

No player should be able to choose the manager for whom he will play when asked to represent Scotland. Richard Gough did this and that quite clearly indicates to me that he is not fully committed to his country . . . I notice that while Richard Gough was injured recently Rangers were unbeaten. On his return they suffered a 2–0 defeat at the hands of Hearts. This, following a 0–3 defeat earlier, would indicate he is not indispensable to Rangers either.
Excerpt from a letter written by Scotland boss **Craig Brown** to Rangers fan Peter Campbell, who'd asked why Gough wasn't being selected for Scotland, May 1996.

I've been playing for 15 years so even the simplest defenders can read me by now.
John Colquhoun, May 1996.

If other humans could move their legs as fast as Spenny when he runs, the world 100-metre record would be about three seconds.
Ally McCoist on John Spencer, June 1996.

You were constantly having to tell him to shut up on the park. He had his own ideas about how you should go about disciplining the other players in the team.
Ref **Davie Syme** on Rangers captain Richard Gough, August 1996.

Peter Schmeichel is always picked on because he is always moaning. Brucey is this central figure who is always saying outrageous things. Pally gets the mickey taken for being lazy. Eric sits there and takes it all in and just laughs at them. Sparky never says a word. Ryan tends to be quiet; as does Denis Irwin. Choccy will have a word of wisdom . . . I love going in and hearing the banter and they all wonder what I'm doing there. They think I'm checking up on how they dress in the morning, or if I can smell drink, but I love the banter.
Alex Ferguson on the Manchester United dressing-room, *A Year in the Life – A Manager's Diary*, 1996.

I think someone took the confidence out of my body one night when I was asleep.
Joe Tortolano after being told he was being freed by Hibs, August 1996.

Paolo Maldini couldn't avoid fouling if he was facing Brian, and he's the best defender in the world.
Hearts' **Pasquale Bruno** after being sent off for a foul on Laudrup, September 1996.

I know Celtic's supporters are fed up with the mention of Brian Laudrup's name but I can't get enough of him. He might be Rangers' property but Laudrup looks like my idea of a Celtic player.
Charlie Nicholas, April 1995.

I thought I was bad but compared to me, he was the devil incarnate.
Victor Kasule on Steve Pittman, October 1996. The pair were team-mates at Shrewsbury.

He may not be the most skilful player Rangers have ever had and he certainly can't compete with Baxter in that respect. But no one has ever served them quite like Ally has done. You need a certain type of player to be successful in Scotland and Ally is that player.
Maurice Johnston on Ally McCoist, December 1996.

I remember swapping jerseys with Franco Baresi. What was depressing was that he got a sweat-soaked Scotland number nine while the Italy number six I got in return was not only bone-dry but still smelling of his cologne.
Rangers and Scotland striker **Ally McCoist**, in match programme for 50th cap, March 1996.

I knew within four weeks of Basile Boli and Oleg Salenko arriving that they weren't going to work out. Neither made any attempt to integrate and it soon became clear that both had another agenda.
Rangers manager **Walter Smith**, August 1997.

What I inherited was a guy with a weight problem, a discipline problem and a problem absorbing anything to do with tactics. Two things happened. When I came out of hospital after my little heart scare, Alex Ferguson called me. He told me that if players weren't doing it for me, I should move them on. In Roddy's case, I moved him on to the reserves.
St Johnstone boss **Paul Sturrock** on striker Roddy Grant, January 1997.

You could send two guys wearing balaclavas and carrying baseball bats to chap on his door.
Hibs boss **Jim Duffy** on a new method of stopping Brian Laudrup after the Dane had scored in Rangers' 3–1 win, February 1997.

Our instructions were simple. Get Brian the ball then get out of his road when he got it.
Ally McCoist on Rangers' tactics on Laudrup's arrival, 1997.

When he first came to the club I don't even think the management knew how good a player we'd got.
Andy Goram on Laudrup, 1997.

The little b****** from Motherwell who stamped all over my leg is up the stairs.
Dundee United's **Lars Zetterlund** breaks the news to his team-mates that his side are about to sign Jamie Dolan, February 1997.

Q: Is there a God?
A: There is and he wears number seven for Manchester United.
Hibs' **Darren Jackson** questionnaire answer, March 1997. Eric Cantona was the object of his affection.

He had a strong Border dialect. At one time we had a South African trialist with a guttural accent and he and John became friends. It was like listening to Bill and Ben the Flowerpot Men.
Former Hibs boss **Pat Stanton** on early memories of John Collins, March 1997.

You come across players like Brian once in a lifetime and when you have got them you don't let them go easily.
Manchester United boss **Alex Ferguson** on Brian McClair, April 1997.

Knowing it was my last game at Broadwood, I took a couple of minutes to reflect on the seminal moments of my career. Every début, Old Firm games, that game at Dundee, Prague, Bologna, Belgrade, Barbados, Mostar, Munich, Magaluf. Marvellous.
John Colquhoun looks back as he announces his retirement, 18 May 1997.

I feel honoured to have played alongside some great players and also some awful players who were just great lads.
John Colquhoun retiring, 18 May 1997.

There are some players in Scotland who are sick of the sight of me and I'm sick of the sight of them.
David Robertson quitting Rangers for Leeds, May 1997.

Dylan Kerr: His brother Wan is a better player.
Ally McCoist, pre-Cup Final Player profiles, May 1997.

When he was at Ibrox he crashed so many sponsors' cars he was eventually given a sponsor's dodgem.
Ally McCoist on Falkirk's David Hagen, May 1997.

I genuinely believe that Maurice Johnston was one of the real world-class players that we've had in the last 10 or 15 years.
Agent **Bill McMurdo**, The Absolute Game fanzine, May 1997.

Gareth Evans used to share a house with him [John Collins] and he told me that whenever they were watching telly and the adverts came on, John

would drop on to the carpet and do a few minutes of exercise before the programme started again.
Darren Jackson, August 1997.

It's fair to say I was never a big believer in unnecessary exertion.
Alan Hansen, October 1997.

Watching him [Chic Charnley] is a bit like watching a Quentin Tarantino movie. You know something terrible is going to happen, you're just not sure when.
John Colquhoun on the Hibs midfielder, August 1997.

That kind of goal can only be scored by a special kind of player. But while Pele tried it and failed Charnley tried it and succeeded.
Former Dundee manager **Simon Stainrod** on Charnley's 65-yard goal for Hibs against Alloa, August 1997.

Charnley has the same outrageous football skills as Gazza (well, sort of), but puts on weight faster and is even more mentally unstable. Imagine Colonel Gaddafi summoning the US ambassador to his bedouin tent for a diplomatic dressing-down after F-14s had bombed Tripoli and you've got some idea of how Charnley communicates with referees.
David Bennie, A Season in Hell, 1997.

Writers find it easier to concentrate on the bad side of me rather than the good. I've seen what they've done to Gascoigne here, hammering him when he's been absolutely brilliant and maybe done only one wee bad thing in a match.
Hibs' **Chic Charnley**, January 1998.

Players can't keep anything to themselves: you don't need to spend a fortune on sophisticated electronic listening devices to tap into the secret conversations in any football club. It's much cheaper and faster to buy a player a pint.
Brian McClair, Odd Man Out, 1997.

He's great in the air, a superb tackler, and the best blocker I've ever seen. You can sometimes be watching Blackburn and you're sure the opposition are about to score, but then in steps Colin. For me, that is what sets him apart from every other central defender in the country – and I'm including Gary Pallister and Tony Adams when I say that.
TV pundit **Alan Hansen**, 1998.

Professional footballers are among the sharpest group of people you'll ever meet, and the banter, comments, the slickness of the wind-up and the psychological torturing that goes on is both witty and intelligent.
Pat Nevin, March 1998.

It's no fault of Walter Smith's but when players get the same whip for ten years it can be a case of 'Aye, right, fine'.
Rangers chairman **David Murray**, July 1998.

I've seen players who could have been world-beaters, loads of them, but I wouldn't mention them because it's hard enough for them to accept what they could have done.
Coventry boss **Gordon Strachan**, August 1998.

They walk about with their baseball caps and expensive clothes, living in cloud-cuckooland. They have no experience of real life, no perspective.
Clyde general manager **Ronnie MacDonald**, October 1998.

At some senior clubs, journalists have to wait an hour and a half to get some wonder piece of insight from some peabrain who just wants to get away and meet his bird.
Clyde general manager **Ronnie MacDonald**, October 1998.

I told him he could change anywhere. Unfortunately he picked big Yogi's spot and his gear almost went in the showers. Still, it would have been a good fight.
Hibs boss **Alex McLeish** on new signing Franck Sauzee's introduction to John Hughes, February 1999.

Just walking about the training ground he's a great example, a guideline to how my players should behave on and off the pitch. I've got another two here like that, Nilsson and Steve Ogrizovic, perfect examples of the way you should train, the way you should eat, and the way to behave.
Coventry boss **Gordon Strachan** on Gary McAllister, February 1999.

The most accomplished Scottish player in the world.
John Colquhoun on Paul Lambert, March 1999.

He was here, we made him the best offer he got when he was available, and he seemed happy with it. He left that night simply to talk things over with his wife, and we never saw him again. Actually, he left here with

about nine advisors. You couldn't move in this office for Ginola's entourage of agents.
Celtic managing director Fergus McCann recalls the club's bid to sign David Ginola, April 1999.

He gave the impression that he could play with a gin and tonic in one hand and a book in the other.
Former Liverpool striker David Johnson on Alan Hansen, April 1999.

The whole affair saddened me. I found Paul an immensely likeable man in most respects, although remarkably opinionated and stubborn. I really believe he is a top-class player, although, as I have already indicated, I feel he actually sells himself a little short considering the ability he has at his disposal.
Former Celtic general manager Jock Brown on his problems with midfielder Paul Lambert, in *Celtic-Minded*, 1999.

PRESS

You would need to buy two of them to find out the correct date.
Kenny Dalglish on newspapers, February 1995.

Journalists feel I belittle them.
Kenny Dalglish, *Dalglish – My Autobiography*, 1996.

I supported Motherwell as a kid, but whenever I'm linked with Rangers I'm a lifelong Rangers fan and when I was linked with Celtic I was a lifelong Celtic fan. I've supported lots of clubs if you believe the papers.
Scotland skipper Gary McAllister, September 1995.

It's my belief that many among the media don't understand the laws of the game and that glaring inaccuracies are transmitted in print, on radio and on television by people who are operating in pure ignorance. I'd say if the Scottish press corps took on the Italian press corps on their knowledge of football, our lads would get a terrible beating. The Italians are far superior in their reading and scrutiny of what's happening.
SFA Chief Executive Jim Farry, March 1996.

Ninety-five per cent of the time I'd come in after a game and give someone a hug but that's not such a good story. That's not going to get you a headline in the *News of the World* on a Sunday morning, is it?
Graeme Souness on managing Rangers, April 1996.

I sold a story to *The Sun*. That was wrong. I'm a big boy and I make my own decisions so I have to be able to put my hand up and say, 'I was wrong.'
Former Liverpool manager **Graeme Souness** on selling the story of his heart op to the newspaper hated on Merseyside for its coverage of the Hillsborough tragedy, April 1996. Souness was photographed kissing new girlfriend Karen Levy on the day of the memorial service for the disaster.

According to one newspaper he was supposed to have been running around mad in a hotel. He shrugged his shoulders and said he knew nothing about it. And he was supposedly serving fish and chips one night in a chip shop. He can't remember doing that. Usually he just shrugs and says, 'This is how they sell their papers. I sell papers for them. More than anyone else.'
Ken McGill, producer of TV documentary, *Gazza's Coming Home*, on Paul Gascoigne, 1996.

I'd like to see young journalists being encouraged to go along to training sessions to watch and more fully understand the subject they're writing about.
George Graham, August 1995.

Just because you live by the sea doesn't mean you can swim.
Kenny Dalglish on journalists, *Dalglish – My Autobiography*, 1996.

I think the media in Scotland have a lot to answer for.
Hearts chairman **Chris Robinson**, October 1996.

I felt the Press weren't important, which was stupid. The media are far more important than I ever imagined.
Dundee United chairman **Jim McLean**, December 1996, 25 years after arriving at Tannadice.

Games are only meaningless because that is how they are promoted by journalists, so that is how the public see them. These games are not meaningless to the players or the fans but the media like sensation, and that is the so-called drama of promotion and relegation battles.
Raith Rovers boss **Iain Munro**, February 1997.

Q: What would you be if not a footballer?
A: A binman or a sports journalist.
Falkirk's **David Hagen**, newspaper questionnaire, February 1997.

We got too much praise for that [Sweden] game and arguably, maybe marginally, just a little too much criticism for this one.
Craig Brown on the 0–0 draw against Estonia, *The Absolute Game* fanzine, April 1997.

My ambition is to get about 10–20 pals and buy them a camera each and go and hound the editor, his kids and family, morning and night, for at least a month. Shove the camera in the kids' faces. I hate them. I really detest them.
Paul Gascoigne on the media, 1997.

I went to see Walter Smith and he asked, 'Do you actually like getting in the papers?' I thought for a moment and said, 'Not really.' And he said, 'Well why do you do it?'
Paul Gascoigne, 1997.

They're doing a job. I had a wee spell as a journalist myself and I know they've got to get an angle. So I've got every sympathy with them.
Craig Brown, *The Absolute Game* fanzine, April 1997.

I can't win. Every game I play nowadays I get hammered. Too fat. Too thin. Not beating five players, should have beaten five players. The same old stories.
Paul Gascoigne, 1997.

The long-running saga of Pierre van Hooijdonk's departure was precisely the kind of thing which most other clubs successfully manage to avoid. Pierre and Fergus [McCann] adapted the by now usual Celtic practice of conducting their negotiations in the tabloid newspapers, with Burns cast in the role of anxious bystander haudin' the jaikets.
Alastair McSporran, *The Absolute Game* fanzine, August 1997.

The way the papers go on about the Old Firm all the time is a slap in the face to all the fans who go to Tynecastle and Easter Road.
Rangers chairman **David Murray**, October 1997.

I'm a man of repute now. In fact, I don't know why I'm talking to you lot.
Alex Ferguson to the Press after getting his OBE, January 1998.

When I came up to Scotland all you got was the journalists who had never seen me, talking knowingly and knowledgeably about the type of player I was. But they were talking nonsense, total nonsense . . . I'm probably closer to a player like John Collins than to a tricky winger.
Kilmarnock's **Pat Nevin**, March 1998.

They're far too quick to ridicule managers, coaches and players as well as the game itself.
Kilmarnock boss **Bobby Williamson** on the press, February 1999.

In the late '80s, say, in an average year I would maybe do three television interviews, three national radio interviews. People are doing that in a day now.
Alan Hansen, March 1999.

Players spend their whole career slaughtering the media, then they finish and say, 'What shall I do now? I know: the media. That'll be easy.'
Alan Hansen, March 1999.

A huddle took place. After a press conference is concluded, many of the journalists go into a huddle to decide how they will present the material they have obtained. The huddle members portrayed me as a liar and as someone who had deliberately deceived them over di Canio. I hadn't, but what every editor would have read in most competing papers matched, so they would come to the conclusion that their own reporters had handled the matter accurately. That's what gives each huddle member his safety net.
Former Celtic general manager **Jock Brown**, in book, *Celtic-Minded*, 1999.

I guessed that Murdo [MacLeod] would sell his story to the *Sunday Mail.* Duly doing so, Murdo stooped to depths which surprised even someone who had become totally disenchanted with his modus operandi.
Former Celtic general manager **Jock Brown**, in book, *Celtic-Minded*, 1999. (The irony that most people first read his views in the book's serialisation in a Sunday newspaper was presumably lost on Brown.)

PRESSURE

I don't want to name names, but there were a few big stars in that Celtic team who weren't having any of it when it came to the crunch.
Dixie Deans, July 1994, on his penalty miss against Inter Milan in the 1972 European Cup semi-final, quoted in Tom Campbell & Pat Woods, *Dreams, and Songs to Sing,* 1996. Celtic lost 5–4 on penalties.

On Friday 28 April, 13 days after Hillsborough, we resumed training. I have never seen tackling like it in my life, certainly not on a training ground.
Kenny Dalglish on the aftermath of Hillsborough, *Dalglish – My Autobiography,* 1996.

My greatest worry when I took over was that I might leave being the only Rangers manager never to have won a trophy. You might laugh at that now but it was a genuine fear.
Rangers boss **Walter Smith,** May 1994.

I never spoke about pressure or strain at that time. All I said was that I simply wanted to take a break from football. The Press are the only people who go on about pressure. You have a problem if you can't handle being top of a league table. I don't want to sound blasé or arrogant but I would imagine the real pressure is something that comes along when your side is at the foot of their division.
Kenny Dalglish, February 1996.

I regard Rangers as a privilege, not a pressure.
Rangers chairman **David Murray,** March 1995.

I get to sleep all right. But if I do wake up in the night then my mind is fully awake and I can find myself thinking over every aspect of some problem for an hour or so. I can't just roll over and drop off again.
Celtic manager **Tommy Burns,** March 1996.

The six months leading up to the [1990 FA Cup] final had been a nightmare for me and I couldn't wait until the final whistle on a Saturday. Most players are genuinely excited during the days leading up to the game but I hated it.
Former Manchester United goalkeeper **Jim Leighton,** June 1996.

I came off on Tuesday and there was sweat running down the cheeks of my arse.

Partick Thistle boss John Lambie gives us the gory details as Thistle begin their customary great escape from relegation by beating Hearts 3–1, April 1995.

The people, they might ask Ruud Gullit why he leave Milan and Sampdoria, and he say that his brain, it is bursting because the pressure in Italy is so very strong.

Hearts defender Pasquale Bruno, April 1996.

One guy stopped his car. He said, 'Just watch what you're doing up here, be careful mate.' I said, 'Cheers, mate.' He said, 'Because I'll slit yer effin' throat.' The training didn't go too well that day.

Paul Gascoigne, in TV documentary, *Gazza's Coming Home*, October 1996.

My wife Lorraine forced me to go to the doctor, who diagnosed a businessman's ulcer. The doctor asked if I was worried about things. I said, 'Well, I play for Celtic!'

Peter Grant on his spell signing monthly contracts, January 1997.

I switch off by sitting in the house watching telly. I watch all the garbage, *Family Fortunes*, things like that.

Coventry boss Gordon Strachan, January 1997.

This game is dominated by nerves.

Celtic's Jorge Cadete on Old Firm matches, April 1997.

The first year was torture.

Andy Roxburgh on managing Scotland, April 1997.

At Rangers you're not as good as your last game. You're as good as your last pass.

Richard Gough, September 1997.

You go home after the Chelsea game and you don't sleep too well. You don't really want to pick up the papers but you do. Everything said on the telly is against you. Everyone on the radio is talking about Tottenham's defeat. It affects players more deeply than fans think.

Spurs' Colin Calderwood after a 6–1 defeat by Chelsea, December 1997.

He has 64 caps and played in two World Cup finals. Is he going to feel pressure winning the league in Scotland?
Former Feyenoord defender **John de Wolf** on Wim Jansen's problems at Parkhead, March 1998.

It can do silly things to you, obsession. If you're obsessive and if you don't get to the point you want to achieve you can become a basketcase. I've seen loads of them.
Coventry boss **Gordon Strachan**, August 1998.

PUNCH-UPS

Bremner got up, came over and whacked me on the leg, the one that had been broken. I controlled my temper and just sort of picked him up. He's smaller than me.
Dave Mackay on the famous 1965 bust-up with Billy Bremner, April 1997.

I'm a small bloke and people seem to react to it. If I was 6' 2" I wouldn't have had these problems because no one with half a brain is going to have a pop at you then.
Former Scotland striker **David Speedie**, December 1996.

The referee came towards me and I thought, 'I've got to be sent off here. I've never been sent off in my life but I'll just have to go off here. The referee can't do anything else. Violent conduct, and I'll deserve it.' But I wasn't even booked. Not that I thought I'd got away with anything, because I knew the real trouble would start once the match was over. I was fined two weeks' wages and that cured me forever.
Manchester United's **Brian McClair** on an infamous brawl in a match against Arsenal, *Odd Man Out*, 1997.

I'd have backed Hateley. He had more time in the ring behind him.
Rangers' **Ian Durrant** recalls a fight between Mark Hateley and Duncan Ferguson while at Il Ciocco training camp in Tuscany, in *Blue & White Dynamite – The Ian Durrant Story*, 1998.

I don't think we'd have won the championship that year unless Graeme [Souness] had gone. He hadn't told me of his plans, but I'd read the script. When he told me Liverpool were after him again, I told him to see me in the morning. I spoke to the other directors and decided he would go there and then.
Rangers chairman **David Murray**, November 1994.

We don't have board meetings at Ibrox. To be honest, we did have a board meeting for the first time in years about six weeks ago. We speak regularly, and if things need to be done then we are in contact by phone or at matches. But in this instance, I was concerned that my colleagues were worried about the direction in which the club was heading. So we had a dinner at my offices in Edinburgh, which Walter Smith and Campbell Ogilvie attended. If anyone was unhappy, there was an opportunity for a frank discussion. That's the way we run the club, and there wasn't a problem.
Rangers chairman **David Murray**, November 1994.

I get around 80 letters a week – that's 4,000 a year – from Rangers fans, and I answer each one personally.
Rangers chairman **David Murray**, November 1994.

My best personal friend was chairman of the club; I don't think I ever realised how lucky I was there. I was the second biggest shareholder, we had a brand new ground, we were making money other than from the gates, we were successful and we had done all the hard work. It could all have been so easy. Because we'd done it all so fast, I never really realised what we'd achieved until afterwards.
Graeme Souness, April 1996.

If Ruud hadn't wanted me I would have gone to Rangers.
Chelsea's **Gianluca Vialli**, November 1996.

There's no way anyone will get that job until Walter wins 10 in a row. And then they'll be looking for a big European name. The likes of me will always be looking for a second-strata club.
Raith's **Jimmy Nicholl** on the Rangers' manager's job, April 1997.

Rangers could be one of the top teams in Europe but we just cannot afford to be second to anyone in Scotland. That would be deemed a failure because clubs had finished ahead of us in the league. Auxerre are mid-table but no one complains because they did well in the Champions' Cup. And look at Ajax – in the semi-finals and fourth in the table. But no complaints over there.
Rangers chairman **David Murray**, April 1997.

When things aren't too clever I always wish I was still at Rangers.
Former Rangers defender **Jimmy Nicholl**, April 1997.

I am a true bluenose.
Dane **Tommy Moller-Nielsen** displays his grasp of Glaswegian after being appointed Rangers' first-team coach, 27 May 1997.

Eleven years ago, when we hadn't won a championship for nine years, nobody was worrying about Europe. Then the focus was at a domestic level.
Manager **Walter Smith**, August 1997.

A wonderful club when you're winning and a tough club when you're not.
Skipper **Richard Gough**, October 1997.

How many Scots have they got there at Ibrox now? Two? They're running out buying Englishmen and Italians and Chileans when every kid in Scotland dreams of pulling that blue jersey on.
Former Dundee chairman **Ron Dixon**, February 1998.

It's not about balance sheets – Rangers are a world brand where everything follows from what happens on the field.
Chairman **David Murray**, August 1998.

Last year we made mistakes. Only recently I was discussing it with Walter Smith and we agreed we had maybe been papering over the cracks a wee bit. We over-relied on Laudrup and Gascoigne and we kept the team together too long.
Rangers chairman **David Murray**, August 1998.

Yeah, we've failed in Europe. Yeah, we haven't done this or that. But 17 trophies and a trading profit in 8 of my 10 years isn't bad.
Rangers chairman **David Murray**, August 1998.

Some of last season's Rangers team wouldn't have survived under Dick Advocaat.
Rangers' defender **Tony Vidmar**, January 1999.

It's been disappointing to hear players criticising what happened before when they haven't really achieved anything with Rangers themselves. Tony Vidmar is one of them. He wouldn't have got a game for Rangers during the previous seven or eight years. He could hardly get a game when we were struggling. In three or four years time every one of the boys who left the club last season – and most of them are Rangers supporters – will want the club to continue being successful and even beat the record they created. That's why it's so disappointing to hear criticism from their replacements who haven't done anything for Rangers so far. They should keep quiet and see how many championship they win.
Everton boss **Walter Smith**'s response, January 1999.

REAL WORK

Jim was in tears. It was devastating. But afterwards, I remember him saying how Ravenscraig had closed that same night. There were thousands of people laid off and Jim said, 'Well, that puts it in perspective, you know; it's only a game.' We were all devastated but when you thought about it in those terms, it was nothing really.
Linda Leighton, wife of Jim, on his being dropped by Manchester United for the 1990 FA Cup final replay against Crystal Palace, October 1996.

I've always enjoyed what I've done. I've always loved the game. I could have been one of those miserable guys you see on the Tube hating what they do. Those last few months at Liverpool I was that miserable person on the Tube.
Graeme Souness, April 1996.

Tell me another career where sleeping for two hours in the afternoon is part of your job? Where else can you get sent on holiday with your mates a couple of times a year? You can act as if you're 17 even though you're 32 and everyone accepts it. All they'll do is say, 'Bloody footballers.'
Former Hearts winger **John Colquhoun**, May 1996.

He'd say, 'This is work – this is life, not what you're doing.'
Dumbarton boss **Ian Wallace**, December 1996, recalling trips to the coalface or Rampton High Security Mental Hospital at Nottingham Forest under Brian Clough.

I don't see myself going back to being a house painter. That's how I started out but, like Adolf Hitler, I decided to leave it behind.
John Colquhoun pondering his future after coming to the end of his St Johnstone contract, May 1997.

This is no kidding, but I used to go to work wearing three pairs of socks under my steel toe cap boots, thermal pyjamas, three pairs of trousers, three tee-shirts, two jumpers and two coats.
Celtic's **Darren Jackson** recalling working in a Leith sawmill as a youngster, August 1997.

I remember saying to my missus, 'Just you wait – the phone is not going to stop ringing with job offers.' After four months she gently pointed out that it hadn't rung once.
Alan Hansen on finishing playing, October 1997.

If I hadn't pulled on a football shirt, I would now be a mathematics teacher.
Brian McClair, *Odd Man Out*, 1997.

My immortality would be to be involved with the club when we win the European Cup. To hell with the law.
Rangers vice-chairman (and QC) **Donald Findlay**, March 1998.

I'm changing the way I run my businesses, including Rangers. I've got so many divisions – metal, mining, sports management, football – that I can't have my hands on all of them. I've got a business in New Zealand which sells washing machines and fridges, which turns over $250m, and I haven't even been there in two years.
Rangers chairman **David Murray**, August 1998.

I was up on roofs and building up chimney stacks. But it was the middle of winter that was horrendous: picking up bricks that were stuck to frozen ground and having the skin fleeced from your fingers.
Kilmarnock manager (and former brickie) **Bobby Williamson**, August 1998.

REFEREES

On August 16, 1982 at 3 p.m. precisely, a certain Mr Hugh Dallas blew his whistle for the first time ever to take charge of Bridgework Amateurs v Victoria Amateurs at a local venue in Motherwell and in the short space of 90 minutes I never imagined I could upset so many people. But three red cards and six yellow later, and £6 to the good, I had.
Referee **Hugh Dallas** recalls his beginnings.

I punched the air before going out on to the right wing. When I got there, the linesman whispered to me, 'Choccy, they've scored, we've won it!' I looked at him in disbelief. The ground was full of Celtic fans that day: most of the 17,000 spectators, and one of the officials.
Brian McClair Odd Man Out, 1997, recalling hearing Dundee had scored against Hearts on the final day of season 1985–86, effectively giving Celtic the Premier Division title.

All over the world it would have been a penalty. But at Ibrox it wasn't.
Dundee United boss **Ivan Golac** after his side had been denied a stonewall penalty while 1–0 up at Ibrox, 23 April 1994. Rangers won 2–1.

[Refs in America] are taught to respect entertainment. What's the point in calling a player over to lecture him in centrefield? He might be 32 years of age and have four kids. It's the height of absurdity.
Dundee chairman **Ron Dixon** on Scots referees, April 1994.

I wanted to go public and explain my version of what had turned into a hugely controversial incident. I was amazed when I was told by a referee supervisor, 'Shut up – referees don't make mistakes.'
Former ref **Davie Syme** on the 1986 League Cup final between Rangers and Celtic in which he sent off Celtic's Tony Shepherd then changed his mind, May 1994.

There's very few places I can go now socially. We're like the reverse of superstars. A star is well known and liked. We're well known and loathed.
Ref **Les Mottram**, June 1994.

You might have 46,000 in a stadium, but only three people, including the supervisor in the stand, will be able to claim the same knowledge of the laws as the ref.
SFA Chief Executive Jim Farry, March 1996.

It is absolute nonsense, a suggestion constantly put forward by those whose knowledge of the laws of football could be contained within my toe nail. Our referees are fitter, more informed, more tactically aware now than they've ever been.
SFA Chief Executive Jim Farry on criticism of referees, March 1996.

There are certain clubs in this country who, in order to deflect talk of their own inadequate performances, blether on about supposedly 'poor' refereeing. It is drivel.
SFA Chief Executive Jim Farry, March 1996.

Willie Miller used to attempt the impossible by playing and refereeing at the same time. If he ever needed a linesman Jim would be a natural for the job.
Former ref Davie Syme on Jim Leighton, August 1996.

The day I had to book Paul Gascoigne for celebrating scoring a goal was the last straw. That was the day I decided to pack it in. My stomach turned but under the system I had to yellow-card Gazza. I was cringing as I did it.
Ref Jim McGilvray, announcing his decision to resign, February 1996. He'd booked Gascoigne against Partick on 10 February.

There is a terrible snobbery which afflicts refereeing. Basically, the higher your professional standing, the greater your chance of becoming a top ref. If a lawyer and a lorry driver are vying for a place on the FIFA list you can bet your bottom dollar the man behind the wheel will miss out.
Former ref Jim McGilvray, February 1996.

If the Scottish FA is accused of creating robots by issuing instructions, then we plead guilty, The set of instructions is called the laws of the game.
SFA Chief Executive Jim Farry's response to McGilvray's criticisms, February 1996.

You do not often hear of a football manager, coach or player admitting good fortune when a decision by a referee goes his way. I don't recall too many of those people saying, 'We were lucky not to have a penalty given against us' or 'We were fortunate Willie wasn't sent off for banging that guy on the head'.

SFA Chief Executive Jim Farry on calls for refs to be able to explain decisions, January 1997.

It has happened to me four times – against Alloa, Kilmarnock, Rangers and again today. I looked at the linesman and made the shape of a TV with my hands. It was my way of telling him that if he watched the game afterwards he would see that I was not offside.

Celtic's Jorge Cadete after an offside ruling against Raith Rovers, February 1997.

I went straight home after the game and had a large one while soaking in a bath.

Ref Hugh Dallas on his Old Firm début in November 1995, in which he disallowed a Rangers goal, awarded Celtic a penalty and booked nine players.

If Rangers win the nine-in-a-row it will be more than coincidence.

Celtic's Jorge Cadete, April 1997.

We are the better team and that is why we win. It is nothing to do with referees.

Rangers' Jorg Albertz's response, April 1997.

I have never yet seen a referee elbow, head-butt or spit upon a colleague.

SFA Chief Executive Jim Farry after criticism of John Rowbotham's handling of the November 1997 Old Firm match where he sent Paul Gascoigne off.

I have not been reported for saying anything I've done on the touchline, apart from this latest one where I was reported for what I said about the referee after the game on television. I wrote to the referee on the Monday and apologised and he accepted that.

Coventry boss Gordon Strachan, February 1999.

I had to say sorry [to the linesman]. Fraser Wishart, who never lies, said it was in.

Clydebank manager Ian McCall on a controversial Darren Patterson equaliser for Dundee United in a Scottish Cup tie, 3 March 1999.

I've had refs coming up and asking, 'What's wrong? You're not shouting at us, Doddsy.'

Dundee United striker Billy Dodds, March 1999. Dodds admitted the change stemmed from the death of his sister Barbara in a car crash in October 1997.

RELIGION

We were founded in 1873 as a Presbyterian Boys Club. To change now would lose us considerable support.
Rangers director **Matt Taylor**, 1967, quoted in Simon Kuper, *Football Against The Enemy*, 1994.

I live my life by my faith. The most important thing in my life is to save my soul. Every day I wake up and say my prayers to live this day as best I can. Everything I have achieved in this life is because of God: I am just an instrument living my life wherever I am taken.
Celtic boss **Tommy Burns**, November 1994.

People don't have to ask me twice about success because I'll not be slow in telling them: it's not come from Thomas Burns but from Jesus.
Celtic boss **Tommy Burns**, November 1994.

The youth team coach said I was the first twelve-year-old to push the Royal Family on to page five.
John Spencer recalls becoming the first Roman Catholic to sign for Rangers, May 1996.

I'm due for retirement in a few years time and some people here are already lining up Craig as a possible replacement.
Hillhead Baptist Church minister **Reverend Bruce Keeble** after Craig Brown delivered an address on the worship of false idols in sport, February 1996.

Rod McDonald was not booked because he blessed himself. He was booked for ungentlemanly conduct because in the opinion of my linesman it was done in such a place and such a way as to inflame the Rangers support in that area of the ground. I have absolutely no problems with a player crossing himself as long as it's not provocative.
Former ref **Jim McGilvray** on booking the Partick Thistle striker against Rangers, February 1996. Ten days later McGilvray announced his retirement from refereeing.

I was always uncomfortable with the Catholic issue because my wife at the time was Catholic and I'd agreed to bring my children up as Catholics. I

didn't go out looking for a Catholic to sign but Mo was available and he was the right kind of player.
Graeme Souness on signing Mo Johnston, April 1996.

The club's a better club for it. I think any half-sensible human being would agree.
Graeme Souness on Rangers signing Catholics, April 1996.

God was blue today.
Hearts goalkeeper **Gilles Rousset** after losing 4–3 to Rangers in an epic Coca-Cola Cup final, 24 November 1996.

After I joined Celtic I was walking down a street in Glasgow when someone shouted, 'Fenian bastard'. I had to go and look it up – Fenian, that is.
Yorkshire-born **Mick McCarthy** recalling life in Glasgow, 1996.

You cannot change the minds of the mindless. But that doesn't mean you just admit that's the way we have to live.
Fergus McCann launching Celtic's Bhoys Against Bigotry campaign, 1996.

I am unaware of any top-class referee who has been involved in refereeing games between Rangers and Celtic who is also a member of our institution. It has become trendy to describe refs as masons in black but there is, unfortunately, a degree of paranoia attached to these statements. Celtic fans will have to look for another excuse.
Jack Ramsay, secretary of the Grand Orange Lodge of Scotland, 7 January 1997, after Celtic boss Tommy Burns complained about refereeing in Old Firm game. Jorge Cadete had had a goal chalked off in the crucial 2 January match, which Rangers won 3–1.

He was a Roman Catholic who often had his rosary beads with him in the dressing-room.
Rangers' **Ian Durrant** on former team-mate Basile Boli, in *Blue & White Dynamite – The Ian Durrant Story*, 1998.

Gentlemen, today we're breaking with tradition at this club – we're signing a Protestant.
Rangers manager **Walter Smith** wryly introducing new Swedish signing Jonas Thern to the Press, July 1997. Rangers' previous summer buys had been Italians.

My great-grandfather wouldn't have been able to imagine such a thing. My grandad would have been furious. My dad was uneasy about it. Myself? I

don't mind who we sign as long as they can play football. And for my son it won't even be an issue.
Rangers fan on the signing of Maurice Johnston, quoted in *Shoot* magazine, December 1996.

There used to be a distasteful side to Rangers' tradition. Now, the old ways are changing.
Rangers chairman David Murray, August 1997.

One of the most insidious examples of Rangers pandering to the prejudices of the Prods was largely passed over by the Press. This was at the finals of the Scottish Schools Cup played at Ibrox on 28 April 1996, a seven-a-side competition in front of 50,000 people at half-time in the crunch Rangers v Aberdeen league decider where Gascoigne scored a hat-trick. The winning team was Christ the King Primary School from Holytown, but they did not play under their own name, being called 'the red team' instead; even references to where they came from were fudged, with Motherwell being preferred to Holytown.
Bill Murray, *The Old Firm in The New Age*, 1998.

Not only would I describe myself as not being anti- any particular religion, given the chance I would scrap the whole lot. Because religion has caused more bother in the history of man than anything else I can think of.
Rangers vice-chairman Donald Findlay, March 1998.

I recall once playing against Linfield, a team known to be strongly Protestant. With a first name of Patrick and my others – Kevin, Francis, Michael – I was expecting a coolish reception, but I couldn't have been more wrong, I have never been made to feel so welcome by a football club in my life. In fact, the only other club who have been almost as welcoming were Glasgow Rangers. So much for the outsider's view of overt bigotry within modern football clubs.
Kilmarnock's Pat Nevin, July 1998.

If you think of all these families that come here – they come for entertainment, they come for a day out. They want to support Celtic. They don't plug into this stuff.
Celtic managing director Fergus McCann, February 1999.

It's fertile ground – these headbangers who drink in the pub all day and then go off to away games at places like Aberdeen – if you've got an IRA sympathiser to wind people up and sing those provocative songs. You can

see, it's just them reacting against the Scottish establishment and annoying the other team. It's not because they believe it, or even have any great interest in the IRA.
Celtic managing director **Fergus McCann**, February 1999.

We asked the SFA, 'What are you doing about sectarianism in Scotland?' They said, 'We don't think there is a problem, except in Glasgow.' But there's a problem in this society in general. They don't see it. We're not talking about football rivalry here, we're talking about hatred.
Celtic managing director **Fergus McCann**, February 1999.

There's a lot of people who are more solid as Celtic supporters than they are as Catholics.
Father Tom Connolly, Catholic Church, February 1999.

Religion is never mentioned in our dressing-room now. The players talk about more important things, like cars and money.
Rangers' press officer **John Greig**, in TV programme, *Football's Foreign Legion*, March 1999.

I do not condone violence and wholeheartedly support the current peace process in Northern Ireland.
Motherwell goalkeeper **Andy Goram**, 8 February 1999, the day after newspapers had accused him of UVF sympathies.

What difference does it make? The Celtic supporters hate him anyway.
Motherwell's **John Spencer**, February 1999. There had been calls for Goram to be left out of the February 21 game against Celtic over the UVF storm. Goram subsequently withdrew himself on the week of the match, which Motherwell lost 7–1.

The songs didn't bother me. My English wasn't good enough for me to understand the words.
Former Rangers midfielder **Rino Gattuso**, March 1999.

You look at the likes of Henrik Larsson coming to Scotland. He seems to be an intelligent man. I wonder what goes through his head when he sees this tribalism.
Former Celtic and Hibs defender **Jackie McNamara**, April 1999.

THE SACK

Received wisdom has it that if it wasn't for our third round victory against Nottingham Forest by a single goal from Mark Robins, following eight games without a win, our Gaffer would have been on his way out.

Manchester United's **Brian McClair** on a job-saving 1990 win for Alex Ferguson, *Odd Man Out*, 1997.

I have no plans for the future but, if there is anybody out there who is looking for an extremely able and successful executive, then I am available.

Former Parkhead Chief Executive **Terry Cassidy** after being sacked by Celtic, October 1992.

For Tommy [Burns] it was a difficult time. He worked through a period when there was a lot of pressure on him in terms of being the man to stop Rangers' charge toward equalling Celtic's nine-in-a-row record. But, in only his second year at Parkhead, to have gone through a full league season and to lose only one match and *still* not win the championship was remarkable. I think it's only happened here once before. He changed the club's fortunes – he certainly made them a far better team – but he knew, as I do, that you have to win, and that never happened for him, so the consequences were that he had to leave.

Rangers manager **Walter Smith** on his Celtic counterpart, August 1997.

Change direction? Where do they want to go? Down the table?

John McCormack after being sacked by Dundee while they were five points clear at the top of Division One, February 1998. A club statement said McCormack was axed because the club wanted to 'change direction'.

He looked across at me and said, 'It breaks my heart to see you leave this club.' As usual, his words were hypocritical, smug and empty.

Celtic assistant manager **Murdo MacLeod** recalls being sacked by Celtic general manager Jock Brown, June 1998.

He has become known as the serial sacker inside Parkhead.

Murdo MacLeod on Jock Brown, June 1997.

They say, in management, that it will happen some day. But I don't believe that. That's negative thinking.

Hearts manager **Jim Jefferies**, who's never been sacked, August 1998.

I've got a five-year contract. If I last five years it will be an absolute miracle.
Coventry boss **Gordon Strachan**, February 1999.

SARCASM

I am the kind of player spectators dislike. My style of play antagonises them. I think it stems from the unfortunate way I run.
Graeme Souness, *No Half Measures*, 1985.

They [his Manchester United team-mates] are always in a hurry to rush off and do any number of important things – like playing with their PlayStations for several hours or buying expensive but tasteless clothes.
Brian McClair, *Odd Man Out*, 1997.

I secretly keep a file of the Simon Donnelly and Derek McInnes 'Young Firm' columns which are printed every week in a Glasgow evening newspaper. They're such a damn good read.
Clydebank player-boss **Ian McCall**, January 1998.

Peter Johnson paid £1.6m and paid me good wages, then four months later sold me for £400,000. He strikes me as a sensible human being and a good businessman.
Motherwell striker **John Spencer** on his former Everton chairman, January 1999.

SCOTLAND V ENGLAND

The media just put them on a pedestal. It really got up our noses, so we were like, 'Let's do 'em, let's fucking show these boys.' And we did. Despite the fact the ref made us wear Leeds' orange away socks. That went against the grain.
Celtic's **Jimmy Johnstone** on the 1970 European Cup semi-final against Leeds.

God, could they play football. They had everything.
Leeds' **Billy Bremner** on the Celtic team which beat them.

They were a good side, but we were a better one.
Jimmy Johnstone on Leeds.

A lot of fuss was made, and even more nonsense written, after Scotland fans dug up some Wembley turf in June 1977. The pitch was about to be ripped up anyway – the Tartan Army just began the job a few days early.
Kenny Dalglish, *Dalglish – My Autobiography*, 1996.

How he never played for Scotland, I'll never know.
Manchester United boss **Ron Atkinson** on Dundee United goalkeeper Hamish McAlpine, after his performance in the November 1984 UEFA Cup third round tie helped United to a 2–2 draw.

I thought something terrible had happened. Then I saw Ally [McCoist] looking to the linesman. He was supposed to be marking me, and was hoping it would be disallowed.
Leeds' **Gary McAllister** on his opening-minute goal at Ibrox, Rangers v Leeds, European Cup, October 1992.

I much prefer 'Flower of Scotland' to 'Scotland The Brave' as our pre-match anthem . . . I'm told 'Flower' can be a bit politically insensitive – sending the English homeward to think again – but that doesn't stop Princess Anne belting it out at every rugby international.
Gary McAllister, *Captain's Log*, 1995.

The game was an embarrassment to the fixture's great past. It was an almost meaningless friendly.
Pat Nevin on playing in the final Scotland v England game in May 1989.

SFA

They're the biggest handicap in this game. If you added up all their imagination you'd fill a small Polish thimble.
Dundee chairman **Ron Dixon** on the SFA, April 1994.

Words can't describe how I feel about the SFA. I thought our biggest problem would be getting a team out of a war zone but the SFA have been the biggest obstacle to the good cause. They have been mean, hardhearted and pathetic.

Charity group Direct Aid's Andy Shaw after the SFA refused permission for a team of Bosnian players to play Inverness Clach, July 1994.

Clach were never in possession of approval from the SFA to play this match. No request was made from the charity in Inverness. Even if it were made now it would be refused. It's like going to Spain for a week's holiday then deciding you want to stay for a fortnight.

SFA Chief Executive Jim Farry's response, July 1994.

It's difficult to walk out on the front steps of this building [the SFA] and tell the world that Graeme Souness has just been suspended for another three weeks and fined £2,000. You could hardly walk out and say to the media, 'I've a great joke for you lads.' The public tended to see me in situations of a disciplinary or inhibitive nature. They weren't exactly meeting me off the park when I was having a good laugh and enjoying myself. I had this double persona, if you like, and the people who knew me used to have a laugh about it because I am usually very facetious.

Former SFA secretary Ernie Walker, April 1995.

There were many occasions when I had to announce things I didn't agree with and it certainly wasn't unusual for me to say to a committee: 'You shouldn't do that.'

Former SFA secretary Ernie Walker April 1995.

We went to the Scottish Stadia Committee – which is basically a group of SFA nominees – and they said, 'Guess what, we have a very good stadium on the south side of Glasgow [Hampden] to rent.' That was a complete outrage not fully appreciated by the public. The stadia committee quango should never have been delegated such powers by the Scottish Office and then have its buddies at the SFA and Queen's Park profit from renting Hampden. It cost us £600,000 to rent and a lot of lost revenue . . . I don't mind dealing with democracy but I do with a quango with a clear conflict of interest.

Celtic managing director Fergus McCann, June 1996.

I'm quite opinionated and I'm not saying that is right, but I would have thought they should have spoken to me. I would have thought the deals that I have done and the level at which I operate in business would have been worth a half-hour chat.

Rangers chairman David Murray on being ignored by the SFA's Think Tank on the game's future, January 1997.

They sit in judgement of you and treat you like a dunderhead.
Former Celtic and Scotland striker **Frank McGarvey** on SFA justice,
February 1997.

During the lap of honour you could imagine the problems it would cause
if players were to collect scarves from supporters. The police have to keep
the track clear.
SFA spokesman **David Findlay** on the announcement banning Cup finalists
Kilmarnock and Falkirk from running to their fans or picking up scarves and
hats at the game, May 1997.

You are allowed the right of appeal on Death Row. Even my wife allows
me to appeal some of her decisions. We must have the same in Scottish
football.
Dundee United chairman **Jim McLean** calls for disciplinary changes, August
1997.

In all the time I was there the SFA never gave me a break. They never so
much as blew me a kiss. Sure, I was a foreigner. But I wasn't one of the
cosseted few and that went against me.
Former Dundee chairman **Ron Dixon**, February 1998.

The central problem in Scotland is the SFA. The SFA know there are too
many teams in Scotland but nothing changes. To be fair to Jim McLean,
he saw that. He said so but he's smart enough to know when he's being a
jerk and to draw back a little.
Former Dundee chairman **Ron Dixon**, February 1998.

We are not claiming malice but we are stating intent. It wasn't a mistake,
it was a failure.
Celtic managing director **Fergus McCann** on the delay in Jorge Cadete's registration which saw the SFA suspend chief executive Jim Farry, 1 March 1999.

I asked Sam Galbraith, an elected minister and representative, to tell me,
a tax payer, what he was going to do to ensure that we have the protection
of the law against an organisation that I am obliged to be part of – the
SFA, which is in a monopolistic position in Scottish football. He refused
to answer the question. He refused to take a view on it. He should have a
view on it and it should be that football is not above the law.
Celtic managing director **Fergus McCann** following the suspension of Jim
Farry over the Jorge Cadete affair, March 1999.

I can't see the SFA being interested in me. It would be like Alex Ferguson managing the England team.
Former FA chief executive Graham Kelly on being linked with the SFA post after Jim Farry's sacking, March 1999.

SOUNESS

I used to go into Bill Nicholson's office every day after training and tell him that I had to be in the first team. He only had Steve Perryman, Mike England and Alan Mullery in midfield. In the end he got fed up with me and sold me to Middlesbrough.
Graeme Souness, April 1996.

I had a few good conversations with Graeme Souness. He gave me useful advice about starting a pension.
Former Aberdeen full-back Stuart Kennedy recalls Argentina '78, quoted in Mike Wilson, *Don't Cry For Me Argentina*, 1998.

The day I went into Liverpool to get my boots, Graeme Souness came over to me – he'd only been at Liverpool about a year – and he said, 'If I achieve a tenth of what you've done here I'll be happy.' And that's the nicest thing anyone's ever said to me.
Former Liverpool defender Emlyn Hughes, 1998.

The hardest, most ruthless player I have come up against in 15 years of top-class football . . . he isn't just hard. There is definitely a nasty side to him.
Frank Worthington on Souness, quoted in *No Half Measures*, 1985.

It became clear he [Souness] couldn't guarantee 100 per cent attention to the Scottish cause in the short term. I am not prepared to compromise therefore I did not select him. He understands my position and we both respect the other's point of view. I'm not playing with words here. Until people say to me they don't want to play they'll be considered. Graeme Souness has never said that to me, he's never even hinted that to me.
Scotland boss Andy Roxburgh on why the Rangers player-manager wasn't in the Scotland squad for a European Championship tie against Eire, February 1987. Souness never played for Scotland again.

[At Ibrox] there would be cans of lager placed in the referee's room for the match official and his linesman after the game. You were there to work but

the atmosphere was never hostile. When Souness arrived all that changed. Even the lager was withdrawn from the ref's room. Yet as soon as he left it was back to normal.
Former ref **Davie Syme**, May 1994.

The pitch didn't have to be a fixed width as long as it was above a certain minimum, so I thought, 'Right, I'll make it the absolute minimum.' On the Tuesday afternoon the Kiev players trained on the pitch when it was the normal size. On the Wednesday night they came out for the match and must have been shocked to discover that, after 15 paces, they were on the touchline . . . it wasn't purist stuff but it was within the rules.
Graeme Souness on the September 1987 European Cup-tie between Rangers and Dynamo Kiev, April 1996.

Graeme's been a bit annoyed I said this publicly, but I honestly believe that eventually the Rangers job didn't offer him the same challenge. He was looking for something else, and that turned out to be Liverpool.
Rangers chairman **David Murray**, November 1994.

I sometimes wonder if, like Lou Macari at Celtic, the club Graeme went back to was not the one he'd left.
Rangers chairman **David Murray**, on Souness leaving Rangers to join Liverpool, November 1994.

I've read things about me and thought, 'I wouldn't like that person.'
Graeme Souness, April 1996.

The Souness era has been blown out of all proportion. The Press didn't like him and the only information people got about him was from the Press. They can poison people's minds.
Steve McManaman on Souness at Anfield, May 1996.

I used to call him 'You old Scottish b*****d'. Did he mind? Of course not. He is like me, we both like a joke off the pitch. He once pushed me in a lake. I was wearing my club blazer, tie and trousers, I had just polished my shoes.
Chelsea's **Gianluca Vialli** on Souness, August 1996.

I would never have thought of myself as a popular player, or as a 'character'.
Graeme Souness, September 1996.

Since moving on from Rangers I've become a better coach, a better man-manager, a better handler of the media and above all a better man. Had I the same maturity, the same grip on life as I have now, I would have had far too much sense to leave a club as great as Rangers.
Graeme Souness, February 1997.

He and his new directors know nothing about football.
Graeme Souness quits as Southampton boss with a blast at new chairman Rupert Lowe, June 1997.

If anyone should be blamed for our situation it is Graeme Souness. I think he has acted out of pure selfishness.
Rupert Lowe responds, June 1997.

I knew I didn't have the same kind of obsession that men like Kenny Dalglish and Graeme Souness have. They're men who can't live without football. They live it and breathe it. They thrive on the pressure. But I can live without that pressure in my life.
Former Liverpool colleague **Alan Hansen**, October 1997.

I found myself thinking, 'I've got to get away. I should be running a club in a bigger country, with twenty good clubs, not just two.'
Graeme Souness on leaving Rangers, January 1998.

STEIN

It must have been a terrible drain on him over the years – and he was a man who didn't know the meaning of the word relaxation.
Billy McNeill, quoted in Tom Campbell and Pat Woods, *Dreams, and Songs to Sing*, 1996.

Supposing I completely detested a player, there would be something wrong with my head if I didn't pick him.
Scotland boss **Jock Stein**, October 1982.

I'll never forget that Auchenshuggle bus. On the nights it made me late for training it was a nightmare. I would sit there shaking, knowing big Jock would give me an almighty rollicking. And he always did.
Celtic boss **Lou Macari**, 1994.

I had a 90-minute train journey to Glasgow two nights a week and a bus ride to Celtic Park, where Jock Stein would flog me round the track for an hour. If we were lucky we'd get a wee game for 15 minutes. I thought it was wonderful. I honestly believe that kept me in the game until I was 35.
Stoke boss Lou Macari on training as a 15-year-old at Parkhead, April 1996.

Class is something you can recognise easily in managers but it's very hard to define. Jock Stein had it. He got it from his stature, the way he spoke and through the authority he commanded over his players and the media. If you could bottle what he had you'd make a fortune.
Former Scotland boss Andy Roxburgh on Jock Stein, April 1997.

It must have been during pre-season training in 1972 and the pubs weren't allowed to open in the afternoon in Scotland then. Wee Jimmy [Johnstone] and I used to share a car together on the way home and we pulled up behind a pub, the Noggin it was called, for a drink. But big Jock had a spy. We chapped the back door and we said 'two lager shandies' to the wee man who was staying on behind the bar. And the phone rang. The wee man behind the bar answered the phone and it was Jim Kennedy, the secretary in charge of tickets at Celtic Park, but big Jock's standin' behind him, listenin' in. So we hear this wee man say: 'Aye, he's here.' He said: 'Somebody's on the phone for you.' So Jimmy takes the phone and by this time Jock Stein's taken the phone off Jim Kennedy and says to Jimmy: 'See you. See you and that big fat bastard. You get your arses out of that place right now.' And we did. We just left our pints standin'.
Ex-Celt Bobby Murdoch on Stein, May 1997.

Stein was the greatest manager ever to draw breath. As a football man, there was no one who came anywhere close to him. He eclipsed Shankly, Busby and all the other legends in the game. He was in a class of his own.
Former Rangers boss Jock Wallace, September 1995, quoted in Tom Campbell & Pat Woods, *Dreams, and Songs to Sing*, 1996.

Without big Jock we would have muddled along, perhaps winning the odd trophy. He electrified the club, just as he had done at Hibs and Dunfermline. Just look, for starters, at how he reorganised our training and tactics. He put a stop to all that running dozens of laps around the track, then going our own way out on the pitch. We were going nowhere until he came to Parkhead.
Billy McNeill, quoted in Tom Campbell & Pat Woods, *Dreams, and Songs to Sing*, 1996.

When anyone writes the history of Celtic in the year 2050 it will be universally acknowledged that the two greatest Celtic servants of all time were Jock Stein and Fergus McCann.
Celtic general manager **Jock Brown**, August 1998.

I couldn't lace his boots – even if I had a pair to play football or manage with . . . the comments were well meant but a wee bit out of place.
Fergus McCann's response, two days later.

How many more times can he put his foot in it?
Lisbon Lion **Jimmy Johnstone** on Brown, August 1998.

STYLE

Bobby Lennox would have his lucky suit. By the end you could almost see your face in the arse of his trousers.
Ex-Celt **Jimmy Johnstone** on superstitions, March 1996.

If you want to wear an earring it's compulsory to wear a dress.
George Graham outlines the dress code at Arsenal to Charlie Nicholas and Graham Rix, 1986.

Gordon Durie says he went to Taylor Ferguson for his latest haircut. It's more like the work of Duncan Ferguson.
Rangers' **John Brown**, May 1995.

Paul's foot is in plaster, and he has to wear a shoe-thing so he can walk. As his image is so important to him, he has managed to get eight shoe-things in different colours to co-ordinate with his various outfits. The trials and tribulations of a fashion slave . . .
Manchester United's **Brian McClair** on team-mate Paul Parker, 1995.

The graphic stripe is a bit dodgy and looks like it's been done by a kid on a computer.
Designer **Jeff Banks** on Clydebank's strip. April 1996.

God gave me this face, although the plastic surgeon did have something to do with it.
Graeme Souness, April 1996.

I've got my team-mates to thank for this – because they're all so ugly.
Ally McCoist's reaction to the news that he had been voted 13th most hand-some man in the world – and top sportsman – in a *Sun* survey, September 1996.

Maybe the small bloke with the ginger hair and the big nose stood out a bit.
Gordon Strachan on being noticed by refs on the Coventry bench, November 1996.

At West Brom we used to dread a windy day because we knew that meant we'd be training in the gym. Big Ron simply refused to train outdoors if it was blowy because it would mess up his hair.
Kilmarnock boss **Bobby Williamson** on working under Ron Atkinson, April 1997.

John Spencer (Queen's Park Rangers): With those tough, builder looks, I imagine him *al fresco* beside a half-built house among bits of wood and empty concrete sacks. No hard hats, but he is wearing a check shirt and torn, dirty jeans.
Duncan Ferguson (Everton): With that natural arrogance which is so plainly Duncan, I imagine a master-servant situation. Obviously he holds the whip.
Extract from a letter listing a gay man's list of favourite footballers, broadcast by DJ Danny Baker, November 1997.

People were very happy to see so many of the Scottish fans wearing their skirts.
Joyce Clay, assistant director of administration in the St Etienne World Cup office, after Scotland's friendly there, November 1997.

I reckon his suit cost more than my house.
Craig Brown, after appearing on TV alongside Glenn Hoddle, February 1998.

I do fear that when someone writes my obituary in years to come I will be remembered for my jackets and not for my 2,000 programmes and 380 match commentaries.
Former Scottish Television anchor man **Arthur Montford**, April 1998.

It wasn't until I saw myself on TV that I realised how stupid I looked.
Celtic's goalkeeper **Jonathan Gould** on his dyed hair, December 1998.

It must have been a long time ago because Andy's still got teeth in the photograph.

Motherwell's John Spencer offers some light relief to team-mate Andy Goram's predicament, February 1999. A newspaper had published a photo of Goram among UVF supporters.

On the pitch, you don't really notice it. You just see a little red head bobbing up and down.

Coventry skipper Gary McAllister on manager Gordon Strachan, March 1999.

I like to be disciplined, punctual when I'm meeting people, things like that. It's a good thing to have in your make-up on or off the pitch.

Celtic's Paul Lambert, March 1999.

SWEARING

Gascoigne is a strange man. In the first leg in Glasgow I was running with the ball and he was shouting at me, 'You f***ing b*****d'. He wasn't even trying to tackle me, just shouting at me as I ran. Why was be doing that? He should be using his energy to tackle me and help his team, not shout and swear. On the way back I looked at him and he made a silly face and stuck his tongue out at me. I just shook my head. That is not the way to behave.

Anorthosis Famagusta midfielder Dimitris Assiotis after facing Gascoigne in the European Cup, August 1995.

I swear constantly. I take football too seriously and I love Scotland so much that logic evaporates into irrational cursing.

Channel 4's Stuart Cosgrove, July 1996.

Don't clap these c****.

Scotland's Ian Ferguson to team-mate Colin Calderwood, as the team depart the pitch to boos from the Tartan Army after the 0–0 draw with Estonia in Monaco, 11 February 1997. The remark was caught by a pitchside microphone.

Journalism now is dominated by yob culture. I've seen it creeping in during the last three or four years. You get papers now printing s-dot-dot-dot and w-asterisk-asterisk-asterisk-asterisk-asterisk. That never happened when I played.

Coventry boss Gordon Strachan, February 1999.

Do you need to be ranting and raving, f-ing and c-ing to be a good manager?
Stand-in Aberdeen boss **Paul Hegarty**, March 1999.

TACKLING

I loved being in Italy, apart from the football. The savagery of defenders was unbelievable, I almost lost an eye in my first game. Against *catenaccio* a chance was so rare you had to take it. I came back half a second quicker and got 34 goals in my first season at Arsenal.
Joe Baker on his move from Hibs to Torino, March 1994.

I have never said one word to him since the day he decked me . . . Am I bitter? Yeah, of course I am . . . To be honest, I don't think I will ever speak to Simpson again.
Rangers' **Ian Durrant** on the October 1988 Neil Simpson tackle that almost ended his career, in book *Blue & White Dynamite – The Ian Durrant Story*, 1998.

Take a good, close look at the expression on Simpson's face. He went in to snap me in two.
Ian Durrant, in *Blue & White Dynamite – The Ian Durrant Story*, 1998.

I remember wondering how he'd react to a good physical challenge. I never got within a yard of him.
Graeme Souness on Zico, April 1996.

In Italy the only thing some defenders want to do is get you stretchered off.
Rangers' **Brian Laudrup**, September 1996.

TOMMY B.

Players had been here for too long without having a future with the club, and there was no sign of a youth policy anywhere. It was like walking into the middle of a cyclone and being expected to stand there, looking unruffled by it all.
Tommy Burns on his first season in charge of Celtic, May 1995, quoted in Tom Campbell and Pat Woods, *Dreams, and Songs to Sing*, 1996.

We will never be pals because we come from two different worlds but each of us is far more appreciative of what the other is trying to do.
Tommy Burns on his relationship with chief executive Fergus McCann, March 1996.

I would like to think I'm personally friendly with every manager in the country, but I admire the way Tommy Burns plays his football. I admire the stands he takes and the team spirit he tries to foster.
Craig Brown, The Absolute Game fanzine, April 1997.

TRAGEDY

The Ibrox Disaster in 1971 was an awful warning that wasn't heeded: there were specific causes for it, but ultimately what was responsible was the way we watch football, among crowds that are way too big, in grounds that are far too old.
Nick Hornby, Fever Pitch, 1992.

Trying to resuscitate someone you know and are very fond of is perhaps the most difficult thing a doctor will face.
Prof. **Stewart Hillis**, August 1998, on attempting to revive Scotland manager Jock Stein after his collapse at Cardiff in 1985.

I will never, never forget 15 April 1989.
Kenny Dalglish on Hillsborough, Dalglish – My Autobiography, 1996.

After seeing so many parents bury their children, my family took on even greater importance to me. Shanks used to say that football was not a matter of life and death, that it was more important than that, but it wasn't to me. I never felt that way, even before Hillsborough.
Kenny Dalglish, Dalglish – My Autobiography, 1996.

I always insisted we used scheduled flights. The players were frightened of those planes and they knew they were dangerous.
Jimmy Bone, formerly manager of Zambian team Power Dynamos, January 1998. Eighteen members of Zambia's World Cup squad were killed in April 1993 when their military plane crashed into the sea off Gabon.

He was a lovely fella, a real character. Even the bastards liked him.
Former Australian goalkeeper **Jack Reilly** pays fulsome tribute to Scots-born
Jimmy Mackay, who'd been killed in a car crash in Melbourne in December 1998.

It's just a game. Two months ago I stood at the graveside of a 19-year-old
player. That puts things in perspective.
Motherwell manager **Billy Davies** as Andy Goram withdraws from playing
against Celtic following alleged UVF connections, February 1999. Motherwell
youngster Andy Thomson had died suddenly on 4 December 1998.

What you are trying to say is that I was a nasty wee bastard on the pitch.
I have changed. And it was what happened to my sister that changed me.
Dundee United striker **Billy Dodds**, March 1999. Dodds' sister Barbara died
in a car crash in October 1997.

TRANSFERS

I bought a lot of players, particularly English players, because you can always
make money on those when you sell them. Because of the position Rangers
have in Scottish football, you always paid a premium if you were buying
Scottish players from other clubs and, if they failed at Rangers, you couldn't
sell them to any other club. But English players were easier to move.
Graeme Souness, April 1996.

I've signed whole teams faster than Victor Kasule.
Hamilton secretary **David Morrison** on the club's 'wayward' former striker,
October 1996.

The night Marseilles sent their representatives to meet Trevor Steven, I had
them in my office and Stuart McCall in the boardroom. We were
approaching a midnight deadline, and couldn't really afford to buy Stuart
unless Trevor left. But a moment came when I had to take the decision to
buy McCall before the Steven deal was done. That's what makes this job.
Rangers chairman **David Murray**, November 1994.

He'd always been a thorn in our side whenever he played against Rangers.
He was a Hungarian international at that time and he went on to become
Hungarian captain after he left. Some things just don't work out.
Graeme Souness looks back on signing Istvan Kozma for Liverpool, April
1996.

The Wieghorst deal was cooked. The first we knew something was amiss was when the Danish club acknowledged receiving an amount considerably less than we'd paid. We agreed to pay £220,000 to the agents who were doing the deal . . . the money went off and a few people took their slice before the Danish club got paid.

Former Dundee chairman Ron Dixon on the December 1992 transfer of Morten Wieghorst from Lyngby to Dundee, February 1998. Lyngby admitted receiving under £77,000 for Wieghorst.

We ended up paying some of the fee to the company representing Banik in the shape of ice hockey equipment that Ron had got from somewhere.

Former Dundee vice-chairman Malcolm Reid recalls the mechanics of the August 1992 transfer deal, negotiated by ex-chairman Ron Dixon, which brought defender Dusan Vrto from Czech side Banik Ostrava to Dundee, February 1998.

Jesus Christ, Durranty, what the f*** are you doing here? Do you realise the state we're in?

Former Rangers team-mate Paul Rideout welcomes Ian Durrant to Everton at the start of his October 1994 loan spell, quoted in book *Blue & White Dynamite – The Ian Durrant Story*, 1998.

Where do you play, son?

Everton boss Mike Walker continues the welcome to Durrant, quoted in *Blue & White Dynamite – The Ian Durrant Story*, 1998.

We were not driven out. I left in a career move. I'm not a violent person but if I got the person who did all this I'd wring their neck.

Mark Hateley on rumours he left Glasgow because he'd had an affair with a friend's wife, May 1996.

Raleigh lives in Tillicoultry and we had a reserve match at Alloa. He invited me and Graeme [Woodward, assistant] round for tea, so we said he could play in the game.

Montrose boss Dave Smith, on the signing of Raleigh Gowrie from Whitehill Welfare, March 1996.

He's costing more in a week than it did for me to buy my first house.

Falkirk chairman George Fulston on new signing Chris Waddle, after he'd scored on his début against Clydebank, 14 September 1996.

On paper it looked good but it didn't work. Whether you call it wrong or disappointing doesn't matter. It didn't work.
Rangers chairman **David Murray** on the 1997 £14.4m spending spree which failed to produce a trophy, August 1998.

Dick Advocaat buys his toys from Harrods. I buy mine from a corner shop.
Motherwell manager **Harri Kampman** after his side, containing eight players costing nothing, lost a last-minute winning goal to a Rangers side whose six buys had cost £25m, 15 August 1998.

You pledge your £100,000, get yourself a mobile phone and you're off, you're a football agent.
Celtic managing director **Fergus McCann** calls for tighter controls on agents, January 1999.

Some clubs would deal with my dog if it means winning the title.
FIFA-registered agent **Jake Duncan** hands back his licence over the unscrupulous nature of football, January 1999.

There are 18 FIFA registered agents in Scotland. If the truth be told, there is only work for about three of them.
Jake Duncan, January 1999.

I felt like going home and dousing myself in four-star petrol.
Motherwell manager **Billy Davies** as the move for Everton's John Spencer runs into problems, January 1999.

It couldn't have been any better if it had been Cindy Crawford on the other end asking me out for dinner.
John Spencer gets the phone call telling him the move to Motherwell was back on, January 1999.

'We've gotta kinda weird situation here: unwilling selling club, unwilling buyer.' These were McCann's words as he pointed out that there was a new, improved contract on offer from Bolton, and that I should go back there.
Former Celtic striker **Andy Walker** recalls managing director Fergus McCann's words over his July 1994 move to Celtic, April 1999.

Fergus would not accept me as a signed player. In our final meeting, I put it to him that I had signed all the relevant forms and contract of employment, passed two medicals and it was time to accept that fact. In conclusion I said, 'There's nothing you can do about it.' His reply left me

speechless. 'Well there is one thing; maybe I could give you some money and you could go away!'
Former Celtic striker Andy Walker recalling being offered money not to sign for Celtic in his July 1994 transfer, April 1999.

With Tommy, we would meet and often exceed his value of a player. With one guy, Tommy thought £850,000 would get him. That proved not to be the case, so we went initially just over a million, then £1.2m and ultimately to £1.35m. Then Tommy comes to me and says Rangers are willing to pay £1.6m so I say 'OK, let them go ahead.' That was almost double our manager's original valuation.
Celtic managing director Fergus McCann recalls transfer moves under Tommy Burns, April 1999. The target was widely held to be Dundee United's Gordan Petric.

TV

I never liked pundits before I became one.
Alan Hansen, 1995.

He has a different language to that of most English-speaking people. I think he tries out some of his expressions on us before using them on television. I remember him announcing that a particular full-back was 'getatable'. I told him it wasn't a word.
Gordon Strachan, then player-coach of Coventry, on Ron Atkinson, February 1996.

It just so happens I've got a lot of friends who play for Rangers.
Scottish Television's Jim White on accusations of Rangers bias, March 1996.

It proved they can't laugh and it appears Rangers have no sense of humour either.
Channel Four documentary commissioning editor Peter Moore after Rangers and the SFA refused permission to show footage of Paul Gascoigne giving ref Dougie Smith the yellow card in a documentary about him, September 1996.

Everyone wanted to show the Tallinn clip of Scotland kicking off, but the bad deal meant we did not profit.
Estonian businessman **Aivar Pohlak**, March 1997, complaining about the business deal the Estonian FA signed with an agent for TV coverage of the infamous game with Scotland.

I cringe when I hear my voice.
TV pundit **Alan Hansen**, April 1997.

I did it and he went, 'It's no' bad, but you're doing me as if I'm from Glasgow. Work out where I'm from and that'll help.'
Impressionist **Alistair McGowan** on his Alan Hansen, January 1999.

He used to say, 'Do you do me yet, do you do me yet?' and I told him that I wasn't going to do him because his voice is so damaging on your throat.
Impressionist **Alistair McGowan** on Andy Gray, January 1999.

US

If there is ever a World Cup for self-destructiveness, few nations will have the nerve to challenge the Scots.
Journalist **Hugh McIlvanney**, *The Observer*, 11 June 1978.

We are a divided nation. Everyone wants to have a bitch at everyone else. It's why we've stood still as a country.
Rangers chairman **David Murray**, November 1994.

Sean Connery once said to me that there are very few celebrities left in Scotland. So many people in the public eye have left – actors, pop singers, film directors – that the football people enjoy the highest profile.
Rangers chairman **David Murray**, November 1994.

Scottish football is not the place to come if you want a quiet life.
Rangers' **Paul Gascoigne**, April 1996.

What is secure? If you're a big-time Charlie and want to do this and that then you need to be really secure but I'm not. I go home, watch the telly, go out occasionally, enjoy a holiday. I'm just normal.
Stoke boss **Lou Macari**, April 1996.

I'd always felt Scottish because of my dad. I'm not bothered about going back to England. I'd sooner rebuild Hadrian's Wall.
Rangers' **Andy Goram**, June 1996.

It's unreasonable to expect that we should be able to beat the champions of France or Switzerland every time. We are a small nation, yet we have a conceit of ourselves way beyond what is achievable.
Hearts chairman **Chris Robinson**, October 1996.

There has always been the anti-hero syndrome in Scotland. It seems that, as a nation, we're almost happier as gallant losers. I'd like us to be lucky winners for a change.
Scotland coach **Craig Brown**, December 1996.

We wanted to show our respect for Scotland in recognition of the part they have played in our history. It was missionaries from Scotland who brought education to our country and we have been grateful ever since. Everyone here loves Scotland and everyone was following the team in Euro '96. I'm sorry if that offends other teams such as England, but that's the way it is.
Gambian First Secretary **BS Faho** on the West African country issuing a postage stamp with Scotland's Euro '96 squad on it, March 1997.

It seems we still have heather in our ears in this country.
Dundee United boss **Tommy McLean** on the Coca-Cola Cup causing Scotland's European representatives fixture problems, August 1997.

I know that there is a certain amount of aggression in Scotland. Perhaps that is the difference between the two countries. The Englishman assumes that no one dislikes him but the Scotsman would not be happy without an enemy.
TV pundit **Jimmy Hill**, November 1997.

I loved it there. I loved the parties and I loved wearing my funny little skirt.
Former Dundee chairman **Ron Dixon** recalls his time in Scotland, February 1998.

Players from other countries have always told me they're taken aback because when they're on the pitch, Scottish or English footballers never shut up.
Scotland's **Colin Hendry**, June 1998.

The guys in senior football haven't got a clue what is happening. They will go and commentate on the World Cup and tell you what Ravenelli is doing wrong but they will not go to Cowdenbeath and look at a guy who plays for an amateur team.
Clyde general manager **Ronnie MacDonald**, February 1999.

I'm seen as an outsider in football. I always have been. After a while, though, you realise that it's not that personal.
Motherwell chief executive **Pat Nevin**, February 1999.

When I first started out I was probably a right crabbit shite but I think I've mellowed a wee bit since then.
Dundee United's **Maurice Malpas** on his own coaching style, February 1999.

Neither of us could head it, neither of us could tackle, my missus was quicker than he was, but we did alright.
Former Liverpool defender **Alan Hansen** on his Anfield partnership with Phil Thompson, March 1999.

Every player in the country who isn't in the side when the real business gets under way next month will have divided loyalties. They won't want to see their team beaten – but nor will they be totally thrilled by a succession of 6-0 wins.
Former Rangers defender **Tom Cowan** recovering from injury, quoted in book, *On the Edge*, 1998.

WALTER S.

If you asked me the most accurate thing I've ever read about myself I would have to say that the person who revealed I'm a Bon Jovi fan got me spot on.
Rangers manager **Walter Smith**, May 1994.

When it comes to negotiations to buy a top player for £2m or £3m, it would be unfair to ask Walter to deal with the fine print of the contract. He's a trained professional football manager and has different skills to offer.
Rangers chairman **David Murray**, November 1994.

I didn't know Walter personally. But I knew he must be Scottish because I used to see him carrying big discount cases of lager back from the supermarket.
Paul Gascoigne recalls his first encounter with his future Ibrox manager [while on holiday in Florida], 1995.

Walter Smith epitomises what I feel a manager should be when it comes to reflecting what a club is all about. He is a first-class individual.
Celtic's **Tommy Burns** on the eve of an Old Firm match, March 1996.

When I walked into the Press conference after the final I thought someone had passed away.
Walter Smith on a subdued after-match conference after the Rangers 4 Hearts 3 Coca-Cola Cup final, November 1996.

I've never meet a manager who has complained and I've always looked at Rangers' performances first and foremost. One of the things I learned from Jim McLean is that he used to have fall-outs with referees but as soon as he went into the dressing-room he never made it a reason why a game was lost. When you do that you offer players an excuse and I've never done that.
Walter Smith, March 1997.

I greatly admire Walter Smith's honesty and his football knowledge.
Craig Brown, *The Absolute Game* fanzine, April 1997.

I've been working in Scottish football, on a coaching level, for the past 17 years, and I've been involved with teams who have won 23 cups, I think I know what I'm doing here.
Walter Smith, August 1997.

After winning 12 cups in the six years I've been the manager here, I can't win in Scotland. As far as people are concerned now, if Rangers win the League or the Cup or the League Cup, then so what? But if we came second in the league, they would be saying, 'Smith out'.
Walter Smith, August 1997. Two months later he announced his decision to quit at the end of the season.

He has carried the managership of Rangers with amazing dignity.
Tommy Burns after Smith announced his decision to quit at the end of 1997–98 season, October 1997.

When he first came to Ibrox he looked like Sacha Distel. Now he looks like Steve Martin.
Ally McCoist on Walter Smith, before the manager's testimonial game against Liverpool, February 1998.

He'll be a hard act to follow. And if Rangers do the double this season, he'll be impossible to follow.
Reading boss **Tommy Burns** on Smith, April 1998. Rangers won neither.

The most successful Rangers manager of all time.
Tommy Burns, October 1997.

WEIRD

I'm a Virgo and I'm told organisation and hard work are strong Virgoan traits.
Billy Kirkwood on his habits as Dundee United manager. Kirkwood admitted brushing the grass on his lawn to keep it tidy and made Tannadice youngsters clean boot studs with toothbrushes.

I love the smell of the grass. I love the smell of the leather and the liniment and I love the smell of my blood when I get a smack in the face.
Former Hibs keeper **John Burridge**, August 1995.

I was humiliated . . . it was like the charge of the Light Brigade.
Margate goalkeeper **Chic Brodie**, after Ted McDougall scored nine goals against him in Bournemouth's 11–0 November 1971 FA Cup win over his side. (Clydebank-born Chic had a varied career; while at Brentford, Millwall fans threw a hand grenade at him; a collision with the post at Lincoln saw the goalposts collapse; then his career seemed to be finished when a dog ran on the pitch at Colchester and he fell trying to avoid it, shattering his knee-cap.)

I remember coming back from America with Celtic on one of our trips and he said to me that he wanted to quit and become a lorry driver. I said there were loads of lorry drivers but only one George Connelly.
Billy McNeill on Connelly, November 1996. Connelly quit Celtic at 27 but the job as a lorry driver never materialised.

I don't like being on my own because you think a lot and I don't like to think a lot.
Paul Gascoigne, in TV documentary, *Gazza's Coming Home*, October 1996.

I'd like Celtic to be the top team this season. They play attacking football, have good players and they have nice shirts.
Hearts' **Pasquale Bruno's** reasoned argument on Celtic's title chances, 1996.

The stupid forget but never forgive, the naïve forgive and also forget, the smart forgive but never forget.
More from the mighty **Ivo Den Bieman** of Dunfermline (the man who referred to Montrose as both a 'chicken factory' and 'reminiscent of a Chinese woman's volleyball team'), September 1996.

I come from Bonnybridge, which is the UFO capital of the world and my granny says she saw one from her kitchen window, a bright light which hovered a couple of hundred feet above her then took off at great speed. Mind you, she does like a brandy.
Falkirk's **David Hagen**, February 1997.

I went through a phase of eating Lion Bars during games but since I switched to Rolos our form's been much better.
Labour MP **Douglas Hamilton** on supporting Falkirk, May 1997.

I can walk on my hands round a penalty box, something I learned when I was a PE teacher.
Scotland coach **Craig Brown**, October 1997.

Let me recommend shopping to any young professional who feels they are in danger of going off the rails. Cheaper and with less risk of personal injury than a punch-up outside a nightclub, you very rarely end up with a hangover.
Brian McClair, *Odd Man Out*, 1997.

I only play football for fun. Cooking is more important to me now and my restaurant will be filled with people who love my cooking.
More surrealism from former Hearts defender **Pasquale Bruno**, after being substituted in his first trial match for Wigan, February 1998.

As soon as I got to Serie A, I missed Dens Park. In fact, I wish I had gone to Dundee when I left Poland instead of Eintracht Frankfurt.
Dariusz Adamczuk on his November 1993 move from Dundee to Udinese, March 1998.

I always take my right boot off at half-time as the circulation around the big toe isn't too good. I like to give it a little wiggle.
Leicester's Matt Elliott on superstitions, March 1998.

Q: Why would you want to be an accountant?
A: Believe it or not it can sometimes be exciting. Honestly, it's all about keeping everything in order and to get everything completely right takes a bit of time and effort.
Celtic's Harald Brattbakk, October 1998.

I thought the SFA was like that from the age of four because my gran told me.
Norwich's Peter Grant, 2 March 1999, on Celtic accusations that SFA chief executive Jim Farry delayed the registration of striker Jorge Cadete.

THE WIFE

On the rare occasions he took me out he talked about nothing but football and the good and bad points about players. By the time I left him, I knew more about soccer than most managers.
Danielle Souness on life with (and divorce from) Graeme, quoted in *The Lad Done Bad – Sex, Sleaze & Scandal in English Football,* 1996.

Give her the most romantic night ever . . . make her feel she's the most special person in your life . . . better than a dozen red roses . . . she couldn't ask for more. Take her to see Paris Saint-Germain against Glasgow Celtic tonight.
Ad in *l'Equipe,* 19 October 1995.

[Being a footballer] is the best job in the world. The second best is being a footballer's wife.
Scotland skipper Gary McAllister, September 1995.

While you're all here someone is round shagging all your wives.
Paul Gasgoine to journalists besieging girlfriend Sheryl's house, August 1996.

My wife is six, almost seven years older than me. I met her very early in my life, when I was 16 . . . I firmly believe that this age difference has been very important to me throughout my career. Mette's experience of life has proved invaluable.

Rangers' **Brian Laudrup**, September 1996.

I love this woman very much, you know. I've always said that football is such a short career. I've played since I was five and I'll still be playing in a number of years. But I hope that our marriage will last 50 or 60 years – until we're not here anymore. Our marriage comes above everything else.

The uxorious **Brian Laudrup**, September 1996.

It was probably easier to leave my first wife than it was to leave Berwick.

Former manager **Tom Hendrie** on leaving Berwick, October 1996.

I'm just a big softie really. People want to write bad things about me. My wife knows the real David Speedie – quietly-spoken, polite and a doting father. It's just that if anybody fucks about with me the mask comes off and the darker side of me comes out.

Former Scotland striker **David Speedie**, December 1996.

My best-ever signing has been my wife, Marina.

Kenny Dalglish, *Dalglish – My Autobiography*, 1996.

[Cantona] once said: 'A football club is like a woman. One leaves when one has nothing else to say . . . ' I wish I could make deeply profound statements like that, but [wife] Maureen would never let me get away with spouting such sexist twaddle.

Brian McClair, *Odd Man Out*, 1997.

Nothing would make me turn back the clock, because not finding Karen in my life would be an unpayable price.

Graeme Souness on wife Karen, February 1997.

I was speaking to Alex Ferguson recently and we agreed that we did not bring up our kids, it was our wives who did that on their own and that is a disgrace.

Dundee United chairman **Jim McLean**, August 1997.

[Jorge] Cadete was an immature depressive character, totally under the influence of a domineering lady.

Celtic general manager **Jock Brown** at the club's 100th AGM, 4 September 1997.

I came home recently and heard all this laughter coming from the front room. It was my wife watching an old interview I did in 1979. I must say, I never thought I looked that bad.
TV pundit **Alan Hansen**, October 1997.

I always feel quite lucky going into a game if Catherine has just shaved my head. Every time she did that at Oxford I seemed to score a goal.
Leicester's **Matt Elliott** on his wife's influence, March 1998.

Q: You spot a mate's missus snogging another bloke in the corner of a nightclub. Would you tell your pal?
A: Aye, definitely. In fact, I've done it in the past.
Clydebank defender **Kenny Brannigan** confesses, newspaper questionnaire, February 1999.

WISE WORDS

There is a frenzy in Scottish football. They run and run when sometimes it would be better to slow down, to think about where they run and why.
Johann Cruyff, 1974.

High intelligence and football fanaticism seldom go together.
Poet **Hugh MacDiarmid**, in a letter to *The Scotsman* newspaper, 8 May 1978, quoted in Mike Wilson, *Don't Cry For Me Argentina*, 1998.

Charisma comes from results and not vice versa.
Scotland coach **Craig Brown**, 1993.

You can look like a worldbeater for 89 minutes but one mistake and you're a tube.
Airdrie goalkeeper **John Martin**, March 1995.

You can only pish wi' the cock ye've got.
Premier Division manager explaining – presumably – that his resources are limited, 1995.

It is one of the game's unwritten laws that players always seem better when people look back at them.
Kenny Dalglish, February 1995.

If I was to describe my real personality, I would have to think back to what Alex Ferguson once told me. He said, 'In this game, never go looking for confrontation, it will always find you.' And it has.
Rangers boss **Walter Smith**, May 1994.

Some people will be upset by our findings. There might be a wee man near Wishaw who has run his local team and gained a certain standing in the community as a result but if he is confusing ten-year-olds by shouting about 'marking space' then he will have to be upset.
'Think Tank' chairman **Ernie Walker**, 16 August 1995.

A great player can do great things, but a great fit player can do greater things more often.
Scotland skipper **Gary McAllister**, September 1995.

We live in our own wee world in football but it's so insignificant.
Celtic boss **Tommy Burns** on the eve of an Old Firm match, two days after the Dunblane Primary School massacre, March 1996.

The announcer congratulated me on making it seven-in-a-row. Then he said, 'I'm sure Walter will agree with all of us: let's make it 10.' What would a visitor from another country make of it? He'd be standing there thinking people had missed something, What happened to eight and nine?
Walter Smith as Rangers headed for their eighth consecutive title and Old Firm rivalry gathered momentum, March 1996.

The Premier League [in England] is a frightening place to be these days if you're not 6' 2" and 13 stone.
Graeme Souness, April 1996.

One of the great things about being Scottish in the '90s is that you know with absolute conviction and certainty that your team are going to win fuck all.
Author (and Hibs supporter) **Irvine Welsh**, August 1996.

I signed up ten years ago because I saw so much misery all over the world and I decided to help because I am such a lucky man. It is easy to be blind and say, 'It is not our problem', but I honestly believe governments must do something to help these countries.
Hearts goalkeeper **Gilles Rousset** explaining why he is godfather to a Rwandan youngster, Buhilike Munyamahugo, November 1996.

I've never seen a player move faster than the ball.
Hibs' Ray Wilkins on accusations that he's too slow, December 1996.

Footballers are like Rolls Royces and fur coats – if you want the best you have to pay the going rate.
Dundee United boss Tommy McLean, March 1997.

I understood something very early in my career: a footballer must learn to forgive quickly.
Kilmarnock goalkeeper Dragoje Lekovic, May 1997.

If players do it on the park, they get away with murder off it.
Agent Bill McMurdo, *The Absolute Game* fanzine, May 1997.

All the kids coming up – just have a look at me and some of the daft things I did when I was starting. Be very, very careful that it doesn't turn round on you. It will be hard to get out of.
A reflective **Paul Gascoigne**, 1997.

I've never fallen out with a coach or a player. But plenty of them have fallen out with me.
Manchester United boss Alex Ferguson, quoted in *Odd Man Out* by Brian McClair, 1997.

Boys, there's not an empty hospital bed. The mortuaries are all full. You are lucky not only to be here with a job and your health, but to be playing professional football.
Motherwell assistant manager Frank Connor in team talks in the 1980s, quoted by ex-Motherwell winger John Gahagan in after-dinner speaking, 1990s.

I wouldn't have touched me with a bargepole.
Clydebank player-boss Ian McCall, asked how McCall the boss would have dealt with McCall the player. McCall was, in his own assessment, an 'underachiever'.

A willing volunteer is better than a prima donna reluctant conscript.
Scotland boss Craig Brown, February 1998. His remarks were widely thought to refer to Duncan Ferguson who'd announced his retirement from international football but who was at the centre of a media clamour for a recall.

The greatest players in the world are all good men. I don't think they really cause you a problem. The ones who've got a problem are those who think they're top players.
Coventry boss Gordon Strachan, August 1998.

Players want to come here for more reasons than money. Gordon McQueen once said that 99 per cent of players want to play for Manchester United and the other 1 per cent are liars.
Manchester United boss **Alex Ferguson**, April 1999.

WORLD CUP '98

Of course I'm up for it, but in a way I wish it would never come. Everyone is so up for it, there is such a good feel-good factor about the whole thing just now. Walking down the street everyone is smiling, happy and wishing us all the best. The country is so enthusiastically supportive. But a couple of defeats over in France and it will all change.
Scotland coach **Craig Brown**, June 1998.

We'll be home before the postcards.
Tommy Docherty after the draw put Scotland in with Brazil, Norway and Morocco.

Aye, and so was Tommy.
Craig Brown's response, June 1998 (referring to Docherty's 1954 experience).

There will be entrepreneurs who contribute next to nothing to the game who will be able to retire to the Bahamas on the back of this World Cup.
SFA Chief Executive **Jim Farry**, April 1998, as World Cup ticket problems mount.

I've had to say to our guys, 'Don't be hypnotised by the golden jerseys. They don't win the games. It's the bodies inside that have to be good and be organised.' I've met [Carlos Alberta] Parreira and he told me the people and even the players think the shirt is enough.
Craig Brown, June 1998.

If I worried about an opponent embarrassing me on a football pitch I'd have stopped after the England game in Euro '96.
Colin Hendry on facing Ronaldo, June 1998.

You don't think, 'Christ, I've got to turn up on 10 June and I really don't fancy it.'
Colin Hendry on the Brazil game, June 1998.

Some players manage to gain reputations that they don't deserve. After all I've seen and everyone I've talked to, I'm convinced Ronaldo's reputation doesn't flatter him.
Craig Brown, June 1998.

The referee might say, 'Bloody hell, this is the game everyone's watching, opening game, bloody smokebombs and flares from the stands. If anyone kicks anyone from behind I'm sending them off'.
Colin Hendry on the World Cup clampdown on tackling from behind, June 1998.

I'm a happily married man with three children. I don't dream about other men.
Colin Hendry, after being asked by a Brazilian journalist if he had dreams about Ronaldo, 8 June 1998.

These Scottish players are very ordinary. In fact, they have no names.
Cameroon TV commentator **Hammed Adio** during the Brazil v Scotland game, 10 June 1998.

You get plenty of slaps in the face in this game and it's fair to say this is one of them.
Goalkeeper **Jim Leighton** after losing to Morocco, 23 June 1998.

A performance as flat as Kate Moss's chest.
Kilmarnock's **Pat Nevin** on Scotland v Morocco, August 1998.

Morocco are Brazil without the concentration.
Rangers' **Jonas Thern** after Morocco beat Scotland 3–0, June 1998.

You could not get two more different games. Against Norway I made a goal, against Morocco I lost us one. I hold my hands up and admit I could have done better when Hadda scored. It was my mistake. I know I won't face Hadda's pace too often in the Premier League, but you cannot hide from your mistakes.
Hearts and Scotland defender **David Weir**, August 1998.

More than one Scot asked, 'What's French for *déjà vu?*'
Pat Nevin quotes Scots fans as things take a familiar turn at France '98, August 1998.

It's about time the Scottish fans started supporting us. We're all British and England are still in.

England's (Scottish) assistant boss John Gorman makes a plea as futile as it is bizarre to the Tartan Army, 24 June 1998.

If there's anyone better to take our places we'll step back because we're all supporters and we want the best for Scotland.

Colin Hendry on questions about being replaced, June 1998.

It's not the losing that hurts, it's the hope that kills us. It's the momentary flicker of possibility that inevitably gets crushed.

Garbage singer Shirley Manson on Scotland's exit.

Bordeaux wishes to thank all the Scottish supporters and say 'well done'! We will never forget your 'joie de vivre', the way you know how to have a good time and your sense of fair play. Come back soon. We miss you already!

Full-page newspaper advertisement placed in the *Daily Record*, 24 June 1998, by the Chambre de Commerce et d'Industrie de Bordeaux.

The following quote is not, technically, related to Scotland. But it made a nation very happy . . .

Brian Moore: Do you back him to score? Quickly – yes or no?

Kevin Keegan: Yes!

Exchange between ITV's commentary team as David Batty placed the ball on the penalty spot during England's second round shoot-out against Argentina, 30 June 1998.

The two players concerned, Craig Burley and Gordon Durie, were sleeping a bit.

Craig Brown on Brazil's first goal, December 1998.

They wouldn't have been able to score a 'lucky' goal if they hadn't been in our six-yard-box.

Craig Brown on Brazil's second goal, December 1998.

In every match we had a penalty turned down which the replays confirm we should have had. But I don't want it to sound like sour grapes. The bottom line is that we weren't good enough.

Craig Brown, December 1998.

To watch the BBC Sports Review of the Year, you'd have thought that England would have won the tournament if only Beckham had stayed on.
Craig Brown, December 1998.

You get headlines saying *Fans in Rage At Brown*, but I haven't met an angry one yet. They usually say, 'It was the best three weeks of my life.'
Craig Brown, December 1998.

They played four games and lost two of them. Every time they played a half-decent team – Romania and Argentina – they lost to them.
Ally McCoist gives his verdict on England's World Cup, February 1999.

THE END

You support the best team in the world, and you are the best supporters in the world, so carry on supporting them because they need you.
Billy McNeill says a dignified goodbye to Celtic fans after being sacked, May 1991, quoted in Tom Campbell and Pat Woods, *Dreams, and Songs to Sing*, 1996.

It was me and Kenny Dalglish and the Peruvian striker, Cubillas. We all pissed in the bottle and theirs was a lot clearer than mine . . . all Scotland had to do was appeal and ask for another test, because there was nothing in it, but I've always felt that they were happy to see me out. It meant that they were able to blame someone for all that had gone wrong. I knew I should never have gone.
Willie Johnston on Argentina '78, May 1996.

I had had enough of the daily grind. I didn't want that anymore. I just couldn't be bothered.
Kenny Dalglish on his reasons for quitting Blackburn, *Dalglish – My Autobiography*, 1996.

By the time the law is changed it'll be too late for us.
Airdrie's **Chris Honor** on his contract battle with the club, April 1996. Airdrie had prevented him and team-mate Wes Reid playing for 18 months after they turned down new contracts.

I had played in a reserve match. In the bath afterwards, I was trying to explain to some young lad why he had made a mistake. The kid just looked at me, asked me what I knew, and told me I was finished. I got

out of the bath, put my clothes on and phoned my wife to tell her I was staying in Edinburgh that night. I had a few pints and the next morning I went to Alex [MacDonald] to tell him I wouldn't be coming back.
Hearts' **Willie Johnston** on quitting football, May 1996.

It'll kill me when I'm no longer going out there to entertain the fans. That will be the saddest day ever. I'll have to find something else to replace that. Maybe I'll go the Richard Gere way and become a Tibetan monk and find religion.
Rangers' **Ally McCoist**, June 1994.

Training with kids who think 15 bottles of Hoopers Hooch is a top night out, my motivation was being dragged from a depth that cannot always be relied upon.
John Colquhoun on why he was quitting football, 18 May 1997.

Here lies Owen, he had a ball. What a pity he couldn't pass it.
Motherwell's **Owen Coyle** on what will be written on his gravestone, January 1997.

My mother told me when I was 14 that football was a cruel and vindictive sport run by people with no standards. She was right.
Former Hearts striker **Darren Beckford**, February 1998. The one-time £1m player was working as a milkman at the time.

I'm really upset at the way I left Rangers. Of course I have regrets, about the flute-playing and stuff, but there will be none of that on Teesside. The gaffer's promised to buy me a guitar.
Paul Gascoigne after joining Middlesbrough, 1998.

We were doing so many that we were ending up with big bald patches, even in the middle of summer.
Rangers' **John Greig** explaining why the club no longer allows the ashes of dead fans to be scattered on the Ibrox pitch, quoted in Simon Kuper, *Football Against The Enemy*, 1994.

When I was a kid dreaming of playing for Scotland, I never imagined that one day I would turn my back on playing for my country.
Coventry's **Gary McAllister**, 9 April 1999, announcing his retirement from international football after being booed by Scots fans against the Czech Republic the week before.

INDEX

Adam, Hugh 23
Adamczuk, Dariusz 209
Adams, Gerry 112
Adams, Tony 54, 129, 166
Adio, Hammed 216
Advocaat, Dick 44, 47, 129, 147, 177, 202
Aitken, Roy 28, 161
Albert of Monaco, Prince 80
Albertz, Jorg 13, 76, 79, 146, 148, 154, 181
Alsford, Julian 32
Amoruso, Lorenzo 154
Andersen, Erik Bo 153
Anderson, Donald 66
Andersson, Kennet 136
Anne, Princess 53, 188
Arafat, Yasser 112
Archdeacon, Owen 15, 59
Archibald, Steve 11, 58, 70
Ardley, Neil 113
Armani, Giorgio 59
Assiotis, Dimitris 57, 197
Atkinson, Ron 11, 124, 188, 196, 203
Auld, Bertie 36, 56
Bacharach, Burt 23
Baker, Danny 16, 91, 94, 196
Baker, Joe 198
Ball, Alan 130
Baltacha, Sergei 25, 97
Banks, Jeff 195
Banks, Tony 51
Baresi, Franco 164
Barnett, Gary 105
Bassett, Dave 139, 140, 154
Batty, David 217
Batty, Laurence 15, 16
Bauld, Willie 102
Beckenbauer, Franz 19, 122
Beckford, Darren 219
Beckham, David 83, 218
Beenhakker, Leo 139
Bell, Dougie 15
Bell, Gavin 35
Bennie, David 166
Benson, Harry 125
Best, George 59, 96, 120, 122, 149, 160
den Bieman, Ivo 209
Biggart, Kevin 150
Black, Eric 23, 130
Black, Jim 94

Blair, Tony 70, 73
Blinker, Regi 20
Blue Öyster Cult 110
Boersma, Phil 106
Boli, Basile 164, 183
Bon Jovi 128, 206
Bond, John 134
Bone, Jimmy 39, 199
Bonner, Pat 100, 125
Booth, Scott 151
Borras, Omar 113
Borrows, Bill 68
Bosman, Jean-Marc 17, 137
Bowles, Stan 152
Bowman, Davie 32, 153
Boy George 13
Boyd, Tommy 51, 139
Bradic, Goran 131
Brady, Liam 18, 48, 157
Bragg, Billy 55
Brand, Ralph 155
Brannan, Bob 85
Brannigan, Kenny 212
Brash, Alex 33
Brattbakk, Harald 21, 210
Bremner, Billy 113, 174, 187
Brodie, Chic 208
Brookmyre, Chris 19
Brown, Bob 27
Brown, Craig 12, 27, 28, 30, 42–4, 46, 51, 52, 53, 54, 55, 56, 59, 64, 71, 76, 80, 84, 88, 96, 103, 107, 108, 110, 114, 115, 121, 127, 128, 138, 150, 152, 153, 162, 170, 182, 196, 199, 205, 207, 209, 212, 214, 215, 216, 217, 218
Brown, James 40
Brown, Jock 20, 21, 22, 23, 24, 27, 42, 80, 127, 140, 152, 155, 168, 171, 186, 195, 211
Brown, John 24, 48, 49, 95, 109, 114, 124, 195
Brown, Lauren 24
Browne, Paul 83
Bruce, Steve 71, 72, 74, 163
Bruno, Frank 142
Bruno, Pasquale 142, 159, 163, 173, 209
Bryson, Bill 158
Buchan, Martin 11, 59, 123, 149, 160

Budd, Zola 76
Burgess, Guy 64
Burley, Craig 21, 60, 127, 217
Burns, Kenny 14, 86,150,160
Burns, Robert 94
Burns, Tommy 11, 13, 18, 23, 60, 81, 82, 84, 101, 105, 125, 129, 133, 136, 139, 142, 144, 145, 146, 147, 170, 172, 182, 183, 186, 198–99, 203, 207, 208, 213
Burridge, John 11, 76, 99, 106, 208
Burruchaga, Jorge 133
Busby, Sir Matt 63, 194
Busst, David 63
Butcher, Terry 19, 104, 144, 146
Butler, Lee 33
Cadete, Jorge 76, 80, 81, 98, 110, 118, 137, 145, 173, 181, 190, 210, 211
Caine, Michael 93, 102
Calderwood, Colin 111, 173, 197
Campbell, Peter 162
Campbell, Sol 69
Campbell, Tommy 29
Cantona, Eric 70, 73, 87, 163, 165, 211
Cassidy, Terry 45, 144, 186
Chamberlain, Helen 96
Channon, Mick 120
Chapple, Geoff 16
Charlton, Bobby 149, 158
Charnley, Chic 77, 142, 152, 166
Cherry, Paul 38
Christie, Max 26
Christie, Terry 26, 140
Christison, John 61
Churchill, Winston 118
Clark, John 156
Clark, Kenny 68
Clark, Tom 46
Clarke, Steve 80, 114
Clay, Joyce 196
Clifford, Max 94
Clough, Brian 14, 121, 124, 125, 149, 150, 161, 178
Cole, Andy 72, 87
Collins, Bobby 155
Collins, Gerry 37
Collins, John 17, 40, 49, 58, 79, 80, 134, 142, 165, 171
Colquhoun, John 15, 16, 34, 38,

39, 44, 62, 64, 83, 97, 108,
110, 153, 163, 165, 166, 167,
177, 178, 219
Connery, Sean 59, 204
Connolly, George 119, 208
Connolly, Fr Tom 185
Connor, Frank 127, 214
Connor, Robert 110
Cooper, Davie 60
Cooper, Neale 73, 127
Cooper, Steve 50
Cosgrove, Lady 154
Cosgrove, Stuart 145, 197
Coulston, Frank 153
Cowan, Tom 95, 107, 111, 206
Coyle, Owen 219
Craig, Jim 57, 62, 143, 156
Crampsey, Bob 92
Crawford, Cindy 202
Crawford, Stevie 136
Creaney, Gerry 144
Crerand, Pat 74
Cruyff, Johann 31, 110, 212
Cubillas, Teofilo 218
D'Arcy, Matt 109
Dailly, Christian 160
Dalglish, Kenny 15, 16, 63, 73,
105, 109, 119–22, 123, 127,
143, 161, 162, 168, 169, 172,
188, 193, 199, 211, 212, 218
Dalglish, Marina 211
Dallas, Hugh 147, 148, 179, 181
Dalziel, Gordon 29, 49, 65
Dasovic, Nick 132
David, Hal 23
Davids, Edgar 53
Davidson, Vic 119, 162
Davies, Billy 200, 202
Davies, Hunter 155
Davies, John 79
Deans, Dixie 172
Dempsey, Brian 18, 19, 136
Dennehy, Stephen 67
Dewar, Donald 117
Di Canio, Paolo 20, 80, 81, 82,
142, 145, 171
Di Stefano, Alfredo 56, 120
Di Stefano, Giovanni 112
Diana, Princess of Wales 115, 117,
118
Dickov, Paul 130
Distel, Sacha 208
Dixon, Ron 31, 32, 50, 88, 104,
118, 126, 128, 138, 176, 179,
188, 190, 201, 205
Docherty, Tommy 14, 73, 81, 93,
123, 124, 146, 153, 160, 215
Dodds, Barbara 181, 200
Dodds, Billy 110, 181, 200
Dodds, Davie 109
Dolan, Jamie 164
Donald, Chris 150
Donnelly, Simon 187
Draper, Paul 68

Drewery, Eileen 107
Drinkell, Kevin 128
Duffy, Jim 31, 35, 76, 95, 126,
128, 138, 142, 152, 164
Duguid, Craig 66
Duncan, Jake 135, 152, 202
Durie, Gordon 45, 54, 118, 135,
157, 195, 217
Durrant, Ian 68, 74, 79, 94, 97, 98,
107, 111, 134, 135, 139, 146,
147, 154, 174, 183, 198, 201
Duvall, Robert 61
Eccles, Sheriff Alexander 67
Edwards, Martin 19
Elgin, Countess of 87
Elliott, Catherine 212
Elliott, Matt 16, 153, 210, 212
Eskilsson, Hans 110
Evans, Chris 93
Evans, Gareth 165
Everett, Kenny 28
Facchetti, Giacinto 57
Fagan, Joe 122, 124, 162
Faho, BS 205
Fairclough, Chris 110
Fallon, Jim 31
Fallon, Sean 31
Farningham, Ray 36
Farry, Jim 17, 42, 46, 51, 104,
116–19, 150, 168, 180, 181,
189, 190, 210, 215
Fashanu, Justin 34
Fawlty, Basil 45
Feldman, Marty 79
Fergie (Ian Russell) 65–6
Ferguson, Alex 26, 27, 33, 35, 39,
50, 57, 69–74, 87, 89, 100,
119, 121, 123, 127, 129, 158,
161, 163, 164, 165, 170, 186,
191, 211, 213, 214, 215
Ferguson, Duncan 48, 66–9, 174,
195, 196, 214
Ferguson, Ian 49, 82, 197
Ferguson, Ronald 30
Fernie, Willie 113
Findlay, David 190
Findlay, Donald 45, 178, 184
Fleeting, Bob 45
Fleeting, Jim 40, 41, 84, 126
Forsyth, Alex 62
Fry, Martin 71
Fulston, George 34, 45, 108, 138,
150, 201
Fulton, Steve 75
Fynn, Alex 85
Gable, Clark 121
Gaddafi, Colonel Muammar 166
Gahagan, John 214
Galbraith, Sam 190
Gallacher, John 29
Gallacher, Kevin 153
Garden, Mark 141
Gascoigne, Paul 25, 49, 55, 61,
74, 76, 89–95, 97, 98, 103,

109, 110, 114, 135, 146, 166,
169, 170, 173, 176, 180, 181,
197, 203, 204, 207, 209, 210,
214, 219
Gascoigne, Sheryl 91, 210
Gattuso, Rino 185
Gemmill, Archie 102, 149
George, Charlie 124
Gere, Richard 219
Giggs, Ryan 163
Gillespie, Gary 114
Gillhaus, Hans 78
Ginola, David 168
'Glanvilla, Bruno' 34
Golac, Ivan 32, 58, 157, 179
Goram, Andy 56, 59, 74, 92, 97,
98, 100, 101, 102, 109, 115,
118, 141, 153, 159, 164, 185,
197, 200, 205
Gorman, John 217
Gorman, Teresa 92
Gough, Richard 32, 79, 90, 144,
150, 157, 161, 162, 163, 173,
176
Gould, Bobby 25
Gould, Jonathan 21, 25, 196
Gowrie, Raleigh 201
Grade, Lew 70
Graham, George 40, 49, 129, 169,
195
Grant, Nigel 69
Grant, Peter 19, 38, 125, 146,
173, 210
Grant, Roddy 164
Gray, Andy (Scotland) 14, 24, 95,
204
Gray, Andy (Falkirk) 33
Greig, John 152, 185, 219
Guivarc'h, Stephane 103
Gullit, Ruud 80, 114, 126, 149,
173
Hadda, Abdeljilil 216
Hagen, David 165, 170, 209
Halliwell, Geri 96
Hamed, Prince Naseem 149
Hamilton, Lord 36, 37
Hamilton, Douglas 209
Hamilton, Lindsay 154
Hansen, Alan 16, 26, 40, 41, 49,
50, 65, 75, 89, 98, 120, 122,
124, 127, 129, 149, 150, 161,
166, 168, 171, 178, 193, 203,
204, 206, 212
Hardy, George 123
Harford, Asa 124
Harford, Ray 99
Harris, Ron 123
Harrison, Steve 15
Hart, Tom 150
Hartley, Paul 16
Harvey, David 112
Hastings, Gavin 53
Hateley, Mark 67, 77, 136, 152,
174, 201

Hay, Davie 18, 119
Hayes, David 137
Heath, Adrian 135
Hegarty, Paul 111, 129, 198
Henderson, Willie 107
Hendrie, Tom 211
Hendry, Colin 16, 25, 27, 53, 55, 56, 61, 81, 99, 117, 136, 137, 140, 153, 166, 205, 215, 216, 217
Hendry, Kyle 25
Henry, John 154
Hewitt, John 70
Heyward, Sir Jack 128
Higgins, Tony 36, 39
Hill, Damon 69
Hill, Jimmy 205
Hillis, Stewart 199
Hitler, Adolf 178
Hoddle, Glenn 36, 110, 129, 196
Hodgkinson, Alan 100, 101
Holt, Gary 99
Honor, Chris 218
Hopkin, David 149
Horley, Sandra 92
Hornby, Nick 199
Horsburgh, Alex 52
Horton, Ed 118
Houllier, Gerard 130
Howe, Don 41
Howson, Peter 29
Hughes, Emlyn 191
Hughes, John 12, 167
Hughes, Mark 163
Hume, Bobby 107
Hunter, Eddie 37
Hurlock, Terry 152
Hurst, Glynn 96
Hussein, Saddam 112
Hutchison, Don 99
Huxley, John 121
Imamovic, Velid 115
Ince, Paul 110
Inglis, John 108
Irons, Davie 36
Irvine, Alan 15
Irvine, Brian 106
Irvine, Hazel 108
Irwin, Denis 163
Jackson, Darren 20, 115, 151, 165, 166, 178
Jacquet, Aime 114
Jansen, Wim 20, 21, 22, 127, 155, 174
Jefferies, Jim 34, 48, 186
Jenkins, Iain 155
Jess, Eoin 25, 151
Johansen, Kai 86
Johansson, Lennart 51
Johnson, David 122, 149, 168
Johnson, Grant 111
Johnson, Peter 68, 187
Johnston, Maurice 12, 96, 132–33, 164, 165, 183, 184

Johnston, Willie 37, 41, 95, 113, 142, 143, 156, 218, 219
Johnstone, George 154
Johnstone, Jimmy 41, 56, 133, 187, 188, 194, 195
Jones, Paul 128
Jonk, Wim 100
Jordan, Joe 86, 126
Julius, Vincent 'Tanti' 86
Juninho 90
Kampman, Harri 89, 202
Kasule, Victor 15, 48, 159, 163, 200
Katchouro, Petr 89
Keeble, Bruce 182
Keegan, Kevin 71, 93, 217
Keely, Dermot 44
Keller, Kasey 153
Kelly, Danny 142
Kelly, Graham 191
Kelly, Kevin 18, 48
Kelly, Michael 12, 121, 144
Kennedy, Jim 194
Kennedy, Stuart 160, 191
Kerr, Dylan 76, 165
Kerr, Jerry 33
Kerr, Jim 22, 23, 24
Khomeini, Ayatollah 144
King, Johnny 155
Kipling, Rudyard 159
Kiriakov, Ilian 78
Kirkwood, Billy 208
Kissinger, Henry 148
Klinsmann, Jurgen 37
Knight, Alan 100
Knox, Archie 43, 98, 109
Kozma, Istvan 200
Krivokapic, Miodrag 87, 112, 159
Lambert, Paul 17, 20, 58, 79, 167, 168, 197
Lambie, John 36, 37, 45, 108, 126, 173
Larsson, Henrik 27, 185
Latimer, John 99
Laudrup, Brian 12, 25, 57, 60, 63, 77, 90, 92, 98, 101, 112, 137, 138, 152, 163, 164, 176, 198, 211
Laudrup, Finn 60
Law, Denis 77, 102, 113, 149
Lecter, Hannibal 72
Leighton, Jim 72, 100, 109, 110, 153, 159, 162, 172, 177, 180, 216
Leighton, Linda 177
Leishman, Jim 35, 108
Lekovic, Dragoje 80, 101, 214
Lennox, Bobby 195
Levein, Craig 104
Levy, Karen 169, 211
Lineker, Gary 90
Litmanen, Jari 115
Lovering, Paul 110
Lowe, Rupert 193

Lynam, Des 49
McAllister, Gary 14, 15, 36, 50, 52, 54, 56, 63, 64, 67, 78, 84, 87, 102, 106, 107, 114, 121, 125, 133, 137, 150, 159, 162, 167, 168, 188, 197, 210, 213, 219
McAlpine, Hamish 188
McAnespie, Kieran 65
McAteer, Jason 100, 122
McAvennie, Frank 59, 95, 122, 144
McCall, Ian 99, 110, 111, 128, 138, 181, 187, 214
McCall, Stuart 12, 47, 109, 200
McCann, Fergus 18, 19, 20, 22, 23, 24, 46, 47, 59, 65, 94, 104, 125, 130, 131, 132, 136, 137, 139, 140, 144, 145, 147, 154, 168, 170, 183, 184, 185, 189, 190, 195, 199, 202, 203
McCarthy, Mick 183
McClair, Brian 12, 16, 27, 57, 60, 63, 69, 72, 83, 85, 96, 102, 103, 110, 161, 163, 165, 166, 174, 178, 179, 186, 187, 195, 209, 211, 214
McClair, Maureen 211
McClelland, John 134
McCoist, Ally 12, 24, 48, 53, 54, 55, 61, 75, 79, 85, 91, 96, 97, 102, 103, 107, 109, 110, 115, 118, 127, 128, 135, 139, 145, 151, 152, 153, 154, 157, 163, 164, 165, 188, 196, 208, 218, 219
McCormack, John 50, 186
McDermid, Danny 52
MacDiarmid, Hugh 212
MacDonald, Alex 50, 79, 219
MacDonald, Allan 47, 147
McDonald, Rod 182
MacDonald, Ronnie 41, 75, 129, 141, 167, 206
McDougall, Ted 134, 208
McDowall, Kenny 39
McFarlane, Neil 151
McGarvey, Frank 190
McGee, Alan 64, 137
McGhee, Mark 70, 100, 128
McGill, Ken 169
McGilveray, Helena 95
McGilvray, Jim 180, 182
McGinlay, John 42, 48
McGinn, Jack 119
McGonigle, Maureen 85, 96
McGowan, Alistair 74, 204
McGowne, Kevin 109
McGrain, Danny 119
McGraw, Allan 35, 47, 105, 106, 155
MacGregor, Archie 38
McGrillen, Paul 33
McIlvanney, Hugh 204
McIlvanney, William 87

McInally, Jim 110
McInnes, Derek 154, 187
Mackay, Dave 33, 174
Mackay, Donald 104
Mackay, Duncan 141
Mackay, Jimmy 200
McKee, John 25
McKellar, Dave 100
McKilligan, Neil 151
MacKinnon, Davie 33
McKinnon, Rob 17, 75
McKnight, Allen 126
McLaren, Alan 26, 45, 115, 161
McLaren, Andy 32, 155
McLaren, Billy 29
McLaughlin, Brian 35
Maclean, Donald 64
McLean, George 'Dandy' 29
McLean, Jim 32, 126, 127, 169, 190, 207, 211
McLean, Peter 22
Maclean, Rob 108
McLean, Tommy 32, 37, 80, 83, 127, 205, 214
McLean, Willie 127
McLeish, Alex 17, 69, 167
MacLeod, Ally 43, 107, 113, 124, 156
McLeod, Davie 107
MacLeod, Murdo 22, 36, 140, 155, 171, 186
McManaman, Steve 192
MacMillan, James 63
McMinn, Ted 135
McMurdo, Bill 17, 29, 32, 46, 85, 132, 136, 165, 214
McNamara, Jackie (sen.) 26, 130, 140, 147, 185
McNamara, Jackie (jun.) 26
McNee, Gerry 108
McNeill, Billy 18, 44, 152, 156, 193, 194, 208, 218
McPhee, Kathleen 19
McQueen, Gordon 106, 215
McSporran, Alastair 20, 127, 170
McStay, John 67
McStay, Paul 43, 125, 140
McStay, Willie 22, 23
McVeigh, John 37
Mabbutt, Gary 90
Macari, Lou 18, 77, 119, 125, 133, 134, 135, 136, 143, 149, 154, 156, 159, 192, 193, 194, 204
Mackin, Alan 148
Mahe, Stephane 21, 147, 148
Major, John 56
Maldini, Paolo 163
Malpas, Maurice 66, 83, 206
Manson, Shirley 217
Maradona, Diego 106, 122
Marinello, Peter 41
Marshall, Peter 106
Martin, Brian 53
Martin, Dean 97

Martin, John 28, 101, 212
Martin, Steve 208
Masson, Don 54, 156
Mathie, Ross 153
Mauchlen, Ally 14
Maxwell, Robert 135
Mayer, Andreas 65
Mercer, Wallace 46, 134
Millar, Davie 136
Millar, Jimmy 155
Miller, Charlie 25, 109, 152
Miller, Joe 144
Miller, Willie 161, 180
Millichip, Bert 70
Minogue, Kylie 96
Mochan, Neil 113
Molby, Jan 36
Moldovan, Viorel 128
Moller-Nielsen, Tommy 176
Money, Campbell 111
Monroe, Marilyn 93
Montford, Arthur 196
Moore, Brian 217
Moore, Peter 203
Moore, Vinnie 151
Moorhouse, Jim 32
Morgan, Willie 14
Morris, Desmond 91
Morrison, David 200
Moss, Kate 216
Mottram, Les 179
Mulhearn, Jack 130
Mullery, Alan 191
Mulryne, Philip 89
Munro, Iain 38, 134, 169
Munyamahugo, Buhilike 213
Murdoch, Bobby 75, 194
Murray, Bill 143, 184
Murray, David 44, 45, 47, 59, 64, 67, 77, 84, 85, 88, 92, 104, 124, 132, 134, 136, 137, 138, 140, 144, 146, 157, 158, 167, 170, 172, 175, 176, 178, 184, 189, 192, 200, 202, 204, 206
Murray, Neil 135
Ndaie, Mulamba 113
Negri, Marco 35, 81, 93
Nelson, Garry 125
Nelson, Sammy 63
Nevin, Pat 27, 28, 46, 48, 74, 76, 97, 152, 155, 161, 162, 167, 171, 184, 188, 206, 216
Nicholas, Charlie 11, 14, 18, 25, 40, 45, 60, 83, 108, 124, 125, 158, 161, 162, 163, 195
Nicholas, Claire 60
Nicholl, Jimmy 13 16, 37, 38, 62, 108, 128, 136, 162, 175, 176
Nicholson, Bill 191
Nicol, Steve 114
Nicoll, Kim 51
Nilsson, Roland 167
Nixon, Richard 24
Nostradamus 86

Numan, Arthur 77
Ogilvie, Campbell 46, 175
Ogrizovic, Steve 167
Okehi, Obie 31
Oliver, Gary 109, 118
Oliver, Jim 36
Olsen, Morten 11
Osborne, Marc 101
O'Byrne, Bernard 30
O'Neil, Brian 154
O'Neill, Martin 14
O'Neill, Michael 86
Pageaud, Michel 133
Pallister, Gary 163, 166
Parker, Paul 195
Parkinson, Michael 122
Parreira, Carlos Alberto 114, 215
Paterson, Steve 29
Paton, Bert 80, 127, 153, 156
Patrick, Philip 101
Patterson, Darren 181
Patterson, Jamie 108
Payton, Andy 144
Pearce, Stuart 53, 137, 162
Pedersen, Erik 76
Pele 162, 166
Perryman, Steve 191
Petric, Gordan 149, 203
Philby, Kim 64
Pittman, Steve 15, 79, 163
Platt, David 90
Pohlak, Aivar 204
Poom, Mart 52
Preston, Allan 77
Provan, Davie 103
Puskas, Ferenc 13, 56, 61
Rae, Alex 104
Rafferty, Alex 148
Rafferty, John 30
Ramsay, Jack 183
Ravanelli, Fabrizio 206
Raznatovic, Zelkjo 112
Redford, Robert 136
Redknapp, Harry 77
Reed, Oliver 97
Reid, Alastair 62
Reid, Brian 154
Reid, Charlie 32
Reid, Hugh 53
Reid, Malcolm 201
Reid, Mike 62
Reid, Wes 218
Reilly, Jack 200
Reilly, John 30
Riedle, Karlheinz 21
Rieper, Marc 21, 77, 110
Riley, Eric 130
Rioch, Bruce 95, 157, 158
Rideout, Paul 201
Riseth, Vidar 147
Ritchie, Andy 35
Rix, Graham 195
Robert, Christophe 133
Roberts, Graham 144

Robertson, David 165
Robertson, John (Nottm. Forest) 14, 62, 150, 153, 161
Robertson, John (Hearts) 27, 44, 102
Robins, Mark 186
Robinson, Chris 134, 169, 205
Robson, Bobby 90, 91, 127
Robson, Bryan 98
Rogers, Dave 50
Ronaldo 216
Rough, Alan 36
Rousset, Gilles 183, 213
Rowbotham, John 181
Roxburgh, Andy 13, 40, 49, 68, 71, 80, 88, 107, 114, 124, 125, 129, 161, 173, 191, 194
Royle, Joe 67, 68
Rozental, Sebastian 13, 107
Rush, Ian 50, 120, 162
Russell, Andy 103
St John, Ian 16
Sacks, Saul 86
Salenko, Oleg 164
Le Saux, Graeme 120, 122
Sauzee, Franck 167
Schmeichel, Peter 101, 163
Scott, Hugh 47
Scott, Jocky 34
Sealey, Les 100
Seaman, David 50, 54
Sedgley, Steve 15
Seedorf, Clarence 53
Sekerlioglu, Attila 28, 79
Shankly, Bill 120, 127, 149, 194, 199
Shankly, Bob 43
Sharples, Ena 108
Shaw, Andy 189
Shearer, Alan 15, 55, 68, 120
Shepherd, Tony 143, 179
Shivute, Eliphas 81, 137
Sik, George 43
Simpson, Neil 82
Sinatra, Frank 70
Sinclair, Davie 162
Simpson, Neil 198
Simpson, Ronnie 56
Slater, Stuart 144
Smart, Craig 35
Smith, Dave 159, 201
Smith, David 45
Smith, Dougie 203
Smith, Gordon 47, 105
Smith, Henry 29
Smith, Jim 73
Smith, John 119
Smith, Scott 141
Smith, Steven 90
Smith, Walter 17, 24, 45, 58, 63, 91, 92, 93, 97, 124, 138, 145, 146, 147, 155, 164, 167, 170, 172, 175, 176, 177, 183, 186, 206–08, 213

Souness, Danielle 210
Souness, Graeme 11, 45, 46, 57, 59, 61, 66, 78, 103, 106, 121, 122, 123, 124, 127, 128, 132, 135, 142, 144, 146, 151, 154, 156, 169, 175, 177, 183, 187, 189, 191–93, 195, 198, 200, 210, 211, 213
Southall, Neville 68, 69
Southgate, Gareth 137
Speedie, David 15, 83, 152, 174, 211
Spencer, John 78, 106, 112, 129, 163, 182, 185, 187, 196, 197, 202
Spiers, Graham 67
Stainrod, Simon 31, 75, 150, 151, 166
Stallone, Sylvester 102
Stanton, Pat 41, 70, 165
Steedman, Jack 30, 85, 127
Stein, Colin 41
Stein, Jock 86, 103, 123, 134, 141, 143, 144, 157, 193–95, 199
Steven, Tom 31
Steven, Trevor 74, 94, 200
Stewart, Rod 15, 59, 62, 63, 113, 126
Stone, Steve 90
Strachan, Gavin 16, 26, 61
Strachan, Gordon 11, 15, 16, 26, 41, 46, 60, 61, 64, 72, 73, 76, 83, 88, 96, 99, 112, 123, 129, 138, 139, 161, 162, 167, 173, 174, 181, 187, 196, 197, 203, 214
Struthers, Scott 65
Stubbs, Alan 47, 135, 152
Sturrock, Paul 164
Sullivan, Neil 113
Swales, Peter 18
Syme, Davie 143, 144, 161, 163, 179, 180, 192
Symon, Scot 93, 123
Tannock, Ross 151
Tarantino, Quentin 166
Taylor, Matt 182
Taylor, Rogan 120
Teresa, Mother 118
Thain, Ian 108
Thern, Jonas 137, 183, 216
Thom, Andreas 78
Thompson, Alan 158
Thompson, Phil 206
Thomson, Andy 200
Thomson, Bill 29
Tod, Andy 33
Tortolano, Joe 163
Totten, Alex 39, 126, 127
Traynor, Jim 28
Turkyilmaz, Kubilay 58
Tyson, Mike 142
Ustinov, Peter 68
Vallance, Tom 133

Venables, Terry 55
Venglos, Jozef 22, 28, 130
Vialli, Gianluca 78, 175, 192
Vicious, Sid 13
Vidmar, Tony 177
Viduka, Mark 86, 130–32
van Hooijdonk, Pierre 25, 78, 81, 82, 139, 140, 155, 170
van Vossen, Peter 79, 109
Vrbanovic, Damir 132
Vrto, Dusan 201
Waddell, Willie 30
Waddle, Chris 33, 137, 201
Walker, Andy 47, 140, 202, 203
Walker, Ernie 26, 84, 85, 86, 88, 116, 159, 189, 213
Walker, Mike 201
Wallace, Gordon 12
Wallace, Ian 178
Wallace, Jock 194
Walters, Mark 102
Warhol, Andy 15
Wark, John 102, 157
Warwick, Dionne 23
Watters, Willie 39, 60, 103, 128
Watts, Graham 94
Weaver, Sigourney 153
Webb, Neil 72
Weir, David 216
Welch, Raquel 11
Welsh, Irvine 213
Westwater, Ian 27
White, Jim 113, 203
Whiteside, Norman 97, 162
Wieghorst, Morten 201
Wiggins, Xavier 19
Wilkins, Ray 135, 214
Wilkinson, Howard 11, 100
Williamson, Bobby 13, 35, 58, 81, 89, 139, 171, 178, 196
Wilson, Bill 138
Wilson, Davie 155
Wilson, Geoff 89
Winters, Robbie 142
Wise, Dennis 78
Wishart, Fraser 17, 181
de Wolf, John 174
Wood, Ian 32
Woods, Chris 100, 144
Woodward, Graeme 201
Worthington, Frank 191
Wright, Bishop Roddy 19
Wright, Brian 30
Wright, Paul 154
Wylie, David 101
Yorath, Terry 51
Young, Chick 95, 108, 109
Young, George 63
Young, Willie 109
Zetterlund, Lars 164
Zico 122, 198
Zidane, Zinedine 111
Zola, Gianfranco 76